I Married My Best Friend (♀) to Shut My Parents Up

Story & Art by **Kodama Naoko**

CONTENTS

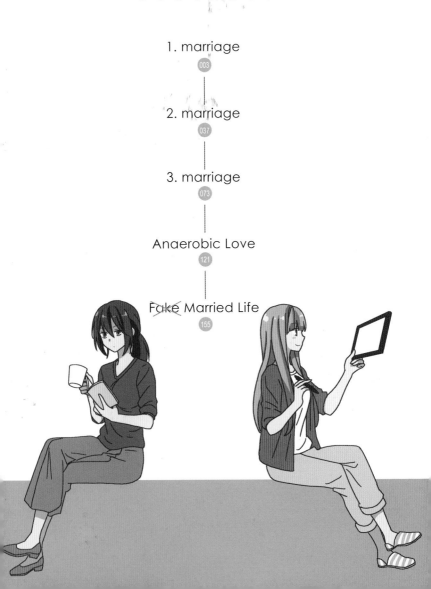

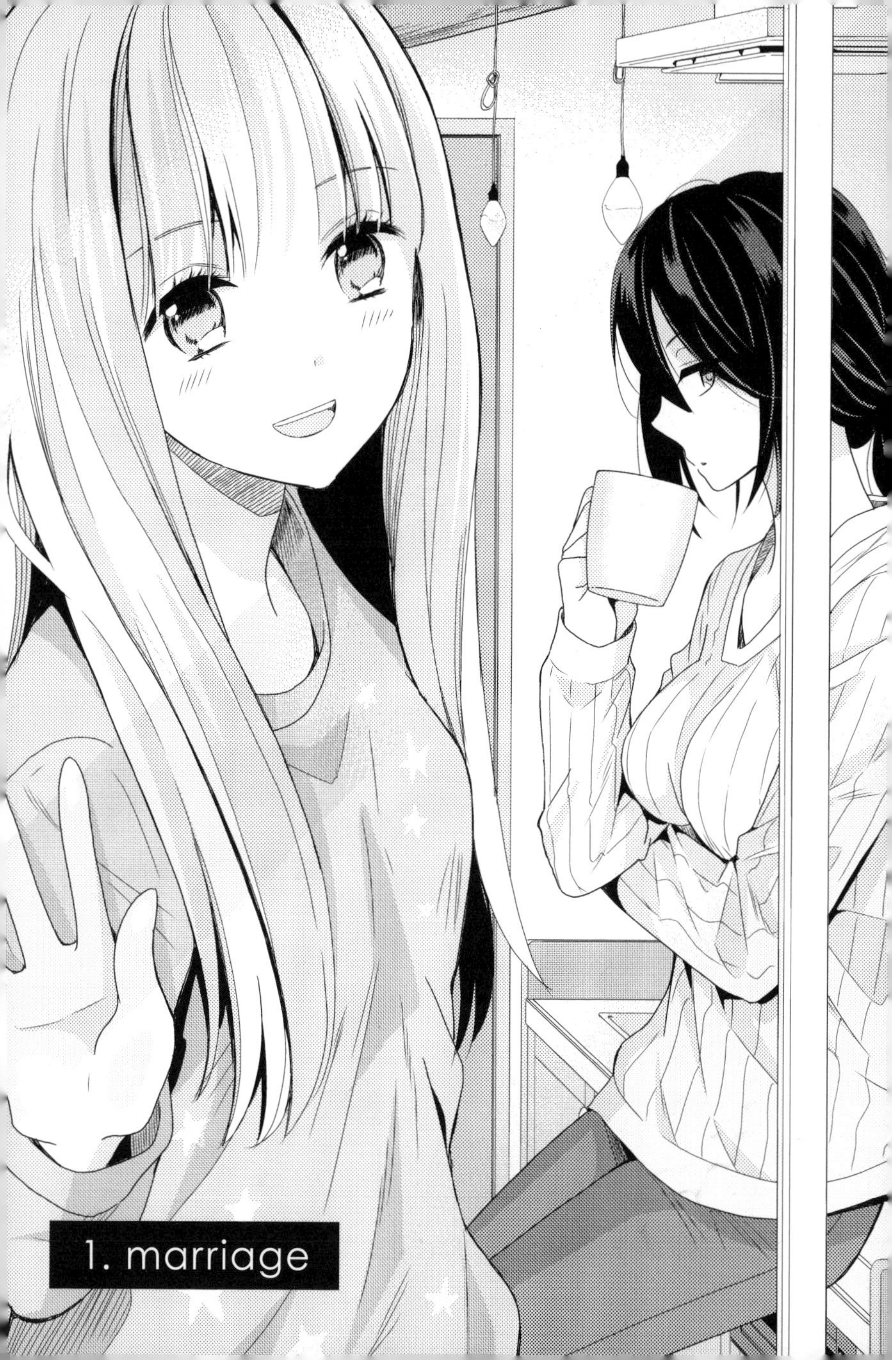
1. marriage

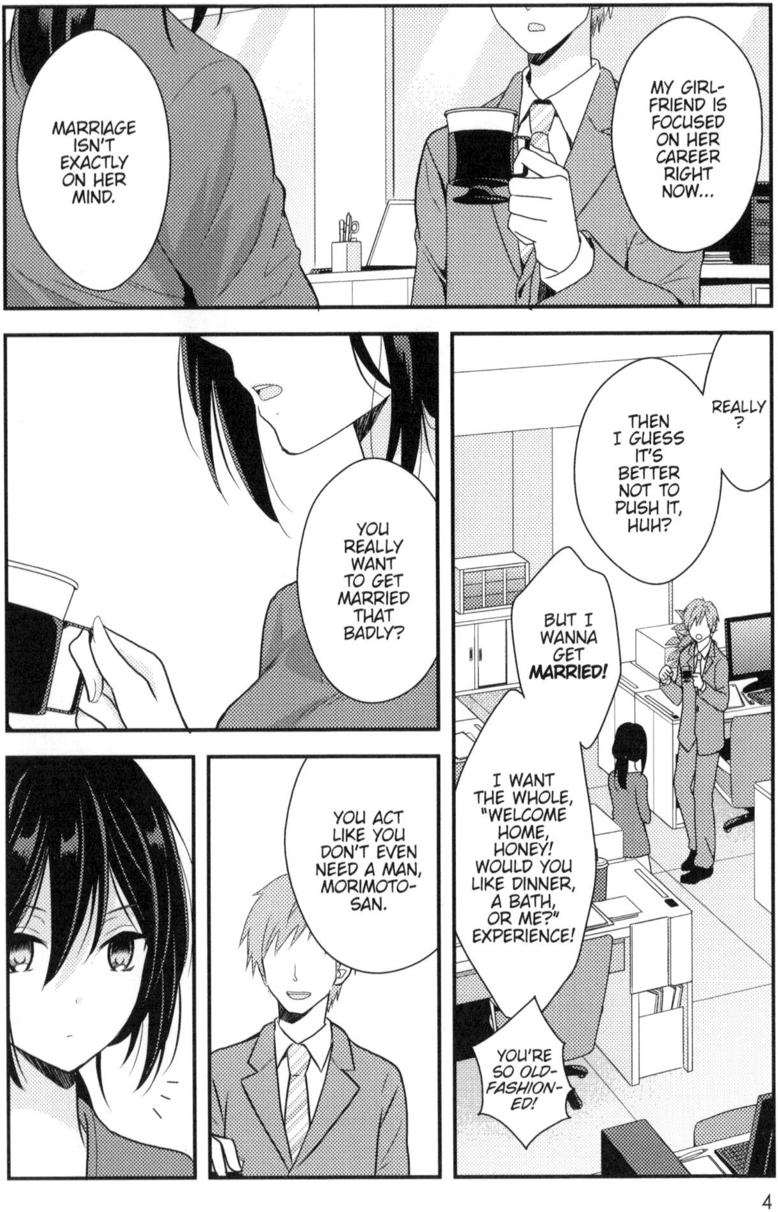
MY GIRL-FRIEND IS FOCUSED ON HER CAREER RIGHT NOW...
MARRIAGE ISN'T EXACTLY ON HER MIND.
REALLY?
THEN I GUESS IT'S BETTER NOT TO PUSH IT, HUH?
BUT I WANNA GET MARRIED!
I WANT THE WHOLE, "WELCOME HOME, HONEY! WOULD YOU LIKE DINNER, A BATH, OR ME?" EXPERIENCE!
YOU'RE SO OLD-FASHION-ED!
YOU REALLY WANT TO GET MARRIED THAT BADLY?
YOU ACT LIKE YOU DON'T EVEN NEED A MAN, MORIMOTO-SAN.

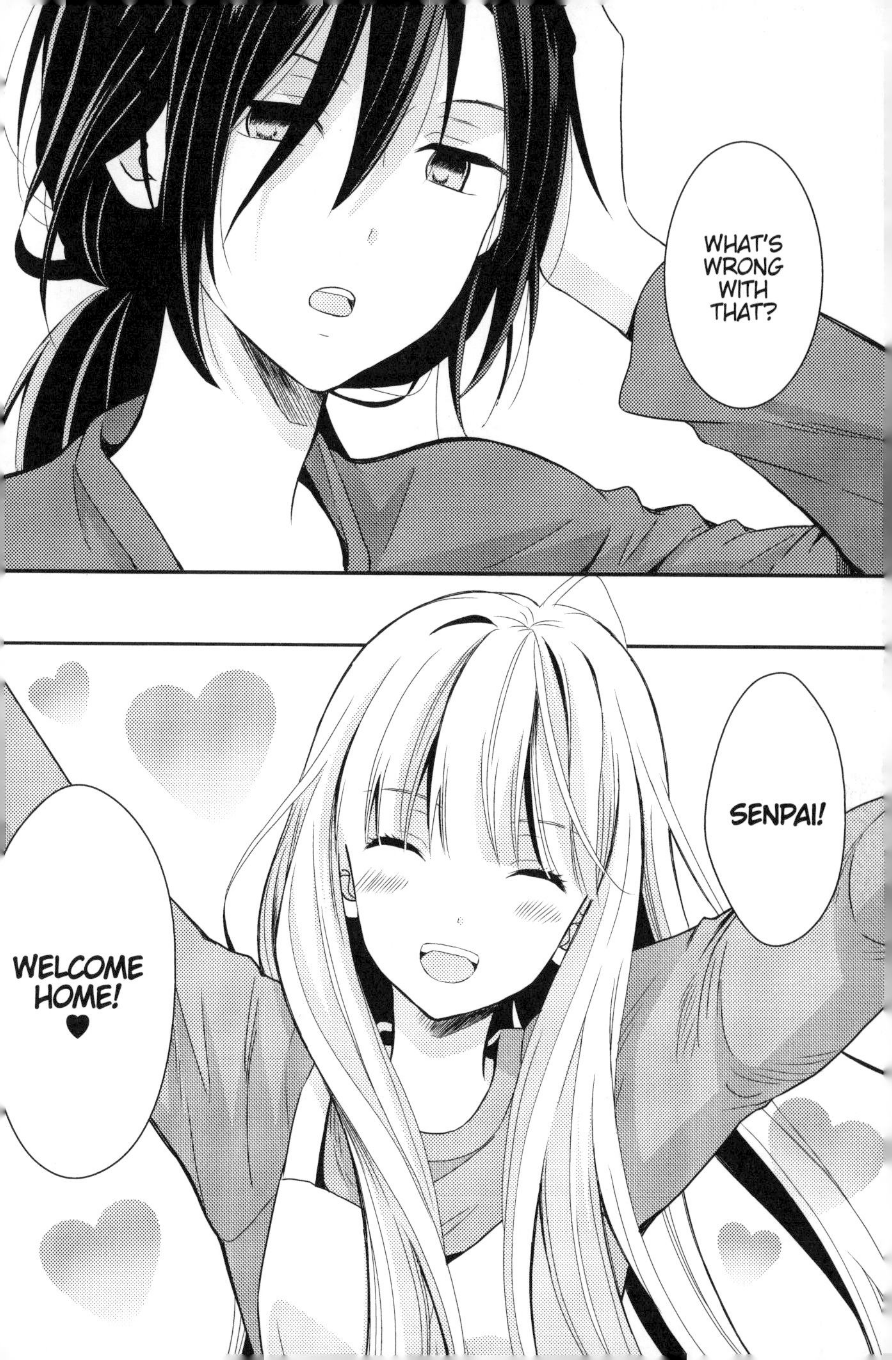
WHAT'S WRONG WITH THAT?
SENPAI!
WELCOME HOME! ♥

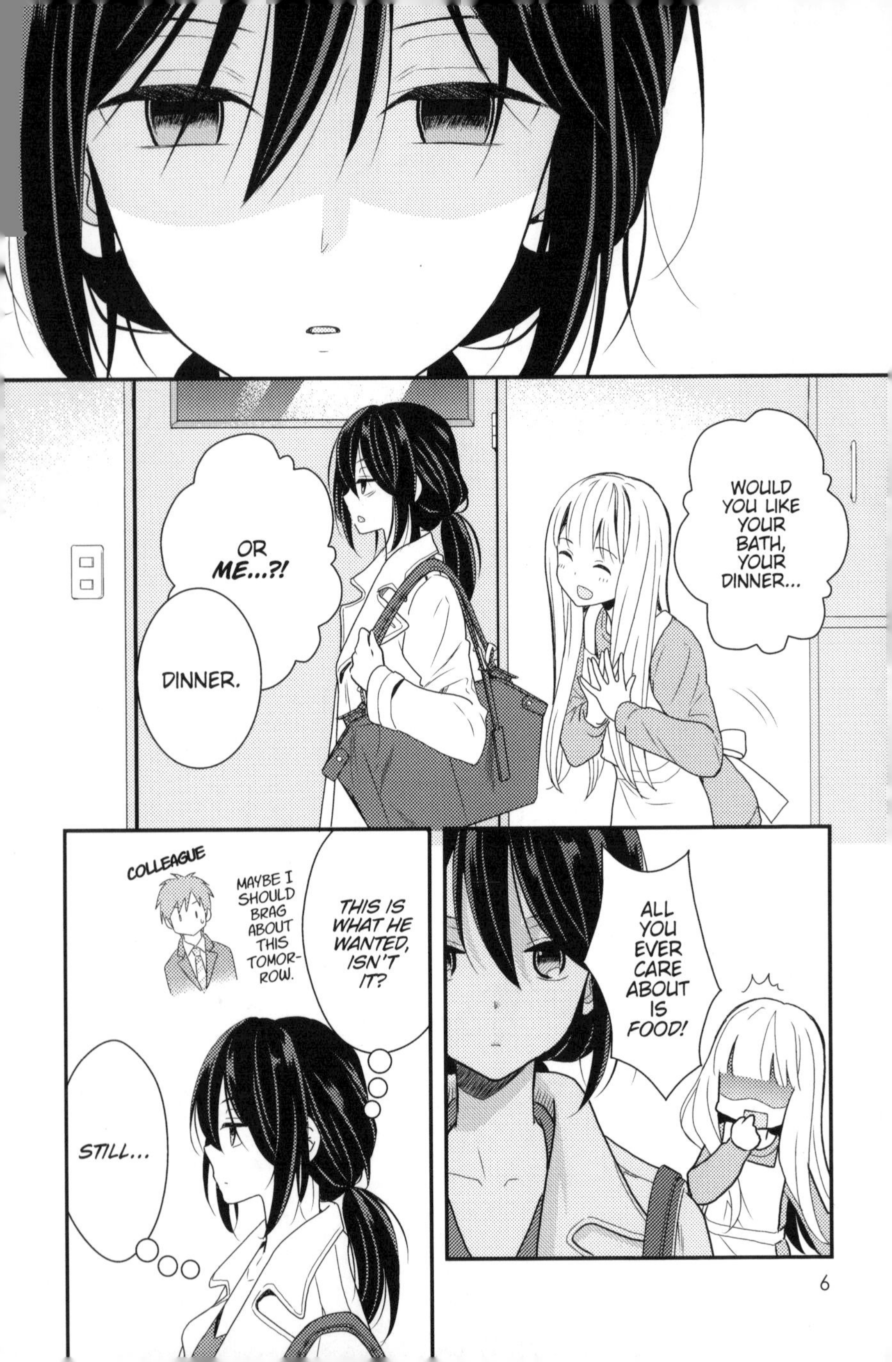
WOULD YOU LIKE YOUR BATH, YOUR DINNER...
OR ME...?!
DINNER.
ALL YOU EVER CARE ABOUT IS FOOD!
THIS IS WHAT HE WANTED, ISN'T IT?
MAYBE I SHOULD BRAG ABOUT THIS TOMOR-ROW.
COLLEAGUE
STILL...

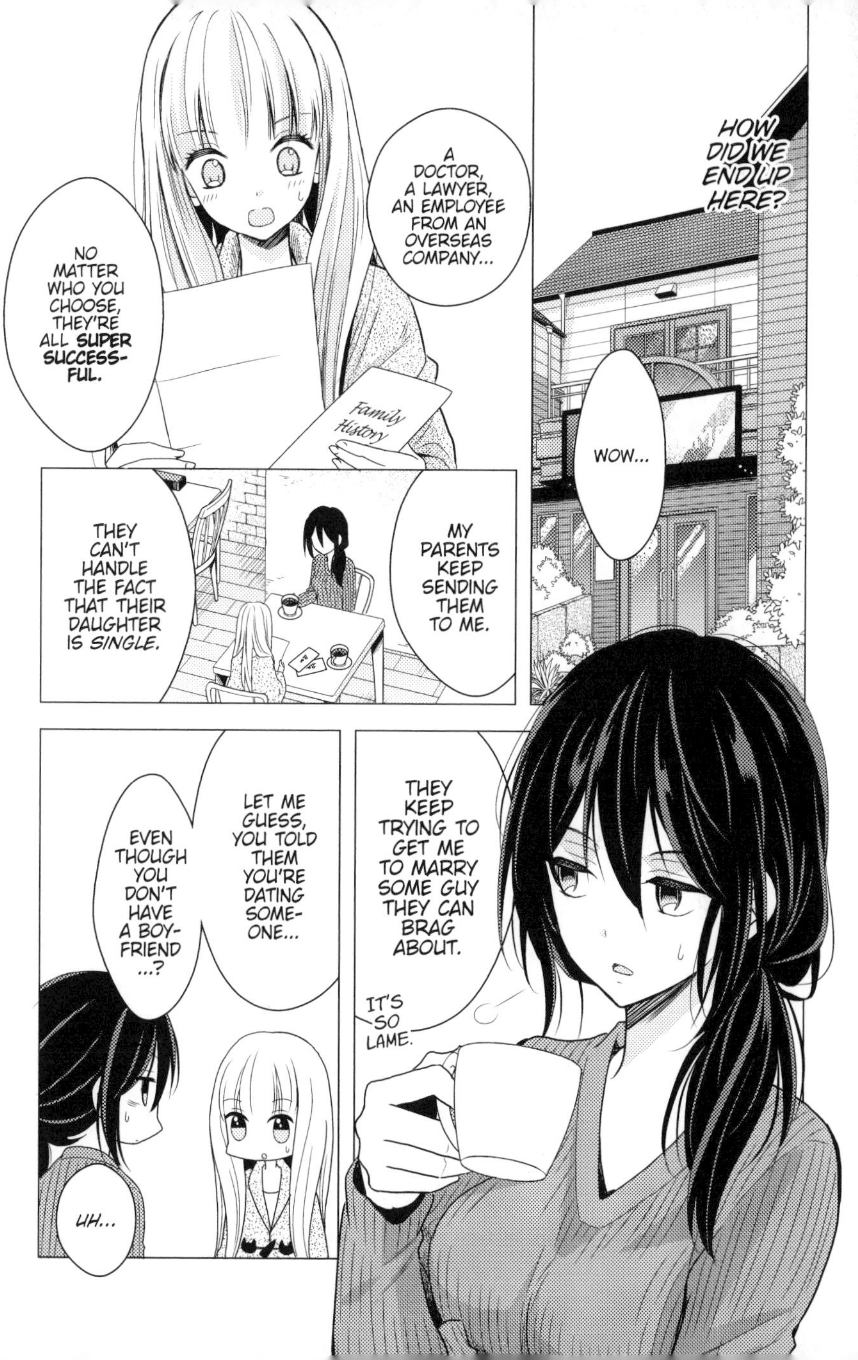
HOW DID WE END UP HERE?
WOW...
A DOCTOR, A LAWYER, AN EMPLOYEE FROM AN OVERSEAS COMPANY...
NO MATTER WHO YOU CHOOSE, THEY'RE ALL SUPER SUCCESS-FUL.
Family History
MY PARENTS KEEP SENDING THEM TO ME.
THEY CAN'T HANDLE THE FACT THAT THEIR DAUGHTER IS SINGLE.
THEY KEEP TRYING TO GET ME TO MARRY SOME GUY THEY CAN BRAG ABOUT.
IT'S SO LAME.
LET ME GUESS, YOU TOLD THEM YOU'RE DATING SOME-ONE...
EVEN THOUGH YOU DON'T HAVE A BOY-FRIEND ...?
UH...

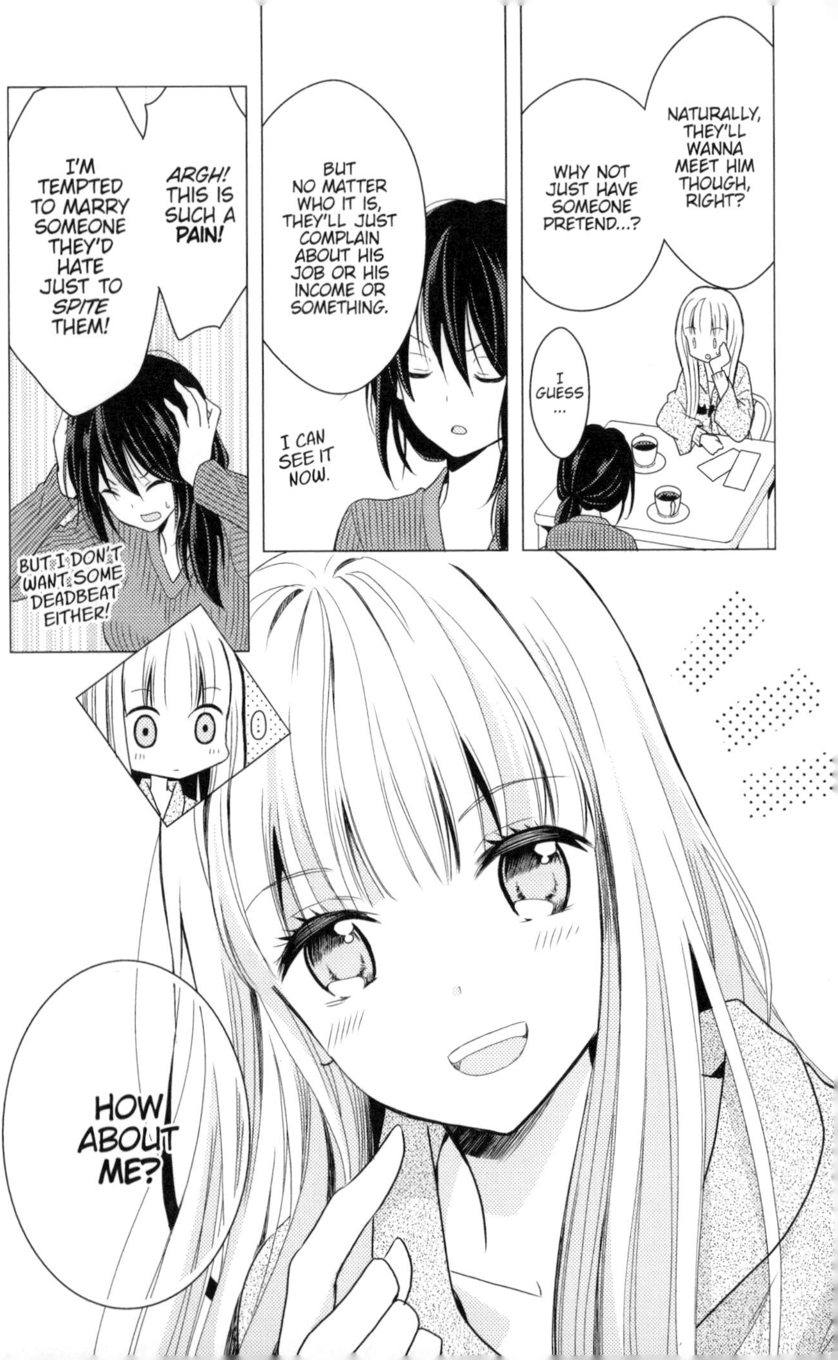

NATURALLY, THEY'LL WANNA MEET HIM THOUGH, RIGHT?
WHY NOT JUST HAVE SOMEONE PRETEND...?
I GUESS...
BUT NO MATTER WHO IT IS, THEY'LL JUST COMPLAIN ABOUT HIS JOB OR HIS INCOME OR SOMETHING.
I CAN SEE IT NOW.
ARGH! THIS IS SUCH A PAIN!
I'M TEMPTED TO MARRY SOMEONE THEY'D HATE JUST TO SPITE THEM!
BUT I DON'T WANT SOME DEADBEAT EITHER!
HOW ABOUT ME?

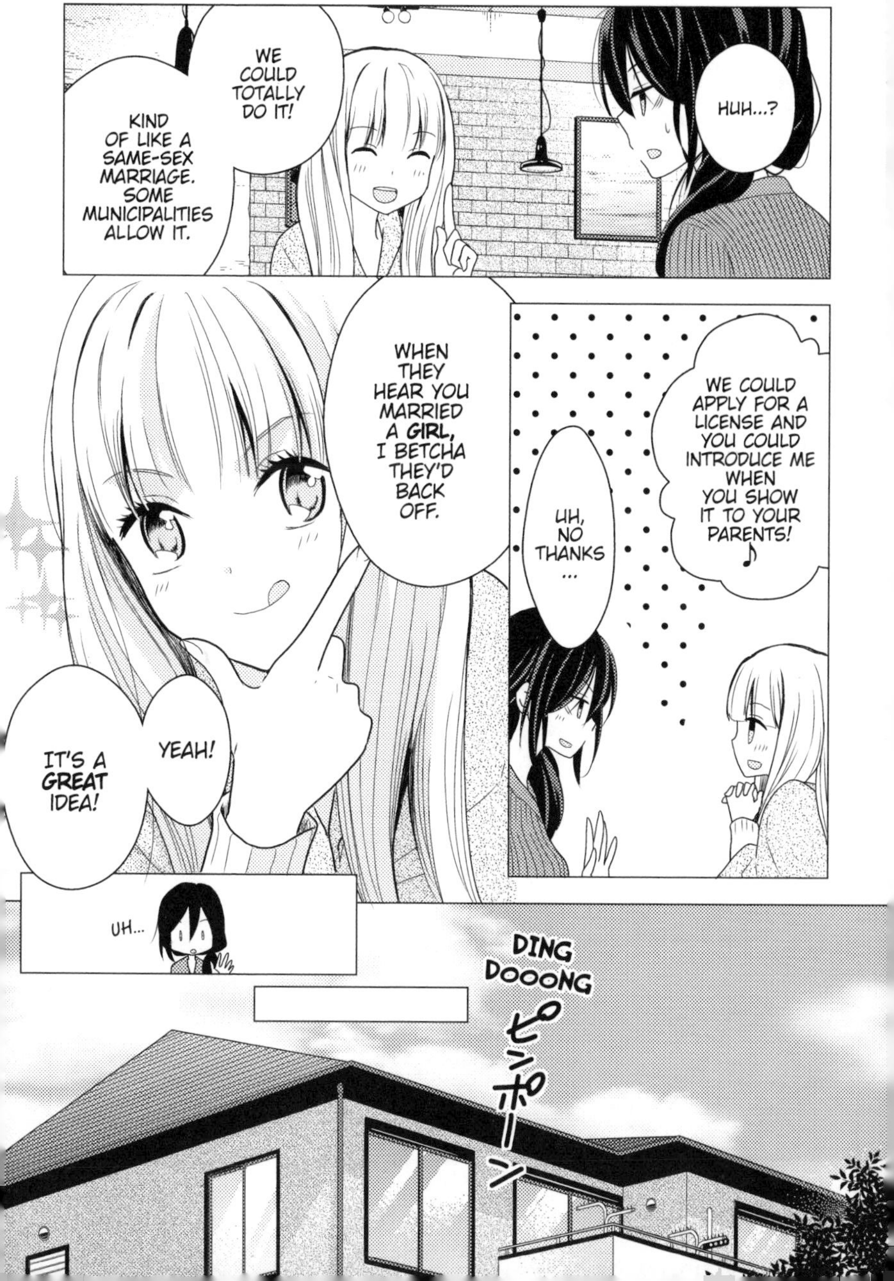
HUH...?
WE COULD TOTALLY DO IT!
KIND OF LIKE A SAME-SEX MARRIAGE. SOME MUNICIPALITIES ALLOW IT.
WE COULD APPLY FOR A LICENSE AND YOU COULD INTRODUCE ME WHEN YOU SHOW IT TO YOUR PARENTS! ♪
UH, NO THANKS ...
WHEN THEY HEAR YOU MARRIED A **GIRL,** I BETCHA THEY'D BACK OFF.
YEAH!
IT'S A **GREAT** IDEA!
UH...
DING DOOONG
ピンポーン

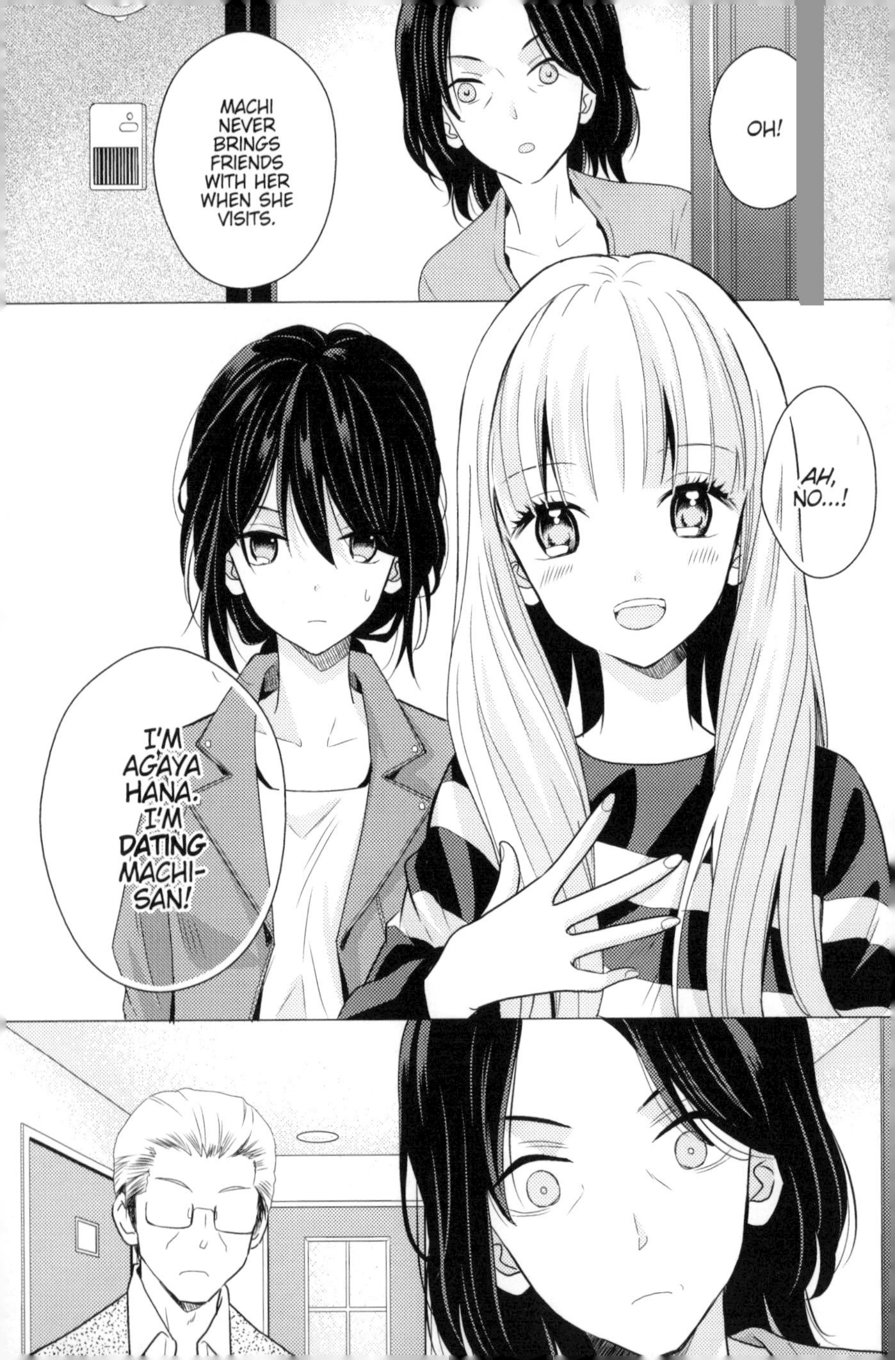
OH!
MACHI NEVER BRINGS FRIENDS WITH HER WHEN SHE VISITS.
AH, NO...!
I'M AGAYA HANA. I'M DATING MACHI-SAN!

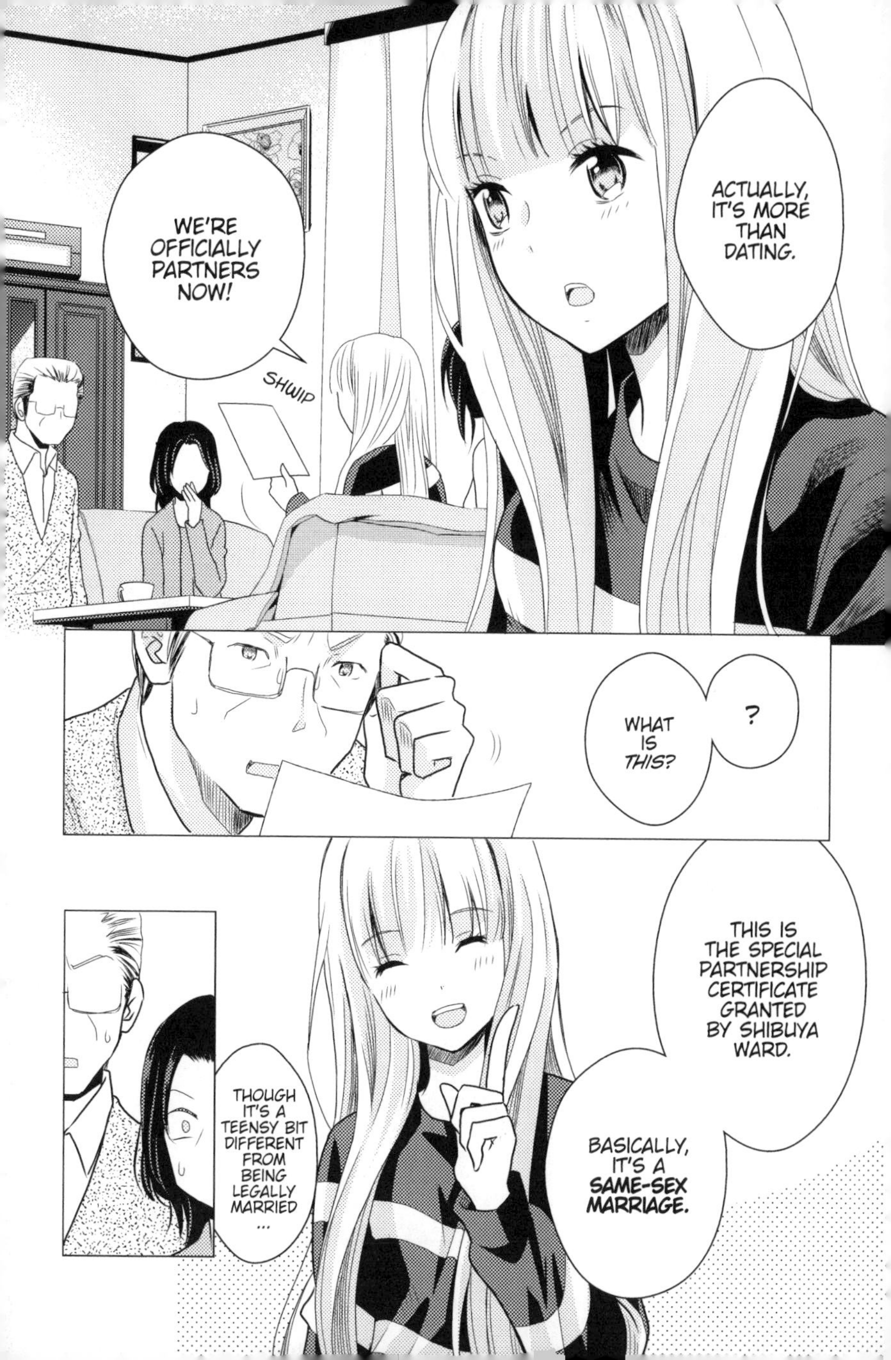
ACTUALLY, IT'S MORE THAN DATING.
WE'RE OFFICIALLY PARTNERS NOW!
SHWIP
?
WHAT IS *THIS?*
THIS IS THE SPECIAL PARTNERSHIP CERTIFICATE GRANTED BY SHIBUYA WARD.
BASICALLY, IT'S A **SAME-SEX MARRIAGE.**
THOUGH IT'S A TEENSY BIT DIFFERENT FROM BEING LEGALLY MARRIED ...

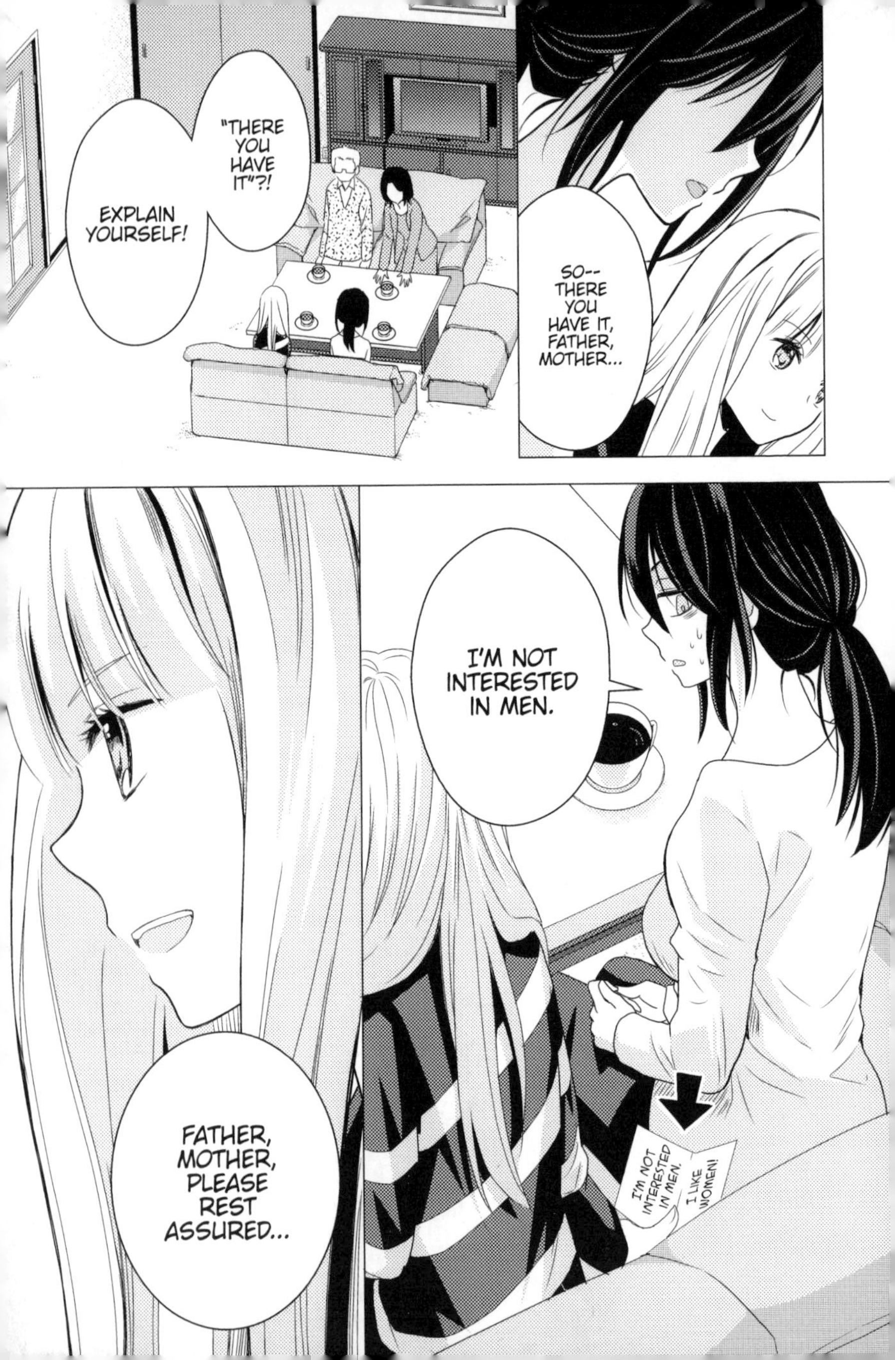
SO-- THERE YOU HAVE IT, FATHER, MOTHER...
"THERE YOU HAVE IT"?!
EXPLAIN YOURSELF!
I'M NOT INTERESTED IN MEN.
I'M NOT INTERESTED IN MEN. I LIKE WOMEN!
FATHER, MOTHER, PLEASE REST ASSURED...

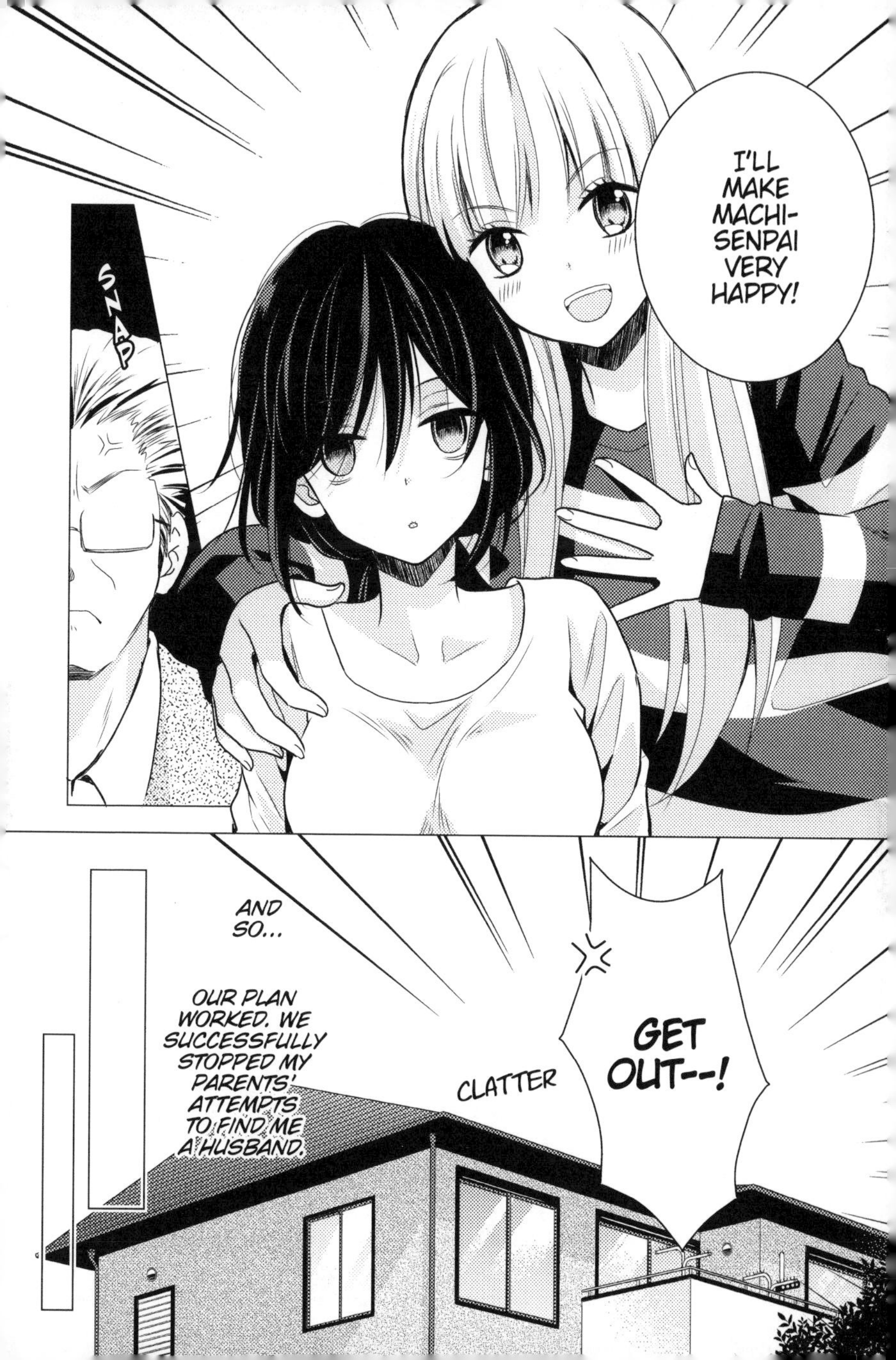
I'LL MAKE MACHI-SENPAI VERY HAPPY!
SNAP
GET OUT--!
CLATTER
AND SO...
OUR PLAN WORKED. WE SUCCESSFULLY STOPPED MY PARENTS' ATTEMPTS TO FIND ME A HUSBAND.

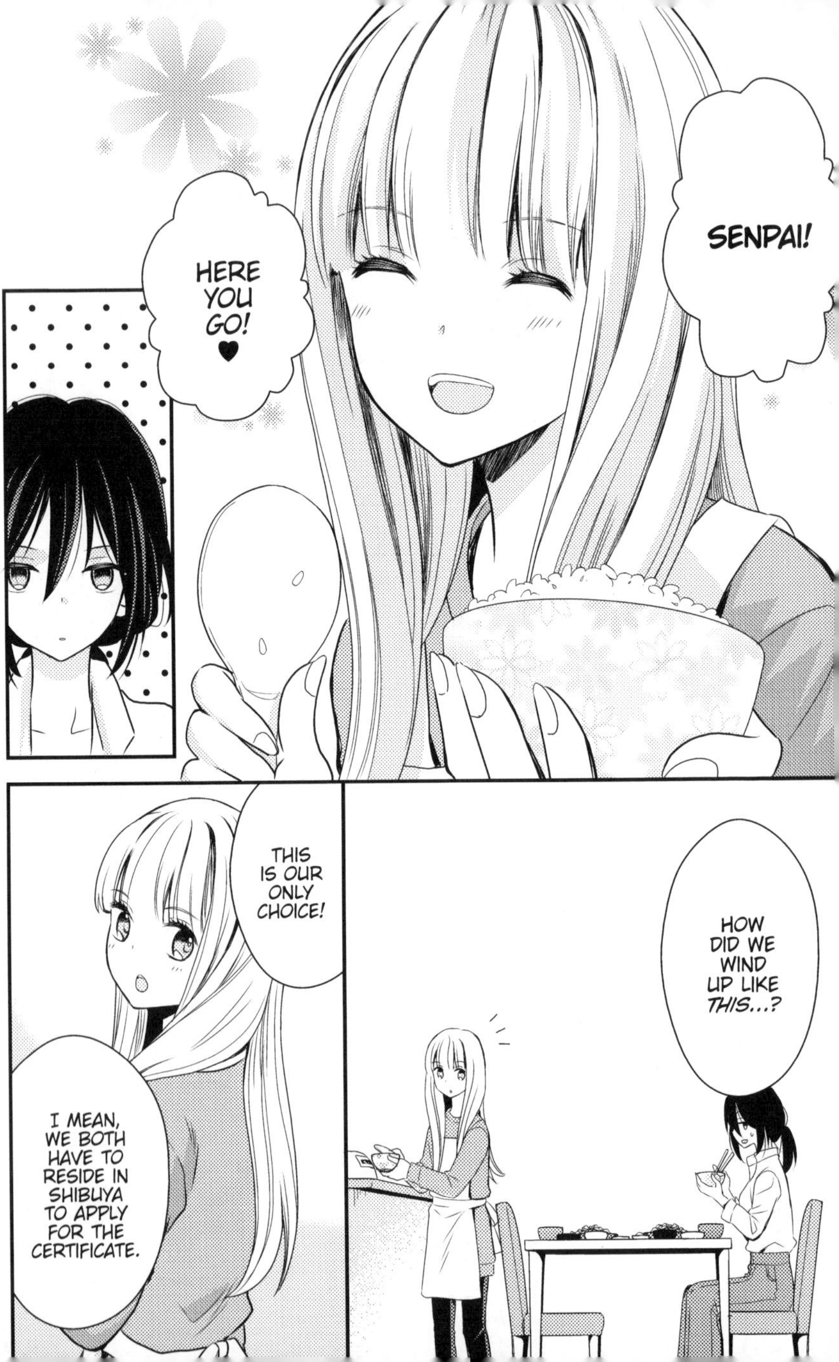
SENPAI!
HERE YOU GO! ♥
HOW DID WE WIND UP LIKE *THIS*...?
THIS IS OUR ONLY CHOICE!
I MEAN, WE BOTH HAVE TO RESIDE IN SHIBUYA TO APPLY FOR THE CERTIFICATE.

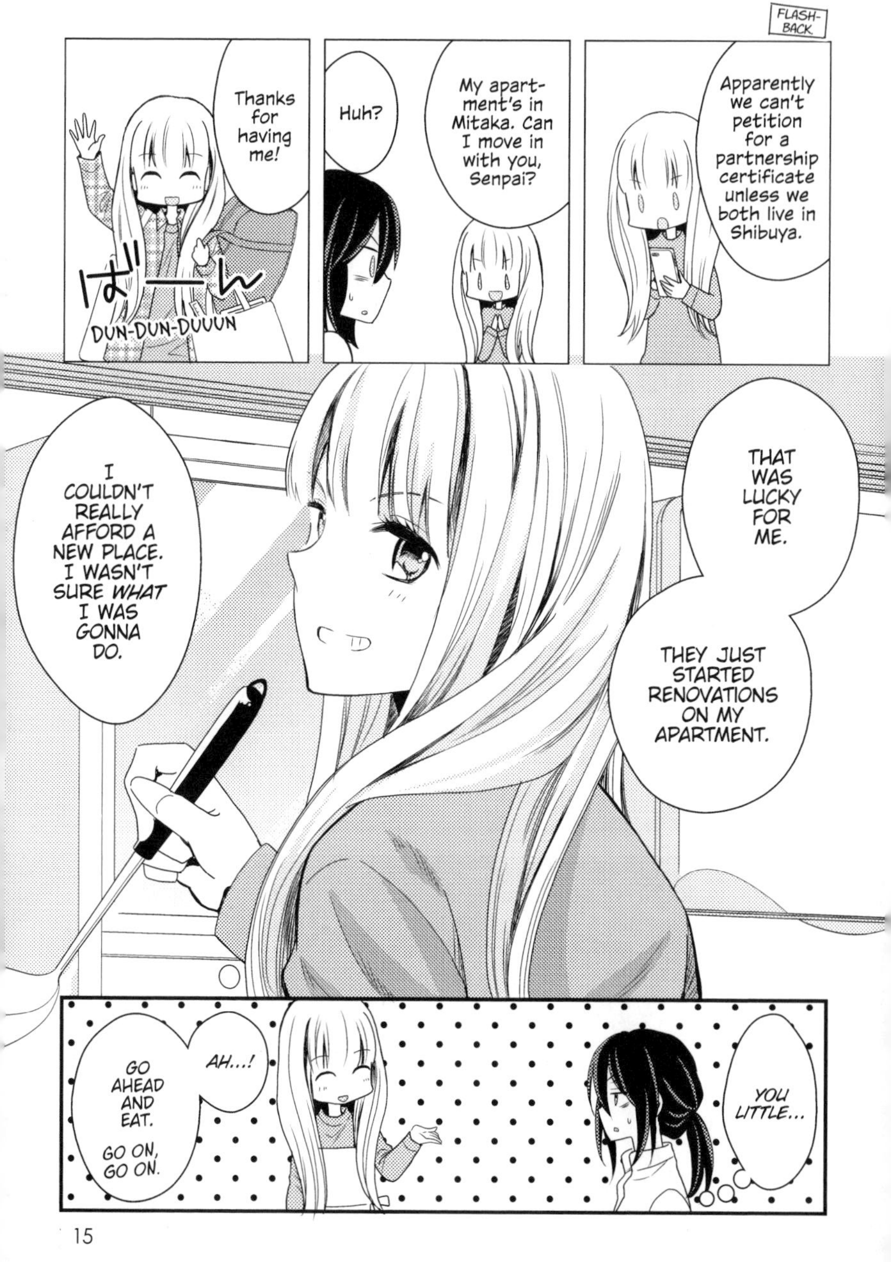
FLASH-BACK
Apparently we can't petition for a partnership certificate unless we both live in Shibuya.
My apartment's in Mitaka. Can I move in with you, Senpai?
Huh?
Thanks for having me!
ばーん
DUN-DUN-DUUUN
THAT WAS LUCKY FOR ME.
THEY JUST STARTED RENOVATIONS ON MY APARTMENT.
I COULDN'T REALLY AFFORD A NEW PLACE. I WASN'T SURE *WHAT* I WAS GONNA DO.
YOU LITTLE...
AH...!
GO AHEAD AND EAT.
GO ON, GO ON.

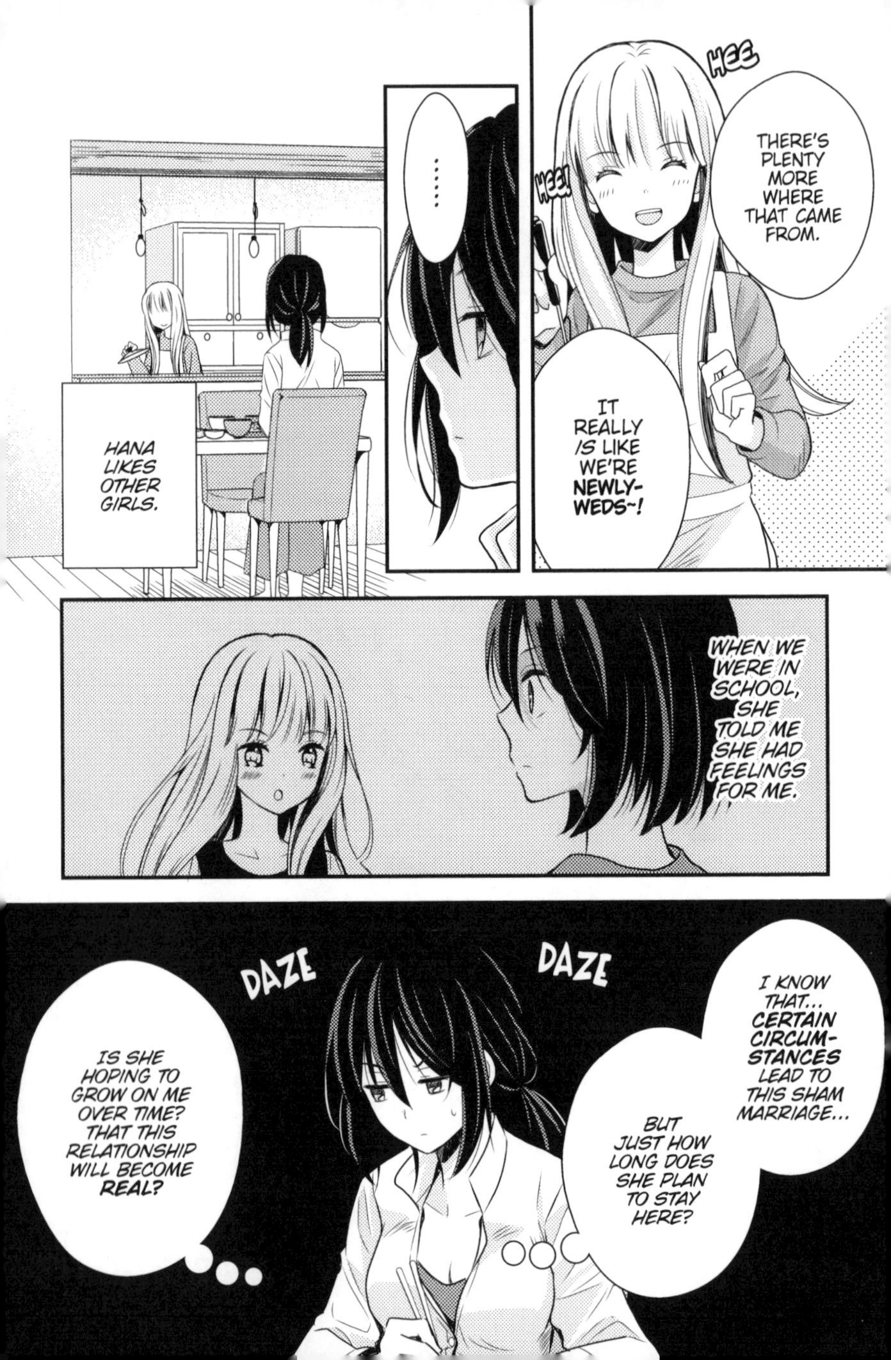
HEE
THERE'S PLENTY MORE WHERE THAT CAME FROM.
HEE!
IT REALLY *IS* LIKE WE'RE **NEWLYWEDS**~!
......
HANA LIKES OTHER GIRLS.
WHEN WE WERE IN SCHOOL, SHE TOLD ME SHE HAD FEELINGS FOR ME.
I KNOW THAT... **CERTAIN CIRCUMSTANCES** LEAD TO THIS SHAM MARRIAGE...
DAZE
DAZE
BUT JUST HOW LONG DOES SHE PLAN TO STAY HERE?
IS SHE HOPING TO GROW ON ME OVER TIME? THAT THIS RELATIONSHIP WILL BECOME **REAL**?

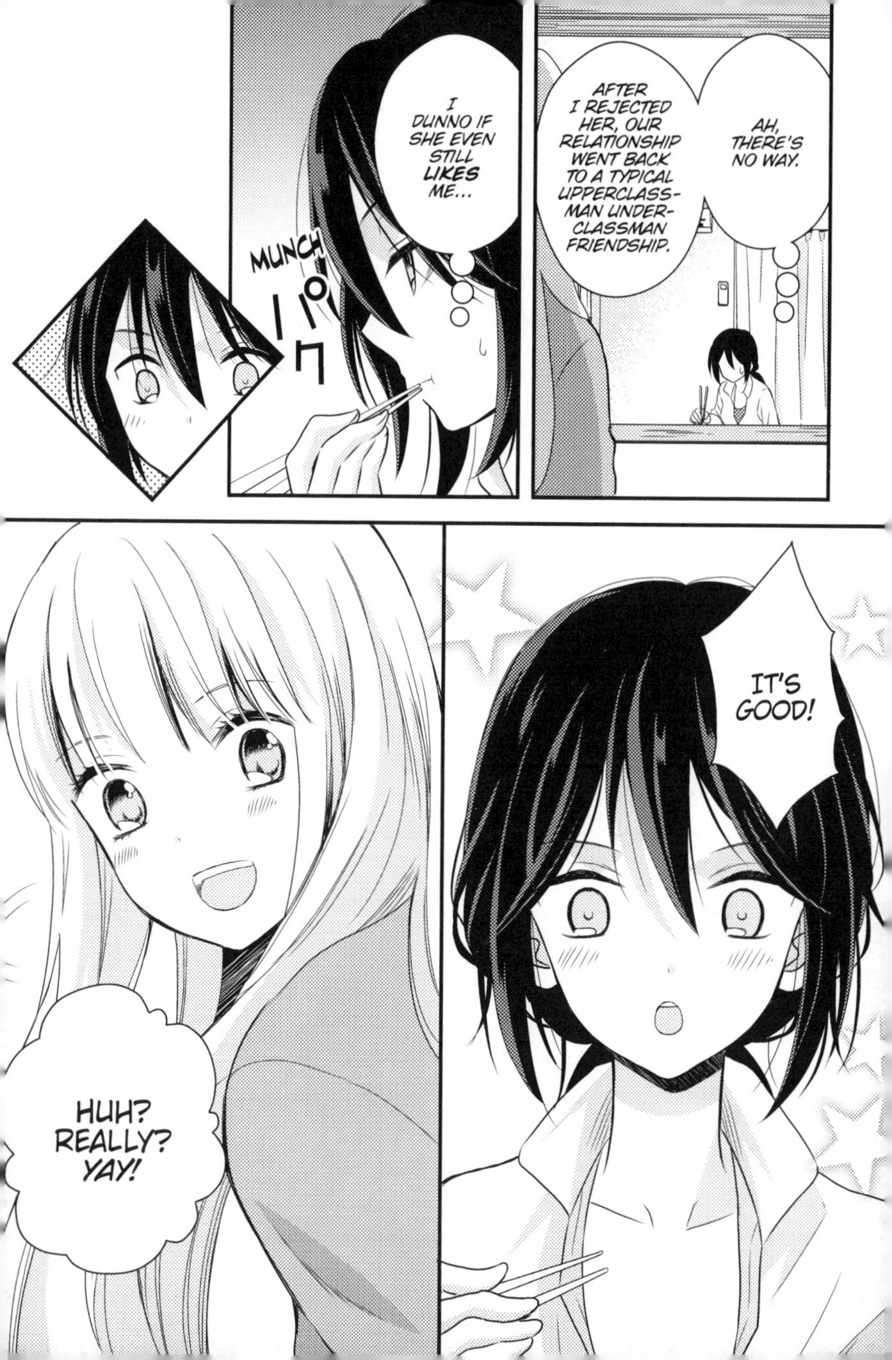

AH, THERE'S NO WAY.
AFTER I REJECTED HER, OUR RELATIONSHIP WENT BACK TO A TYPICAL UPPERCLASS-MAN UNDER-CLASSMAN FRIENDSHIP.
I DUNNO IF SHE EVEN STILL LIKES ME...
MUNCH
IT'S GOOD!
HUH? REALLY? YAY!

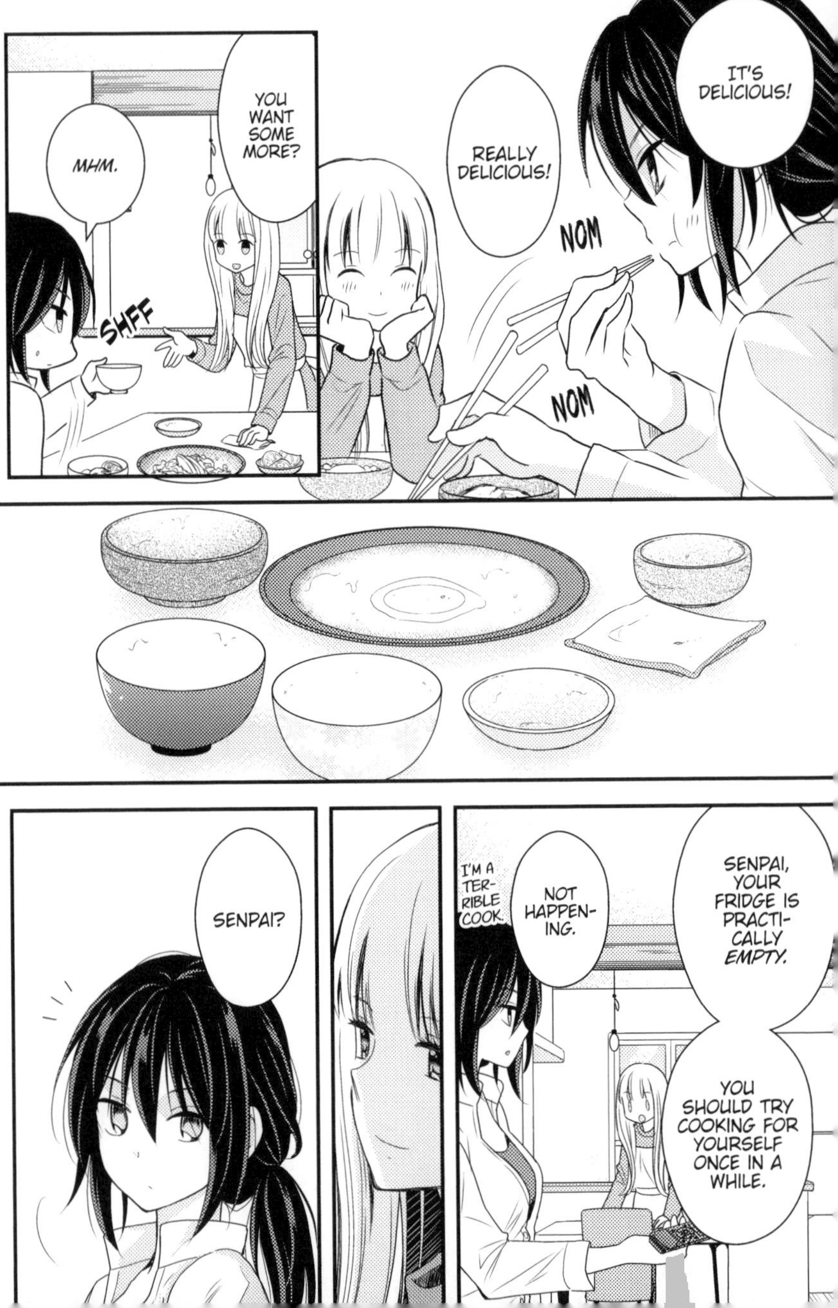
IT'S DELICIOUS!
REALLY DELICIOUS!
NOM
NOM
YOU WANT SOME MORE?
MHM.
SHFF
SENPAI, YOUR FRIDGE IS PRACTICALLY *EMPTY.*
YOU SHOULD TRY COOKING FOR YOURSELF ONCE IN A WHILE.
NOT HAPPENING.
I'M A TERRIBLE COOK.
SENPAI?

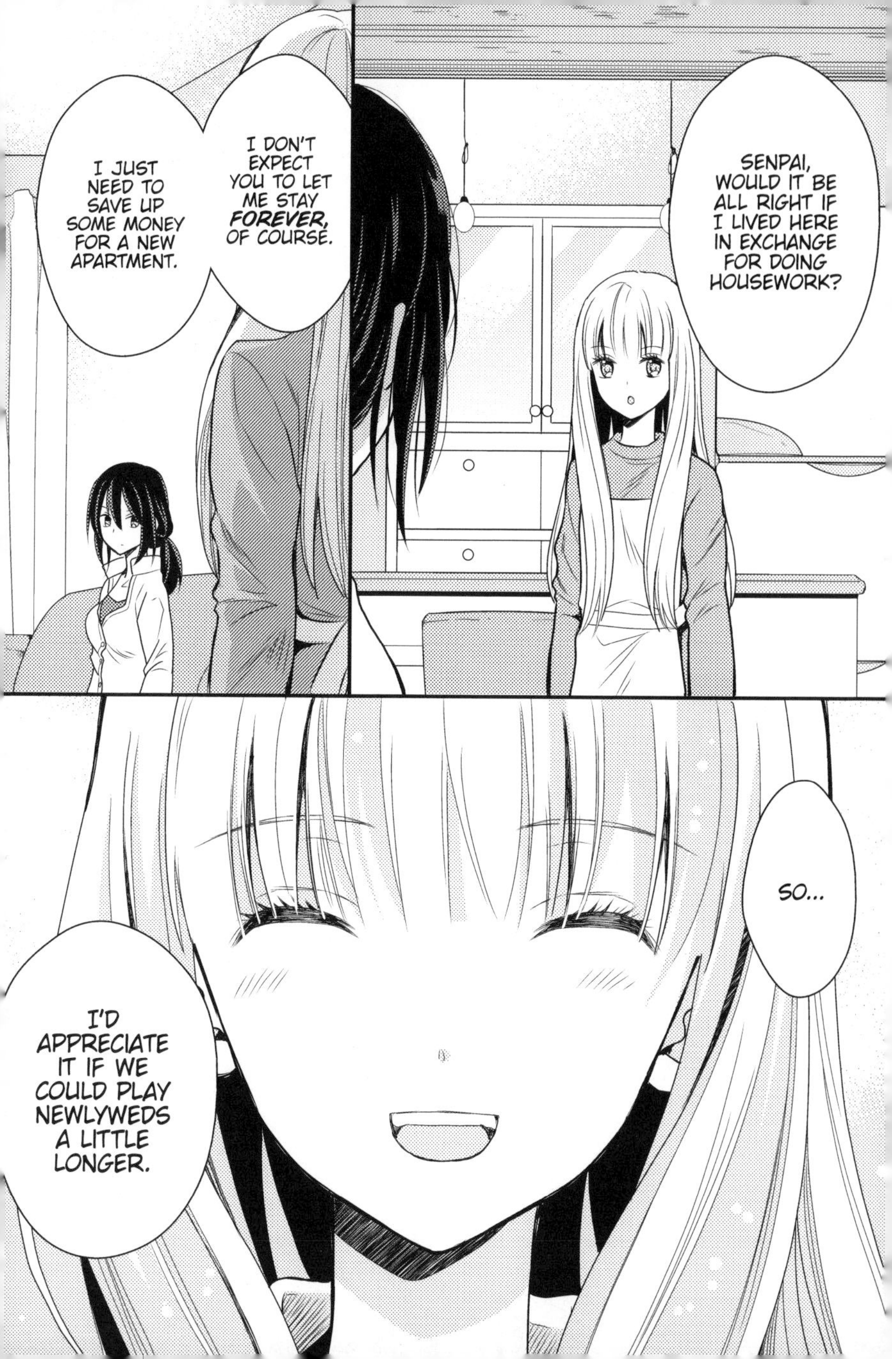
SENPAI, WOULD IT BE ALL RIGHT IF I LIVED HERE IN EXCHANGE FOR DOING HOUSEWORK?
I DON'T EXPECT YOU TO LET ME STAY ***FOREVER,*** OF COURSE.
I JUST NEED TO SAVE UP SOME MONEY FOR A NEW APARTMENT.
SO...
I'D APPRECIATE IT IF WE COULD PLAY NEWLYWEDS A LITTLE LONGER.

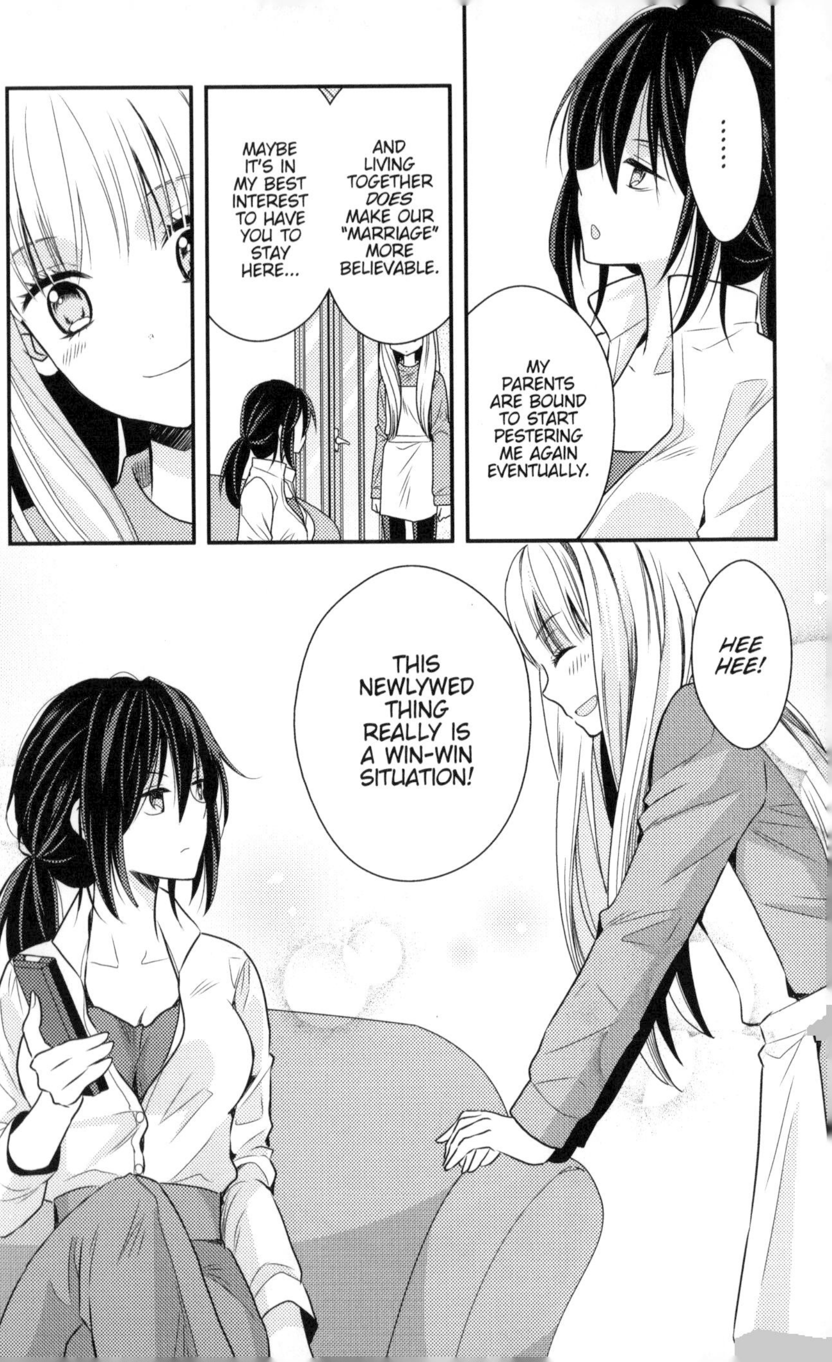
......
MY PARENTS ARE BOUND TO START PESTERING ME AGAIN EVENTUALLY.
AND LIVING TOGETHER *DOES* MAKE OUR "MARRIAGE" MORE BELIEVABLE.
MAYBE IT'S IN MY BEST INTEREST TO HAVE YOU TO STAY HERE...
HEE HEE!
THIS NEWLYWED THING REALLY IS A WIN-WIN SITUATION!

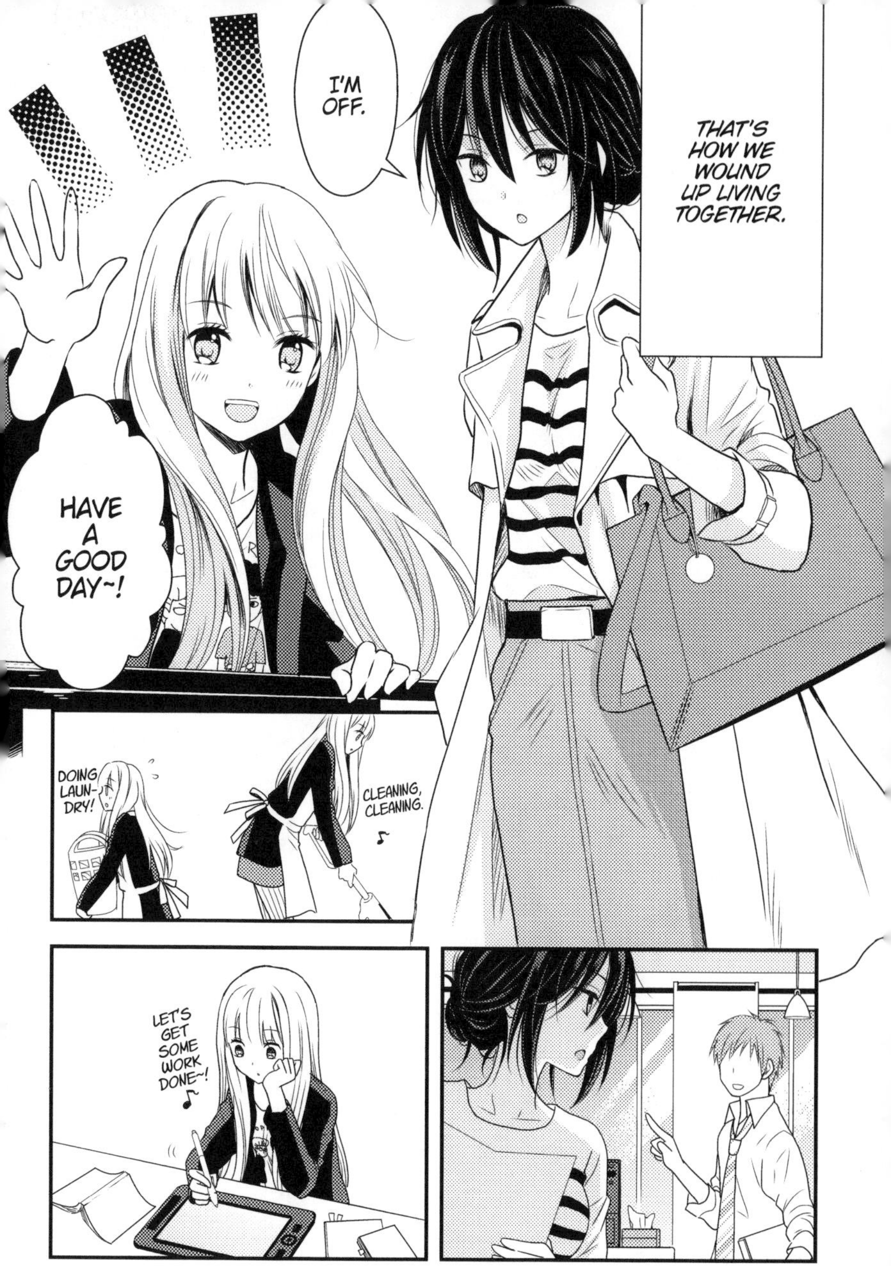
THAT'S HOW WE WOUND UP LIVING TOGETHER.
I'M OFF.
HAVE A GOOD DAY~!
CLEANING, CLEANING.
DOING LAUN-DRY!
LET'S GET SOME WORK DONE~!

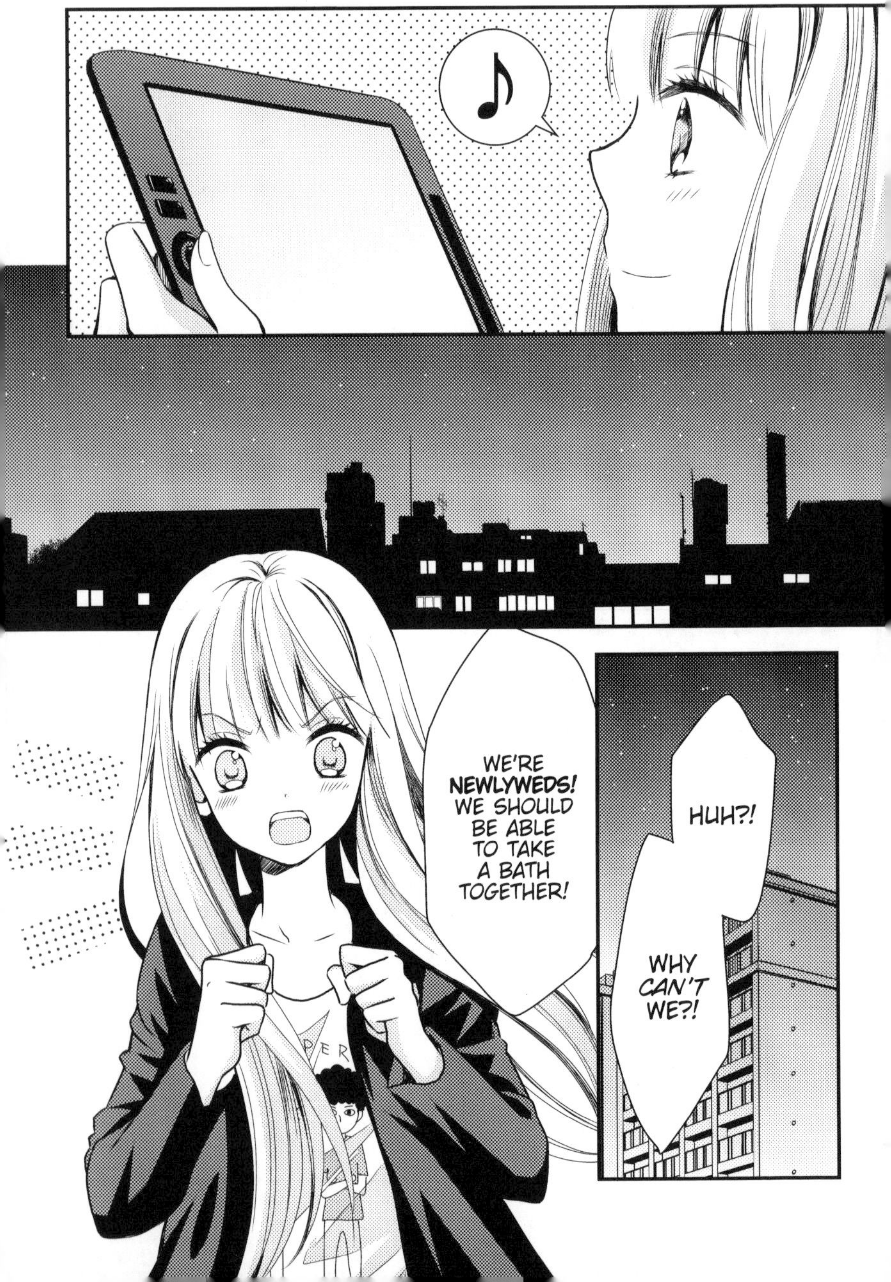
♪
HUH?!
WHY CAN'T WE?!
WE'RE NEWLYWEDS! WE SHOULD BE ABLE TO TAKE A BATH TOGETHER!

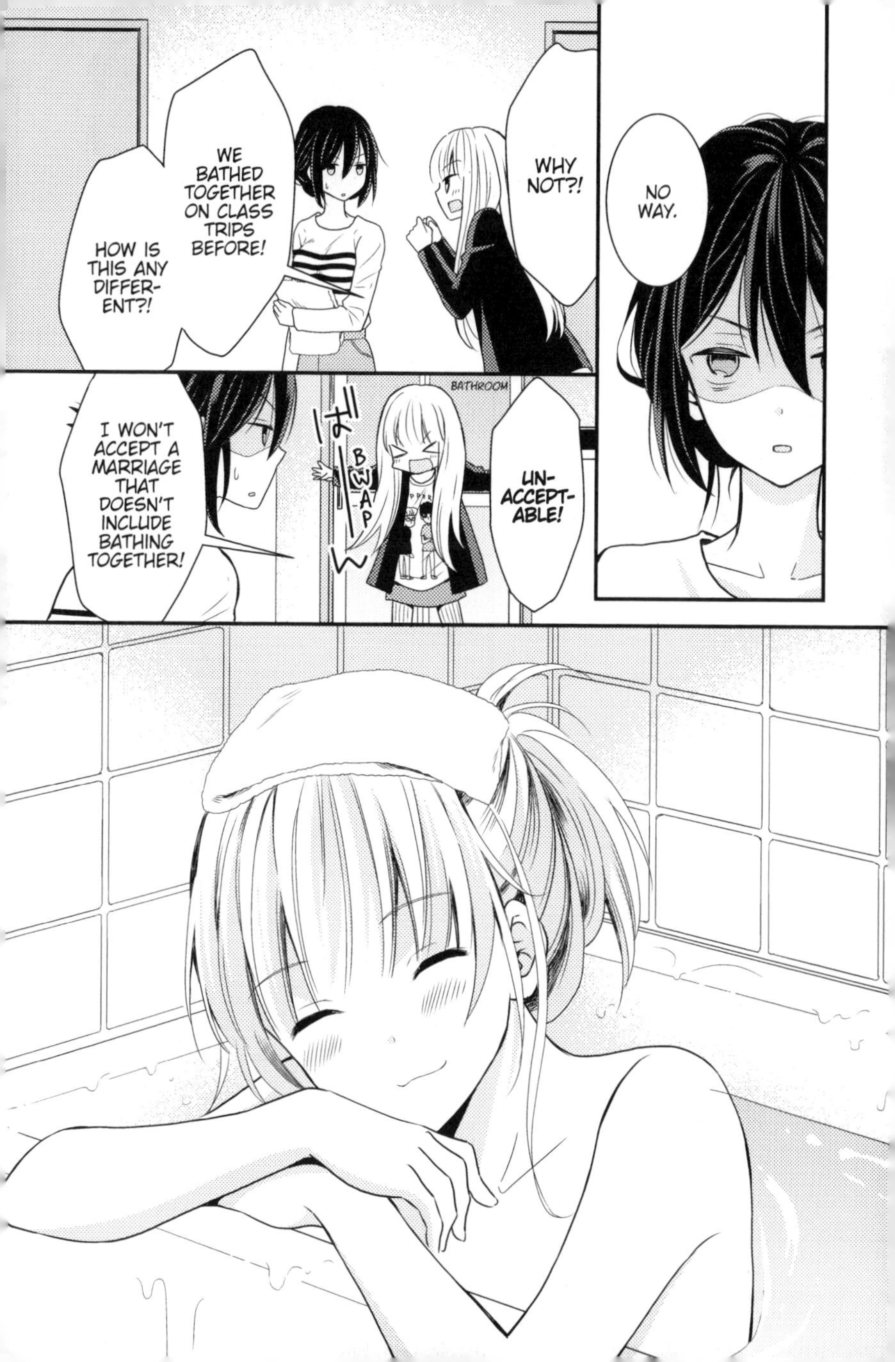
NO WAY.
WHY NOT?!
WE BATHED TOGETHER ON CLASS TRIPS BEFORE!
HOW IS THIS ANY DIFFERENT?!
UN-ACCEPTABLE!
BATHROOM
BWAP
I WON'T ACCEPT A MARRIAGE THAT DOESN'T INCLUDE BATHING TOGETHER!

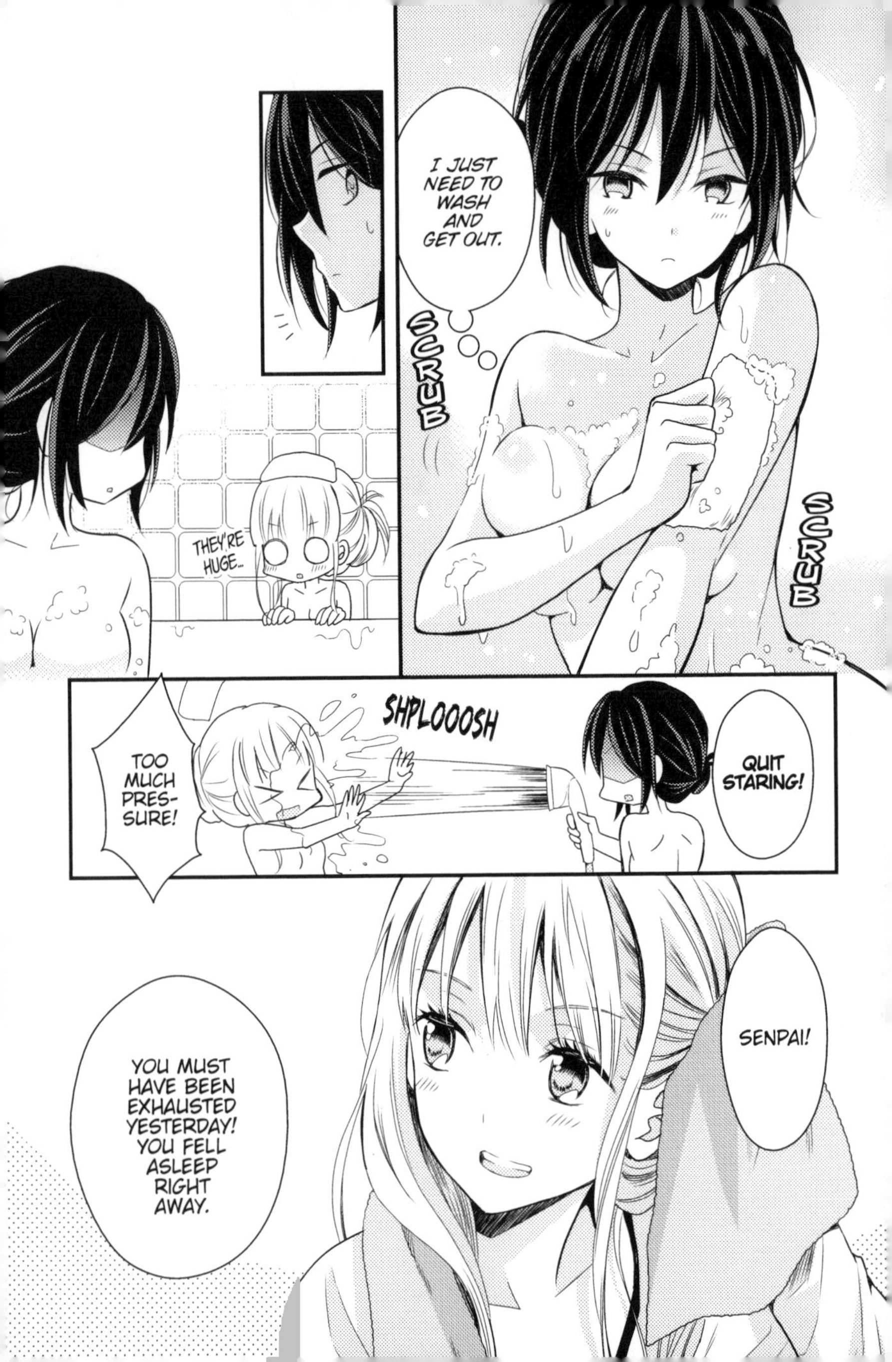
I JUST NEED TO WASH AND GET OUT.
SCRUB
SCRUB
THEY'RE HUGE...
QUIT STARING!
SHPLOOOSH
TOO MUCH PRES-SURE!
SENPAI!
YOU MUST HAVE BEEN EXHAUSTED YESTERDAY! YOU FELL ASLEEP RIGHT AWAY.

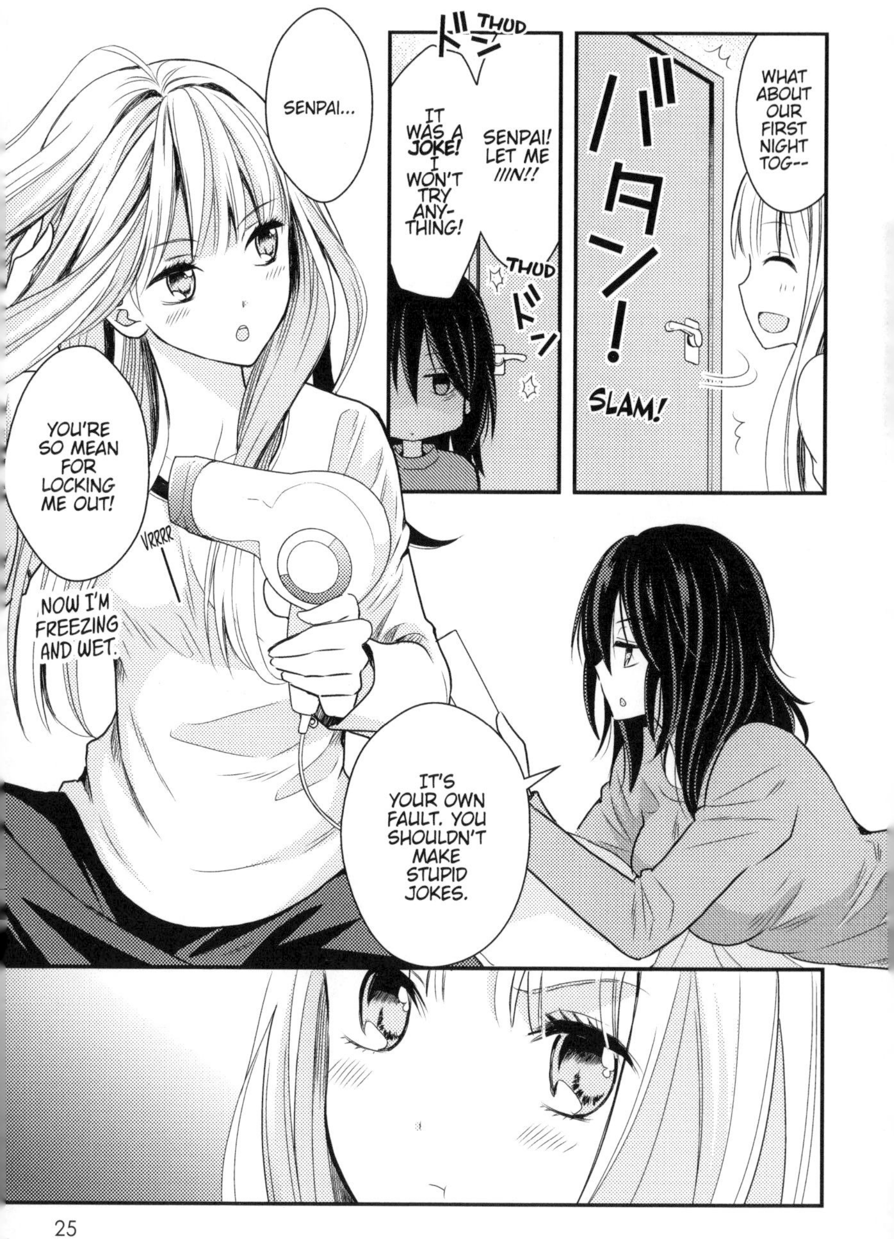
WHAT ABOUT OUR FIRST NIGHT TOG--
バタン!
SLAM!
ドン
THUD
SENPAI! LET ME IIIIN!!
IT WAS A JOKE! I WON'T TRY ANY-THING!
ドン
THUD
SENPAI...
YOU'RE SO MEAN FOR LOCKING ME OUT!
VRRRR
NOW I'M FREEZING AND WET.
IT'S YOUR OWN FAULT. YOU SHOULDN'T MAKE STUPID JOKES.

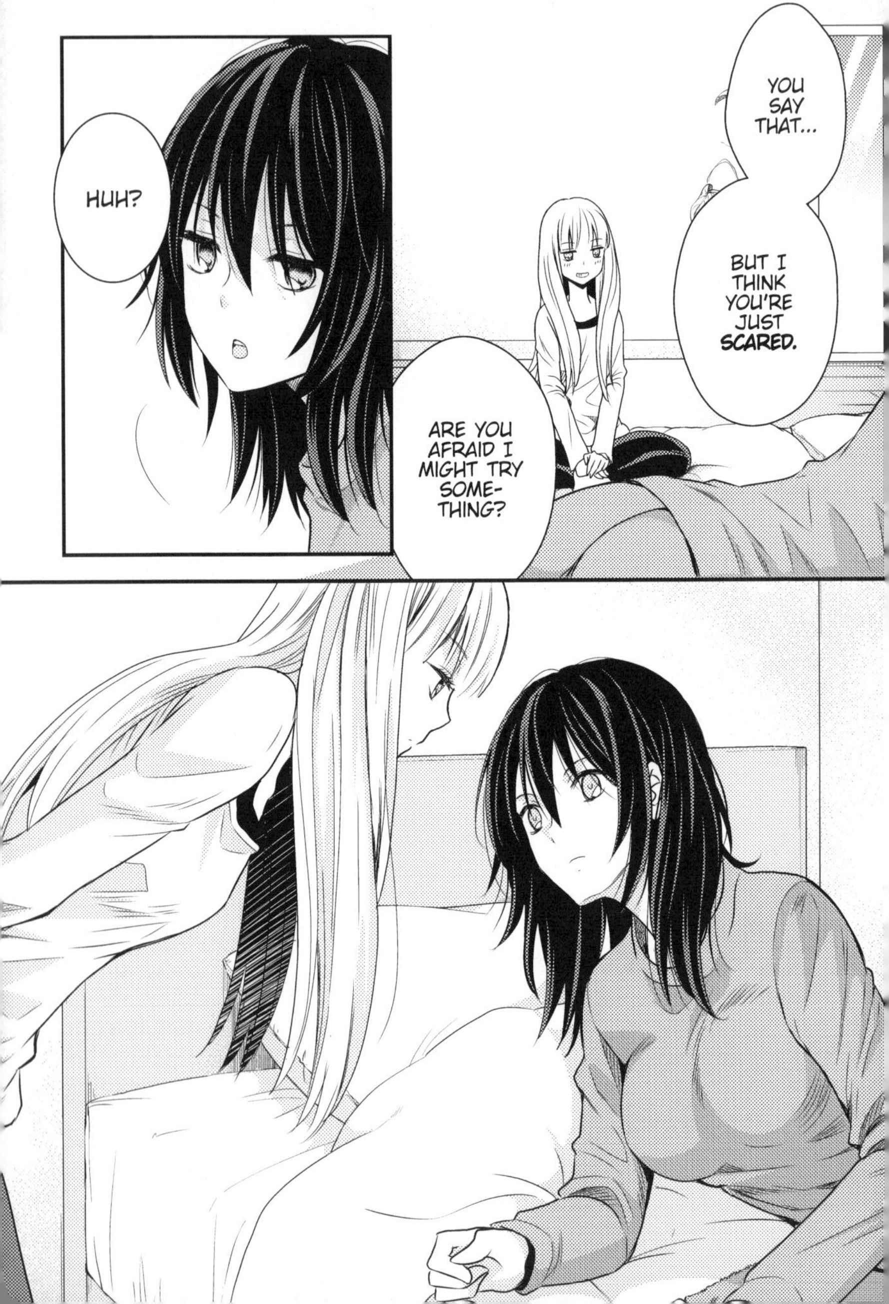
YOU SAY THAT...
BUT I THINK YOU'RE JUST **SCARED.**
ARE YOU AFRAID I MIGHT TRY SOME-THING?
HUH?

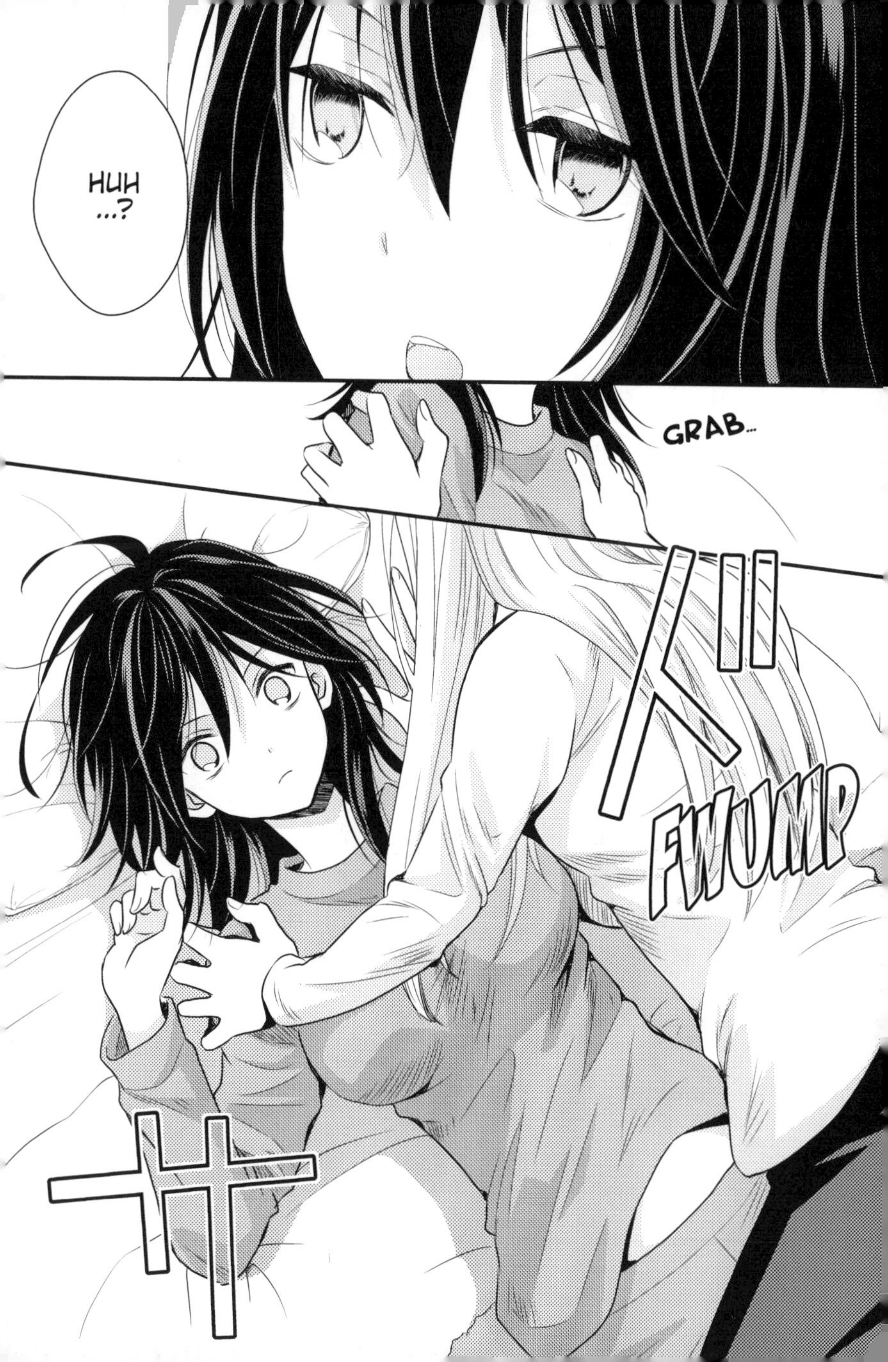
HUH ...?
GRAB...
FWUMP

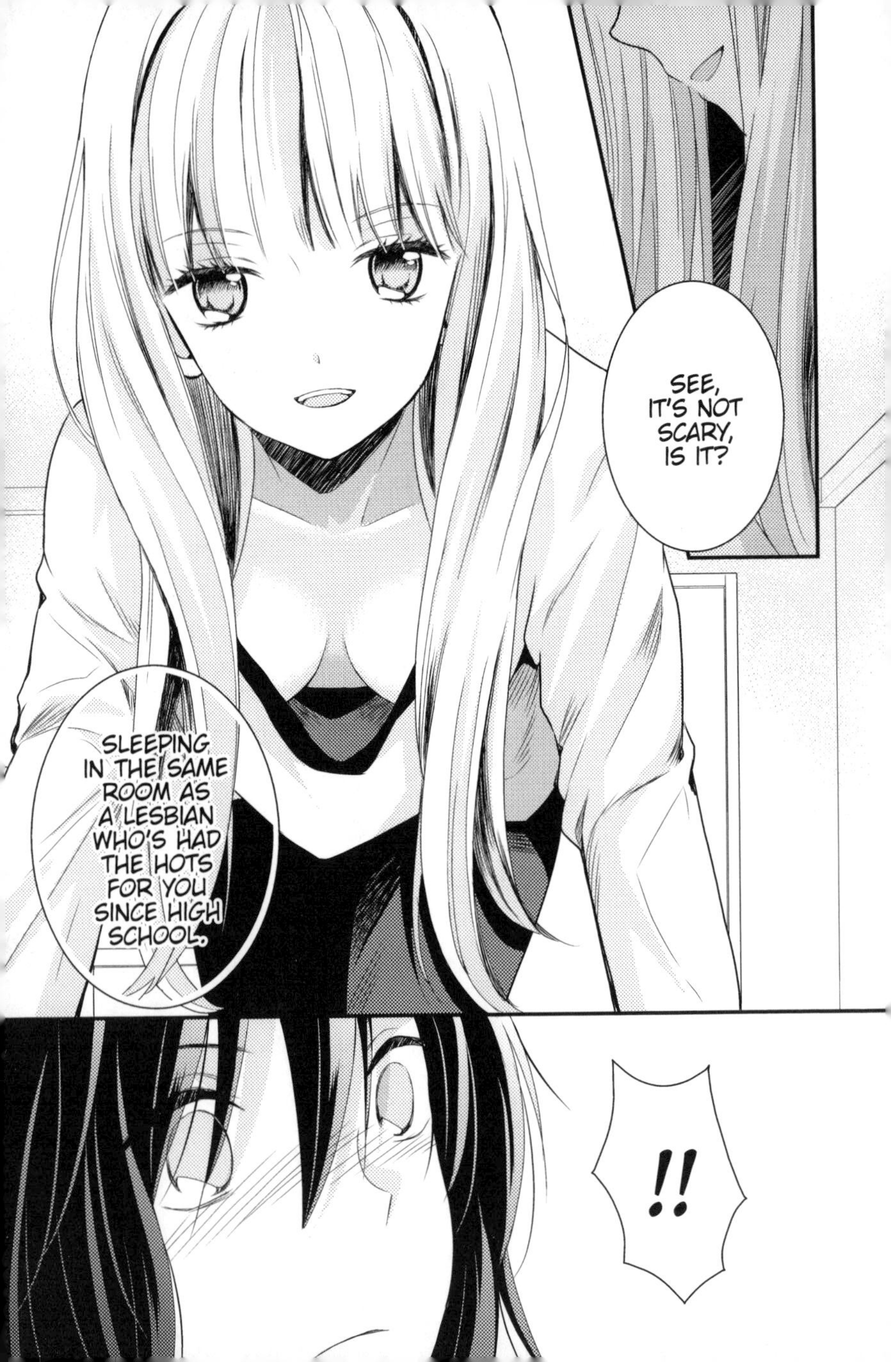
SEE, IT'S NOT SCARY, IS IT?
SLEEPING IN THE SAME ROOM AS A LESBIAN WHO'S HAD THE HOTS FOR YOU SINCE HIGH SCHOOL.
!!

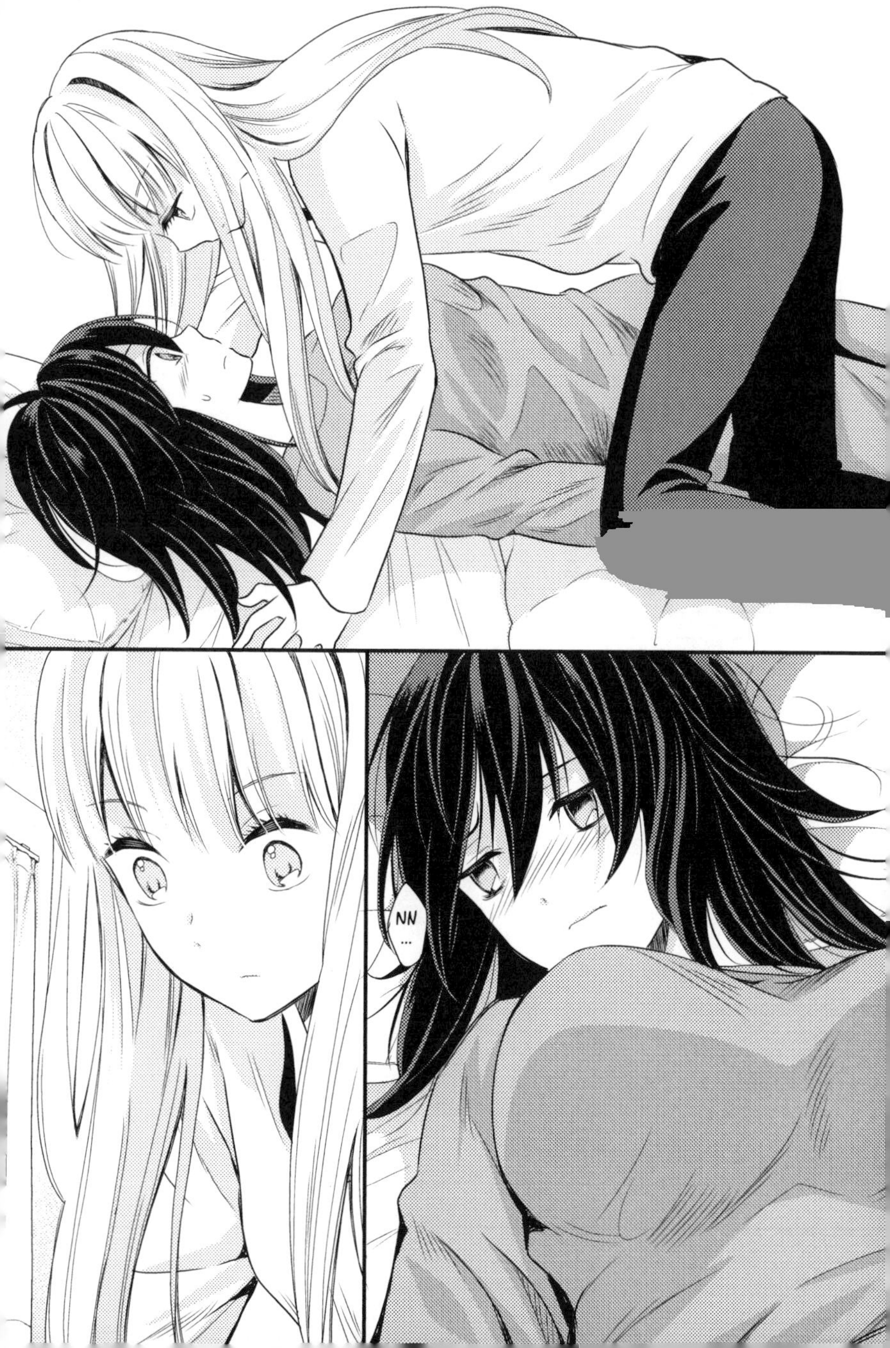
NN ...

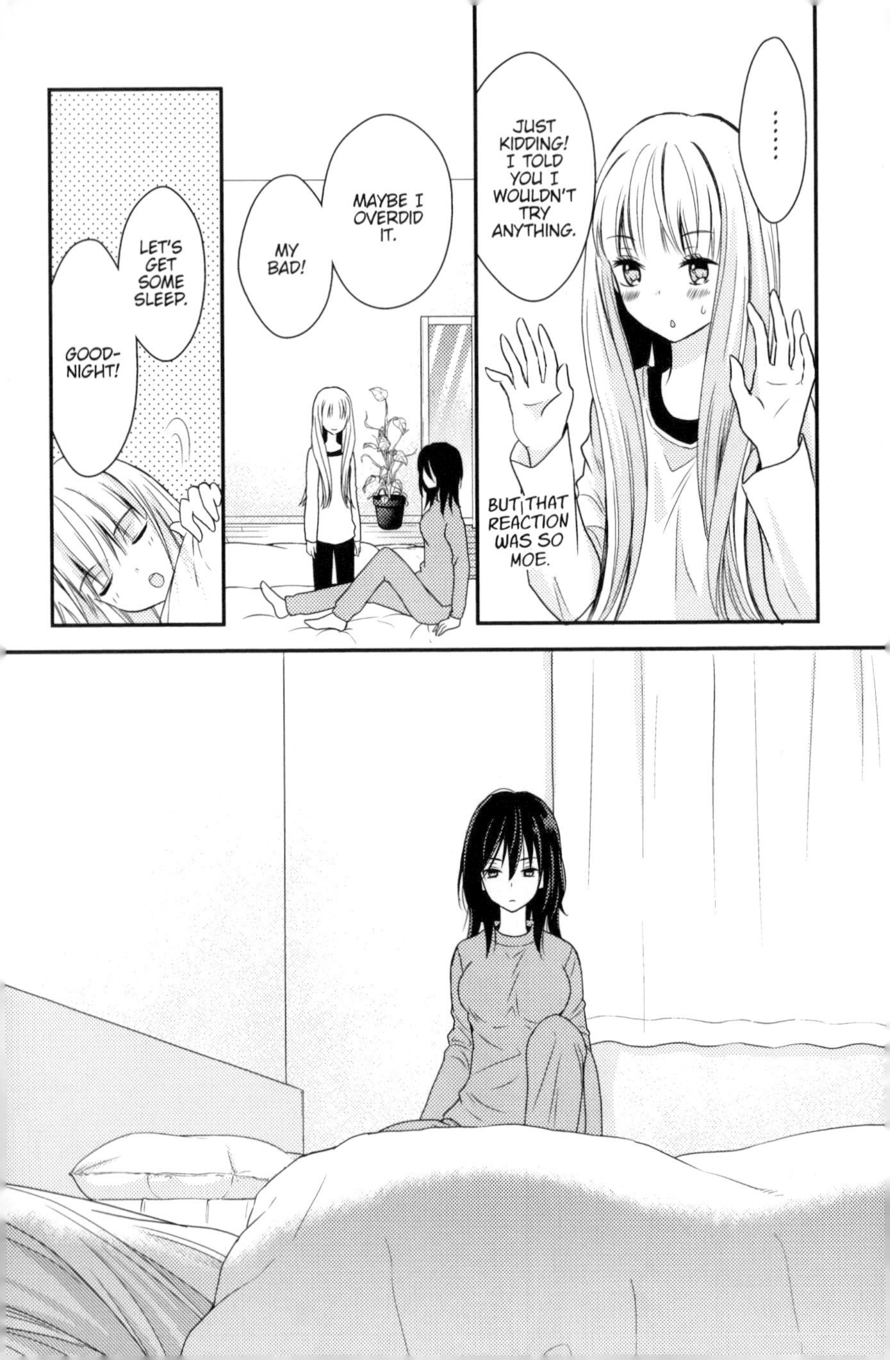
......
JUST KIDDING! I TOLD YOU I WOULDN'T TRY ANYTHING.
BUT THAT REACTION WAS SO MOE.
MAYBE I OVERDID IT.
MY BAD!
LET'S GET SOME SLEEP.
GOOD-NIGHT!

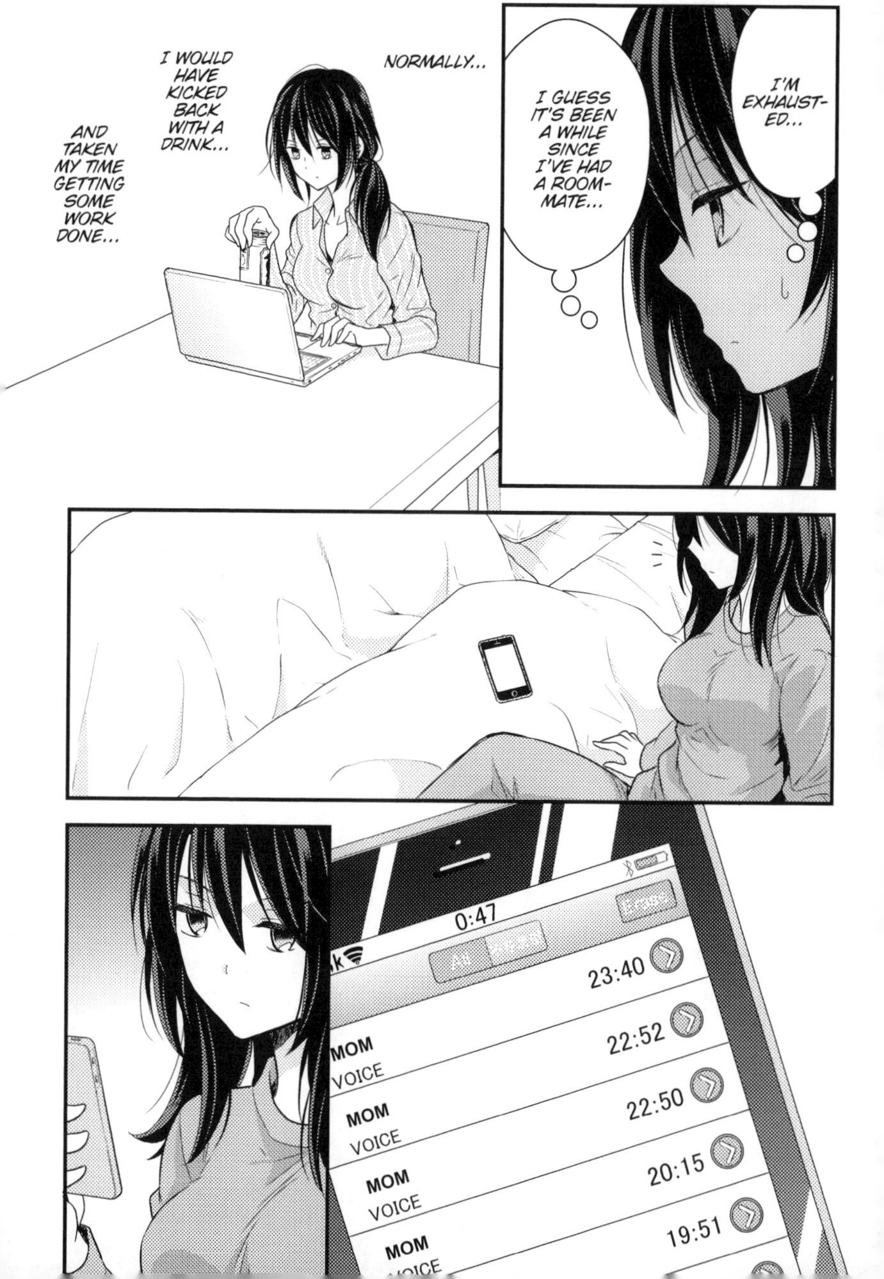
I'M EXHAUSTED...
I GUESS IT'S BEEN A WHILE SINCE I'VE HAD A ROOMMATE...
NORMALLY...
I WOULD HAVE KICKED BACK WITH A DRINK...
AND TAKEN MY TIME GETTING SOME WORK DONE...
0:47
23:40
MOM
VOICE
22:52
MOM
VOICE
22:50
MOM
VOICE
20:15
MOM
VOICE
19:51
MOM

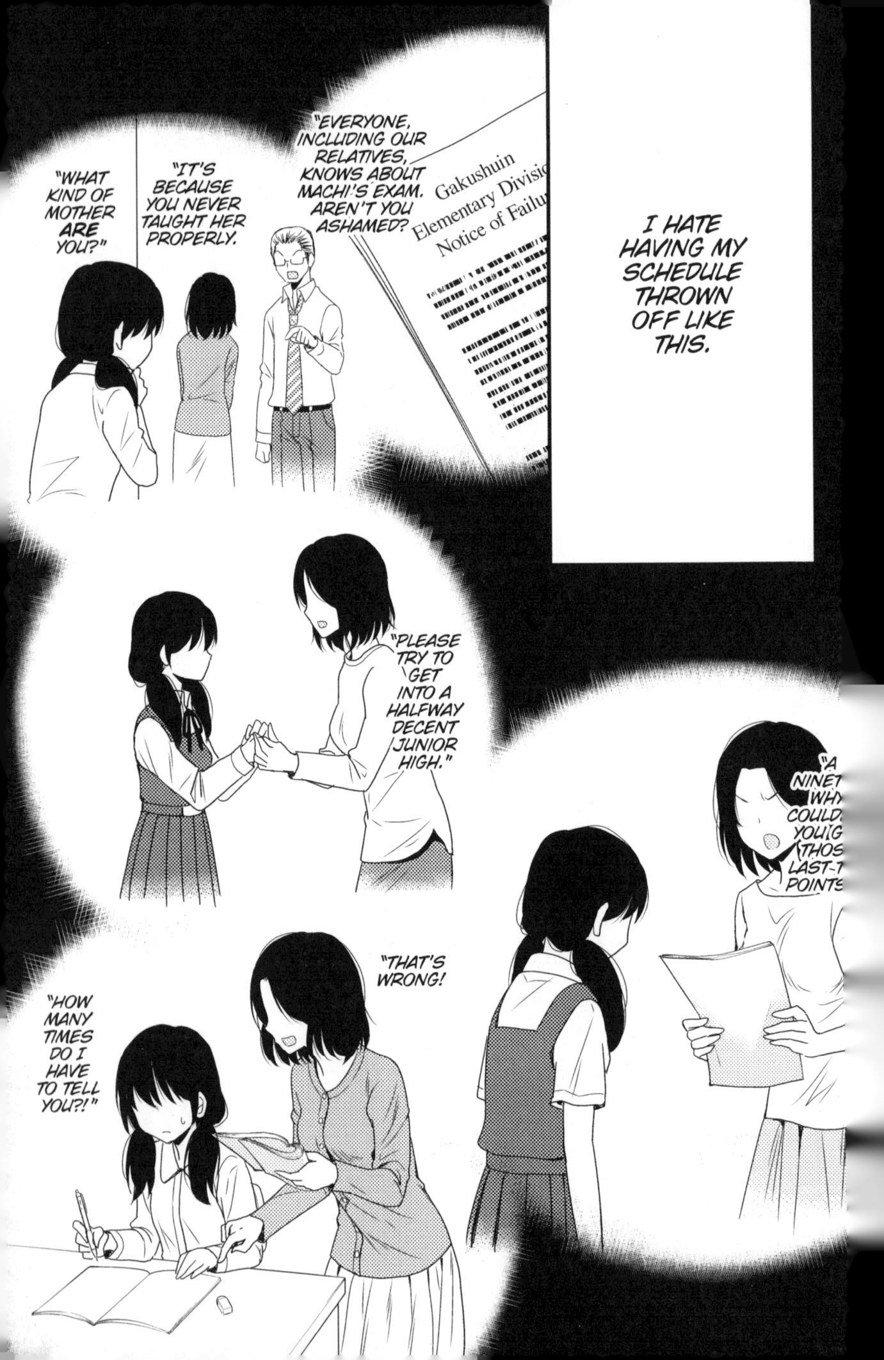
I HATE HAVING MY SCHEDULE THROWN OFF LIKE THIS.
"EVERYONE, INCLUDING OUR RELATIVES, KNOWS ABOUT MACHI'S EXAM. AREN'T YOU ASHAMED?
Gakushuin
Elementary Divisi
Notice of Failu
"IT'S BECAUSE YOU NEVER TAUGHT HER PROPERLY.
"WHAT KIND OF MOTHER ARE YOU?"
"PLEASE TRY TO GET INTO A HALFWAY DECENT JUNIOR HIGH."
"THAT'S WRONG!
"HOW MANY TIMES DO I HAVE TO TELL YOU?!"

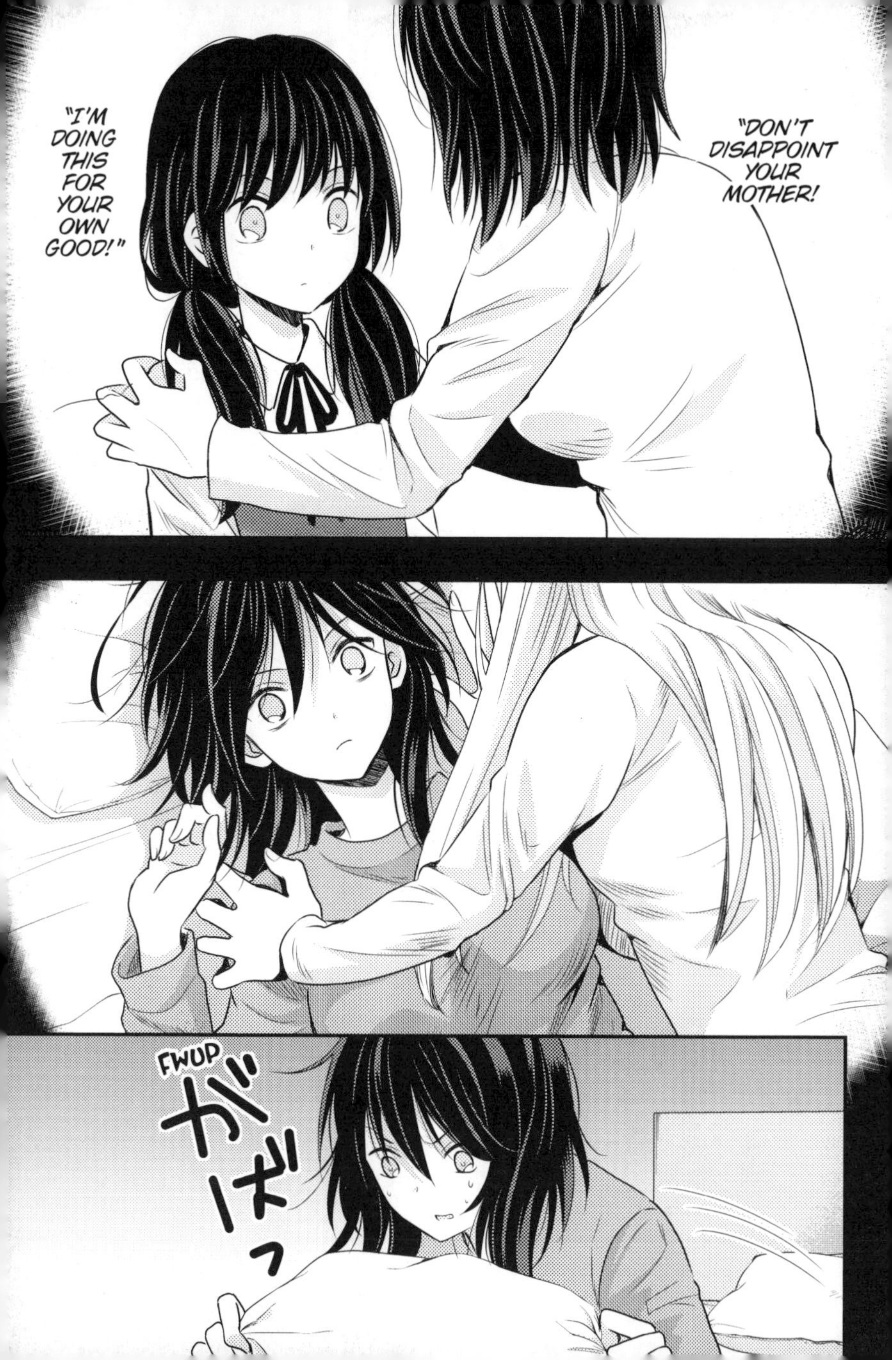
"DON'T DISAPPOINT YOUR MOTHER!
"I'M DOING THIS FOR YOUR OWN GOOD!"
FWUP
ガバーっ

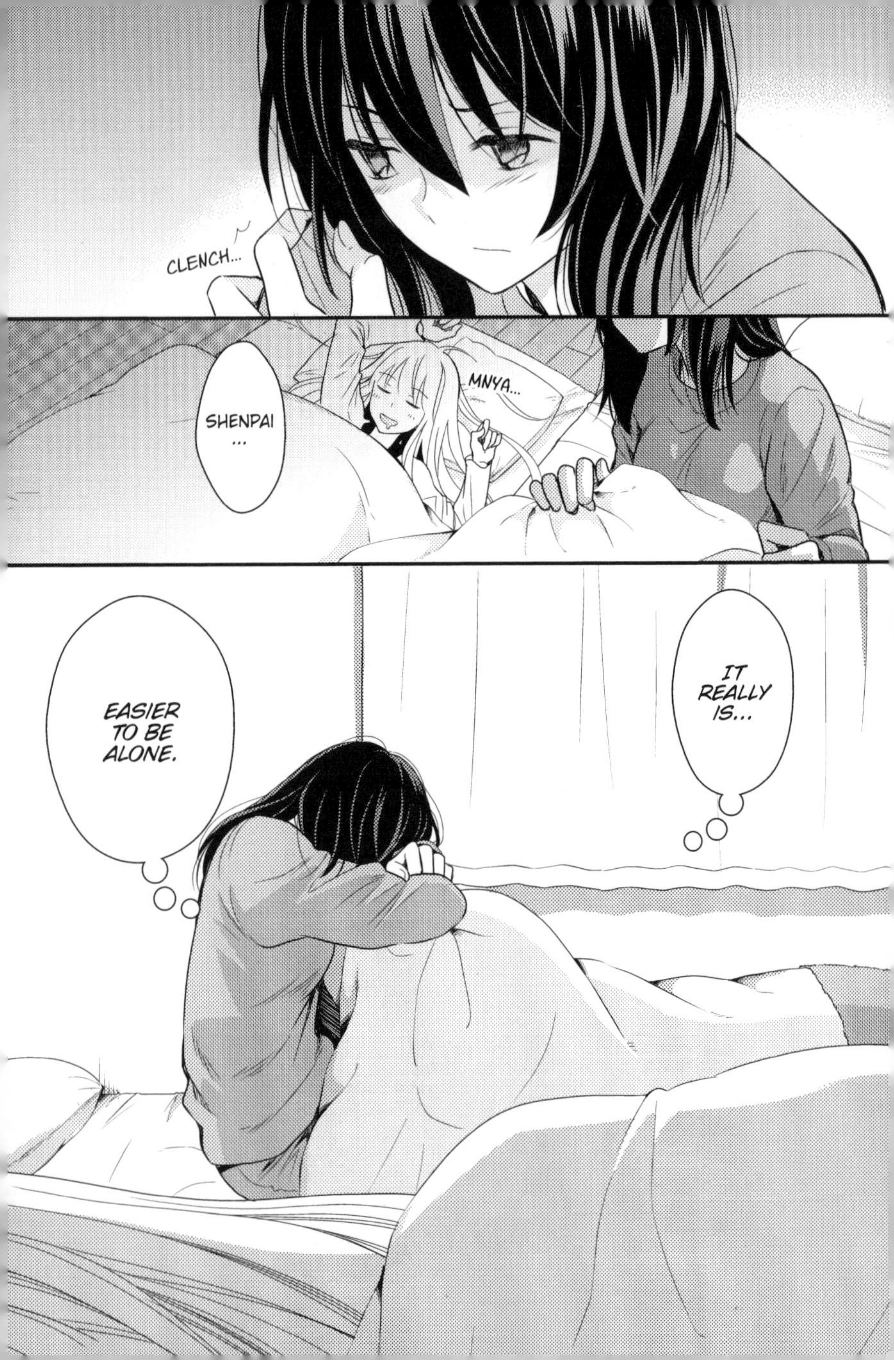
CLENCH...
MNYA...
SHENPAI ...
IT REALLY IS...
EASIER TO BE ALONE.

I Married My Best Friend (♀)
to Shut My Parents up

I Married My Best Friend(♀)
to Shut My Parents Up

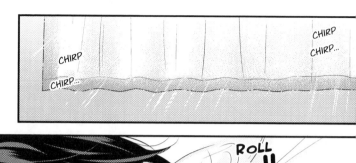

ROLL

CHIRP

CHIRP...

CHIRP

CHIRP...

M...

MY CHEST HURTS...

?!

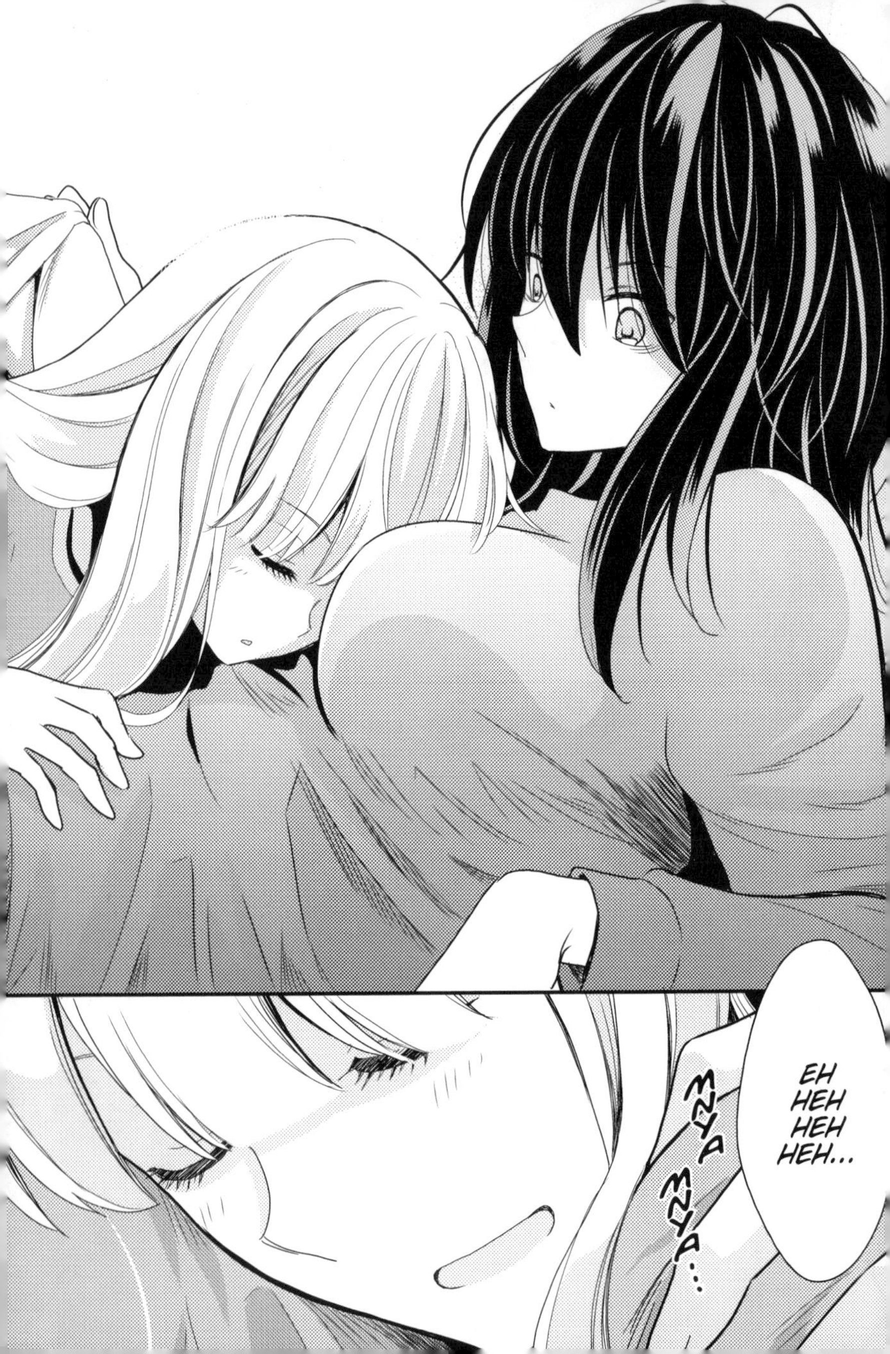
EH HEH HEH HEH...
MNYA MNYA...

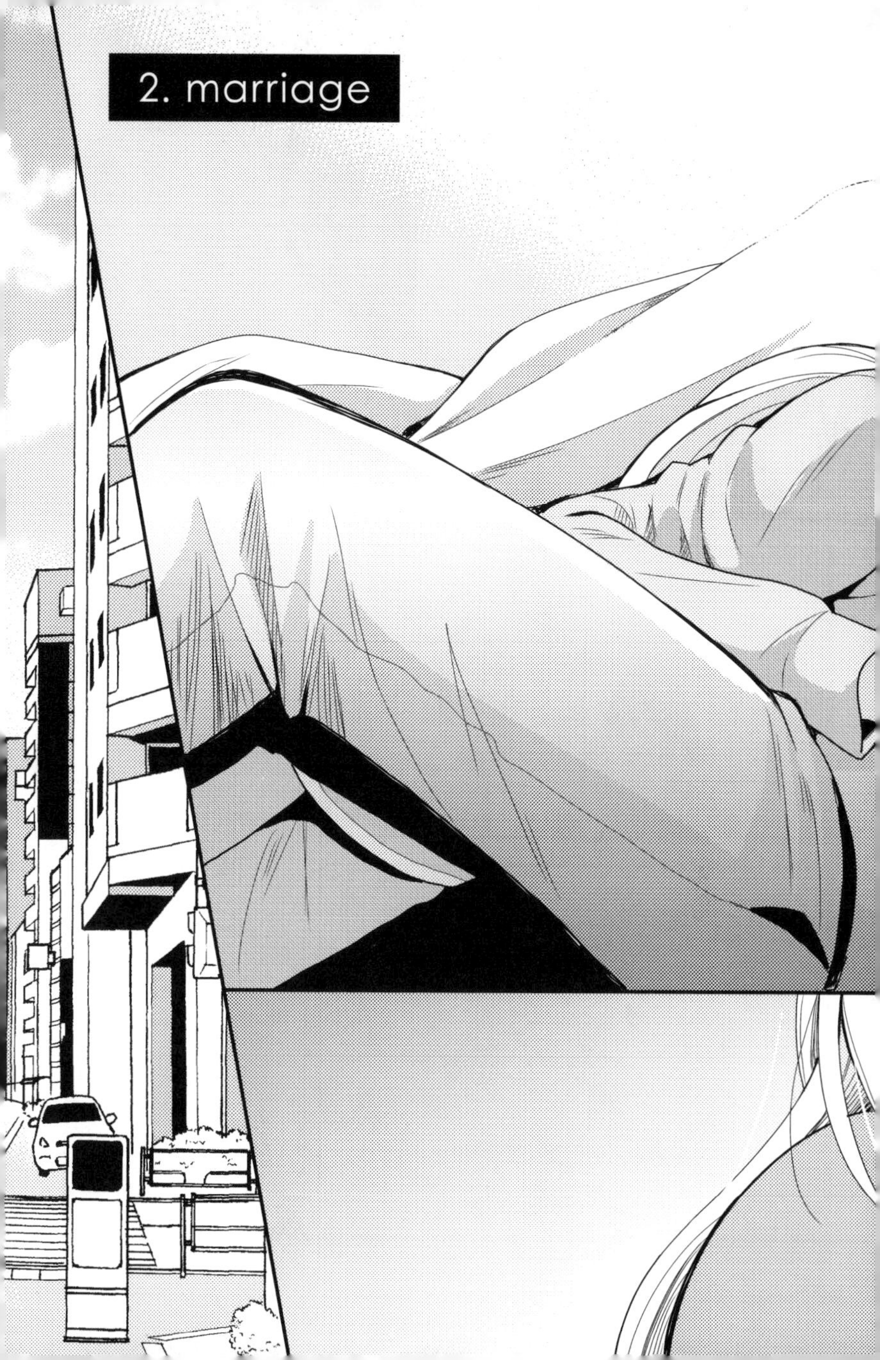
2. marriage

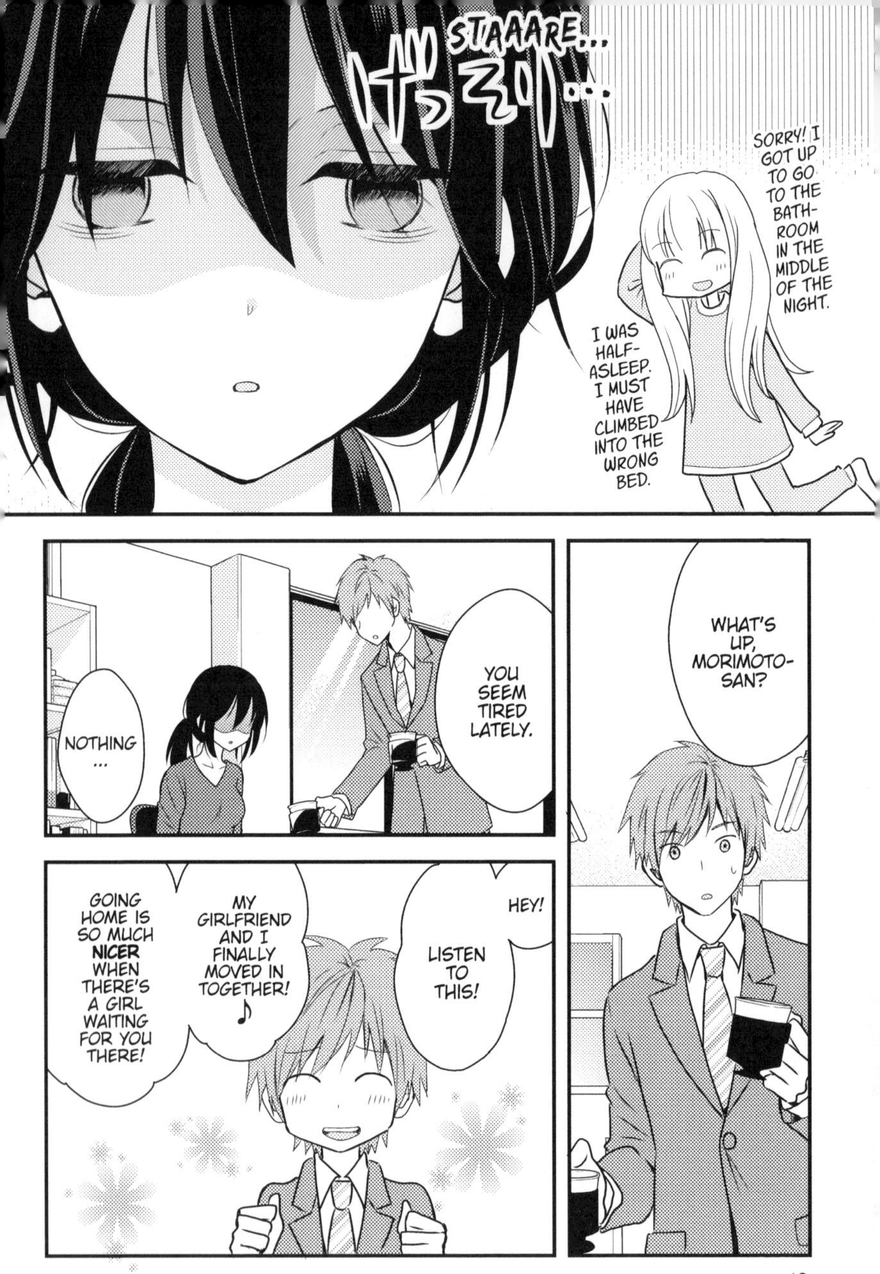
STAAARE...
SORRY! I GOT UP TO GO TO THE BATHROOM IN THE MIDDLE OF THE NIGHT.
I WAS HALF-ASLEEP. I MUST HAVE CLIMBED INTO THE WRONG BED.
WHAT'S UP, MORIMOTO-SAN?
YOU SEEM TIRED LATELY.
NOTHING...
HEY!
LISTEN TO THIS!
MY GIRLFRIEND AND I FINALLY MOVED IN TOGETHER! ♪
GOING HOME IS SO MUCH **NICER** WHEN THERE'S A GIRL WAITING FOR YOU THERE!

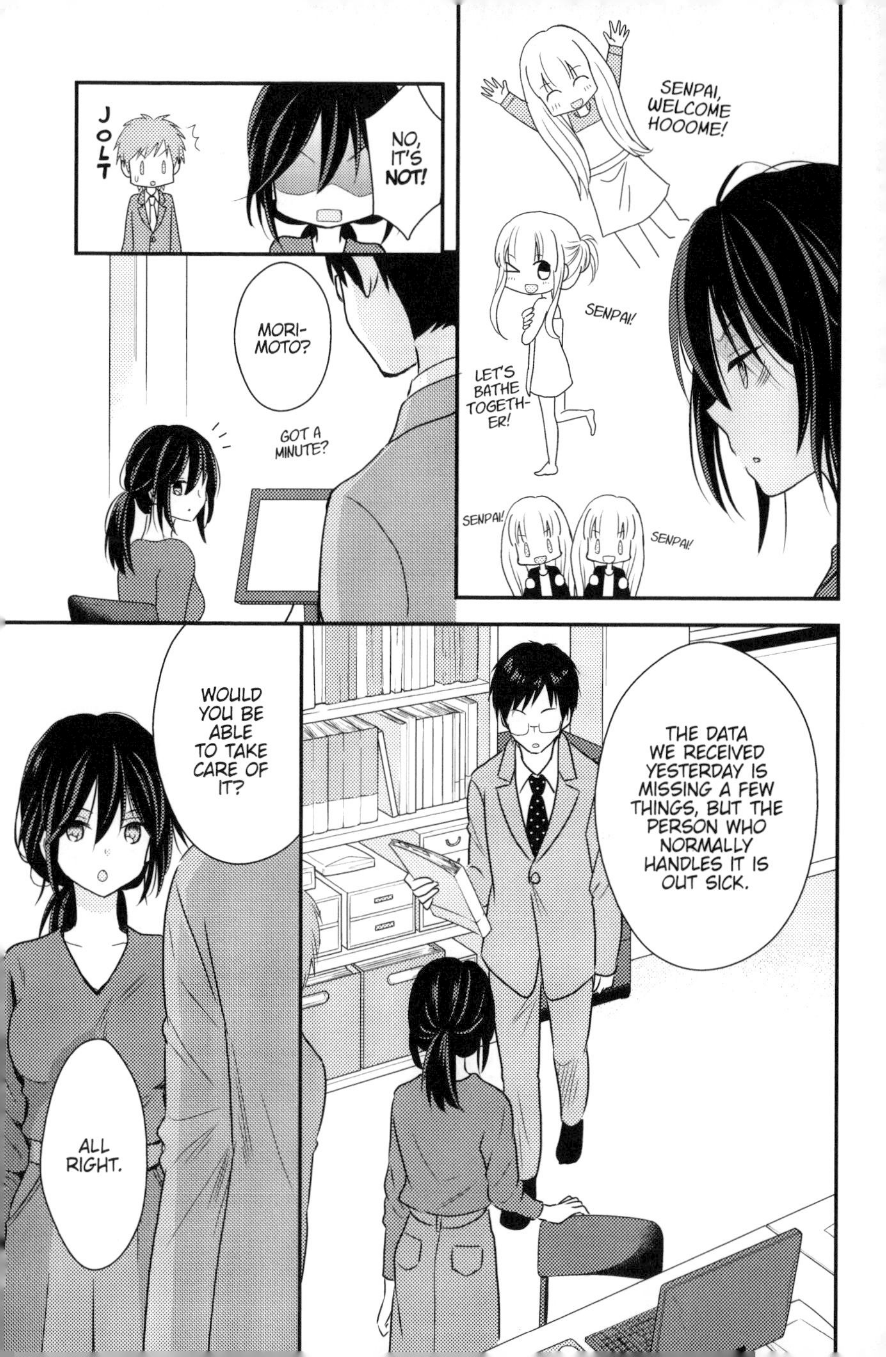
SENPAI, WELCOME HOOOME!
SENPAI!
LET'S BATHE TOGETH-ER!
SENPAI!
SENPAI!
NO, IT'S NOT!
JOLT
MORI-MOTO?
GOT A MINUTE?
THE DATA WE RECEIVED YESTERDAY IS MISSING A FEW THINGS, BUT THE PERSON WHO NORMALLY HANDLES IT IS OUT SICK.
WOULD YOU BE ABLE TO TAKE CARE OF IT?
ALL RIGHT.

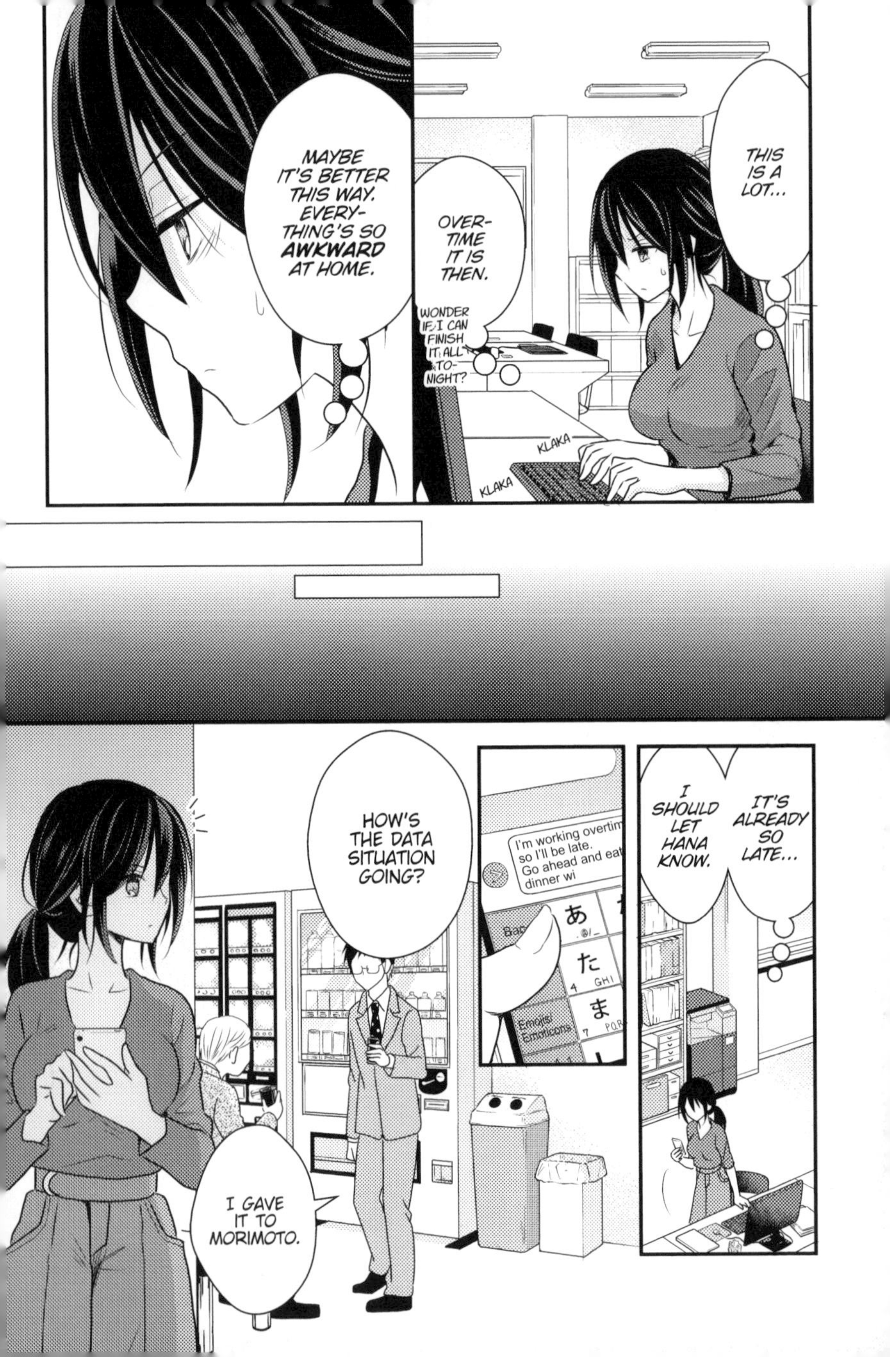
THIS IS A LOT...
OVER-TIME IT IS THEN.
WONDER IF I CAN FINISH IT ALL TO-NIGHT?
KLAKA
KLAKA
MAYBE IT'S BETTER THIS WAY. EVERY-THING'S SO AWKWARD AT HOME.
IT'S ALREADY SO LATE...
I SHOULD LET HANA KNOW.
I'm working overtim so I'll be late. Go ahead and eat dinner wi
あ
た
4 GHI
ま
7 PQR
Emojis/ Emoticons
HOW'S THE DATA SITUATION GOING?
I GAVE IT TO MORIMOTO.

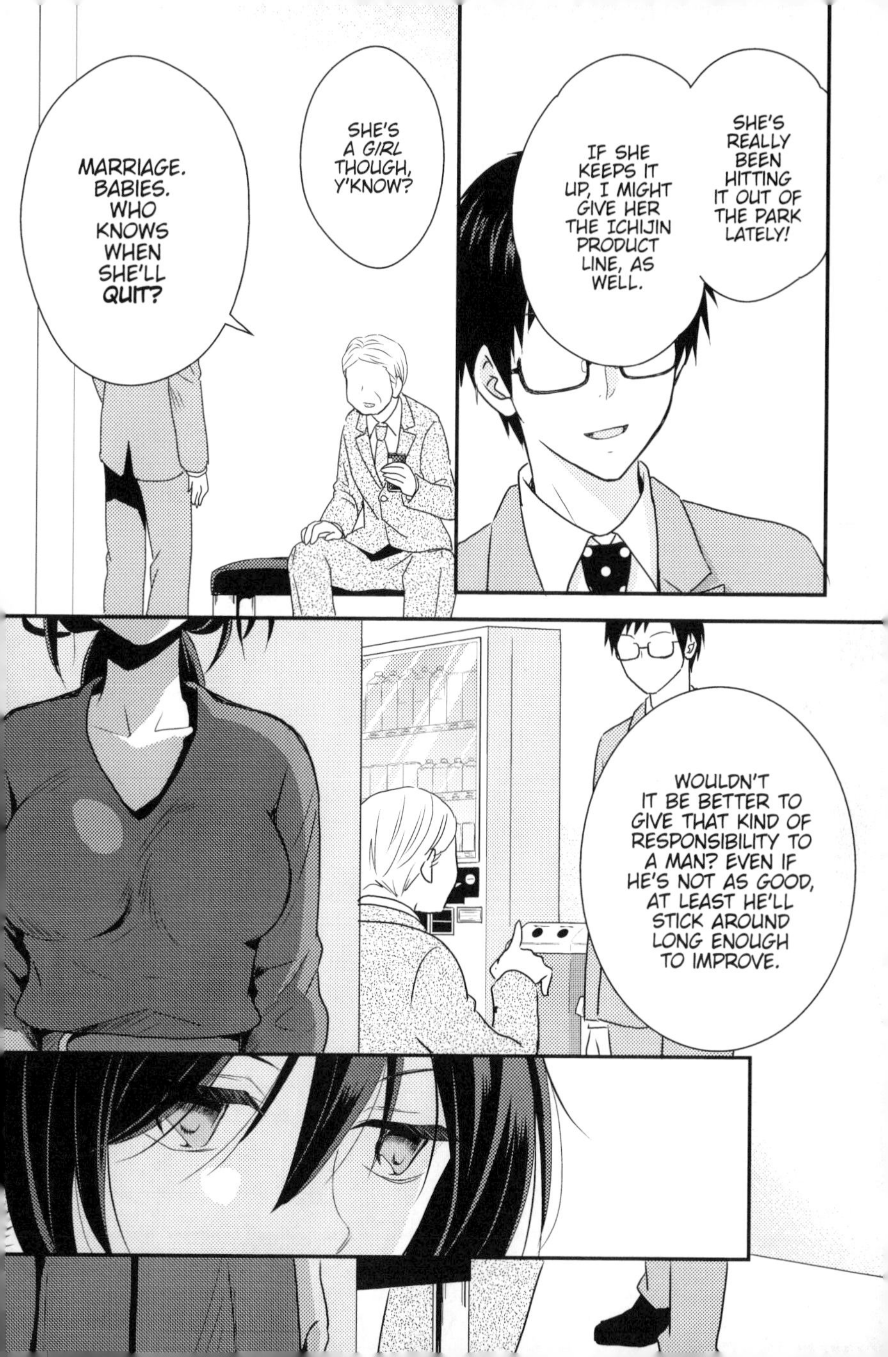
SHE'S REALLY BEEN HITTING IT OUT OF THE PARK LATELY!
IF SHE KEEPS IT UP, I MIGHT GIVE HER THE ICHIJIN PRODUCT LINE, AS WELL.
SHE'S A *GIRL* THOUGH, Y'KNOW?
MARRIAGE. BABIES. WHO KNOWS WHEN SHE'LL **QUIT?**
WOULDN'T IT BE BETTER TO GIVE THAT KIND OF RESPONSIBILITY TO A MAN? EVEN IF HE'S NOT AS GOOD, AT LEAST HE'LL STICK AROUND LONG ENOUGH TO IMPROVE.

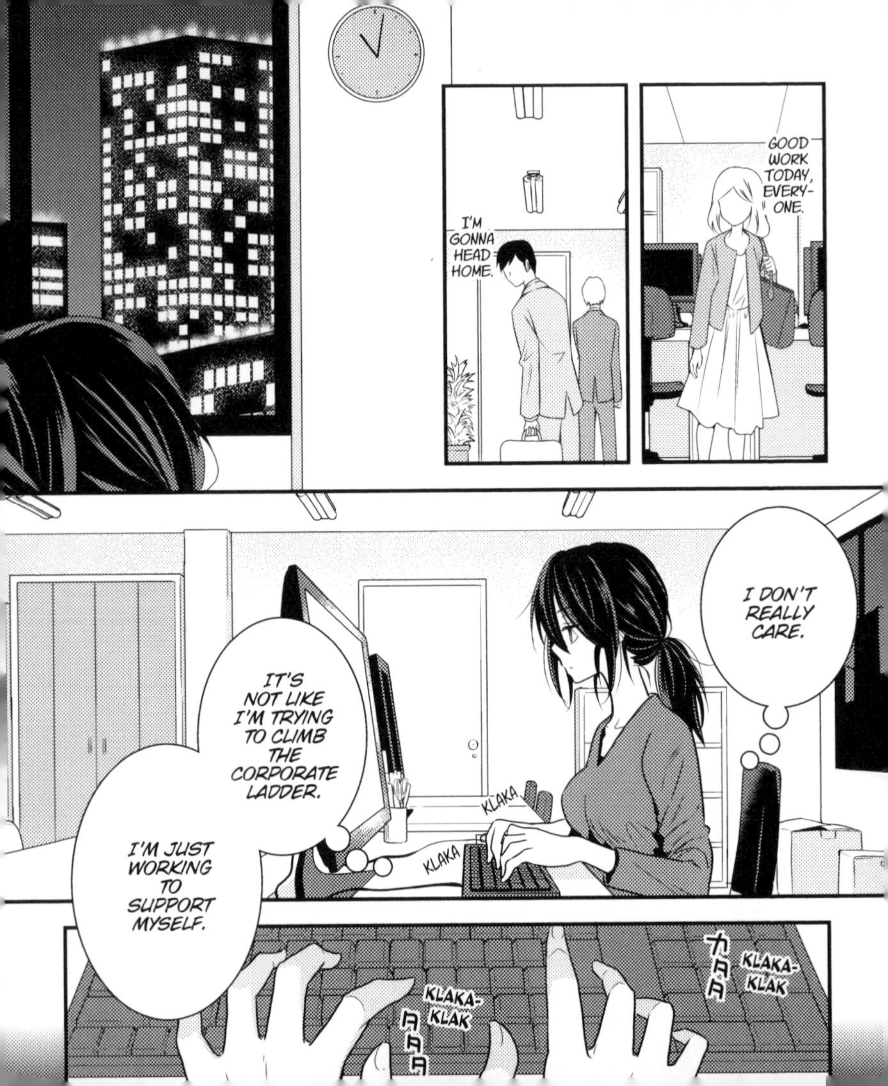
GOOD WORK TODAY, EVERY-ONE.
I'M GONNA HEAD HOME.
I DON'T REALLY CARE.
IT'S NOT LIKE I'M TRYING TO CLIMB THE CORPORATE LADDER.
KLAKA
KLAKA
I'M JUST WORKING TO SUPPORT MYSELF.
カタタ
KLAKA-KLAK
KLAKA-KLAK
カタタ

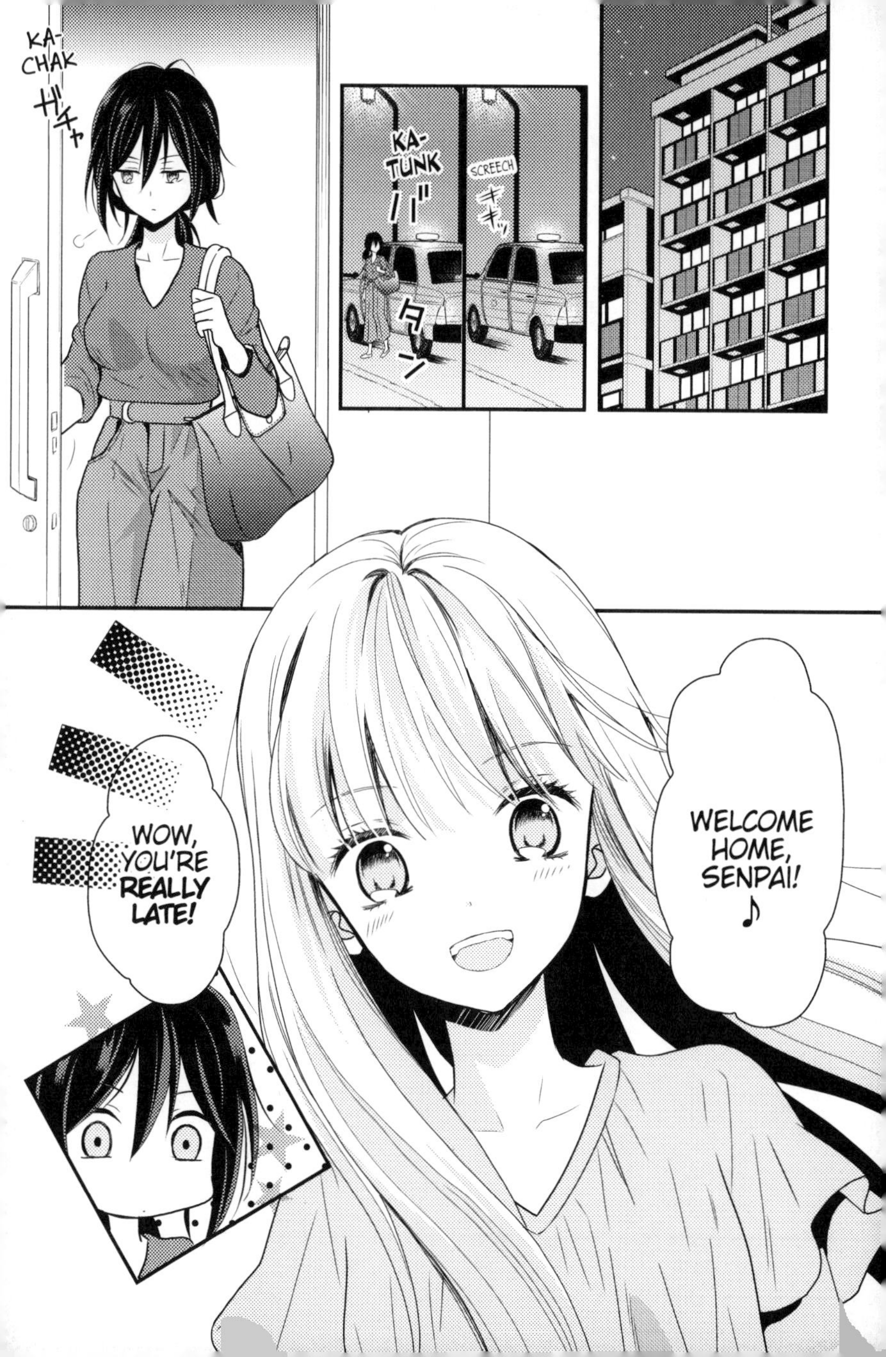
SCREECH
キキッ
KA-TUNK
バタン
KA-CHAK
ガチャ
WELCOME HOME, SENPAI! ♪
WOW, YOU'RE REALLY LATE!

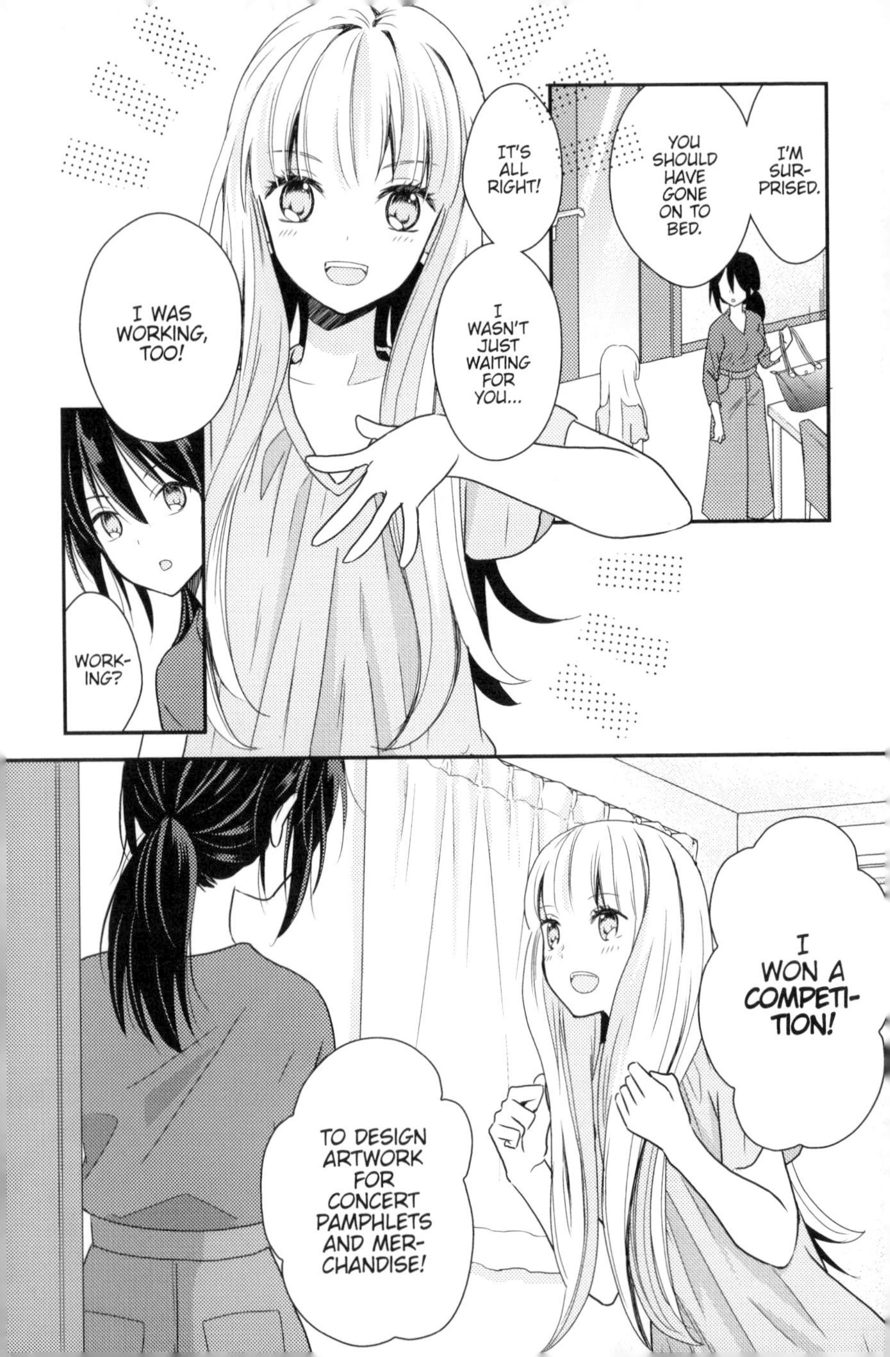

I'M SURPRISED.
YOU SHOULD HAVE GONE ON TO BED.
IT'S ALL RIGHT!
I WASN'T JUST WAITING FOR YOU...
I WAS WORKING, TOO!
WORKING?
I WON A COMPETITION!
TO DESIGN ARTWORK FOR CONCERT PAMPHLETS AND MERCHANDISE!

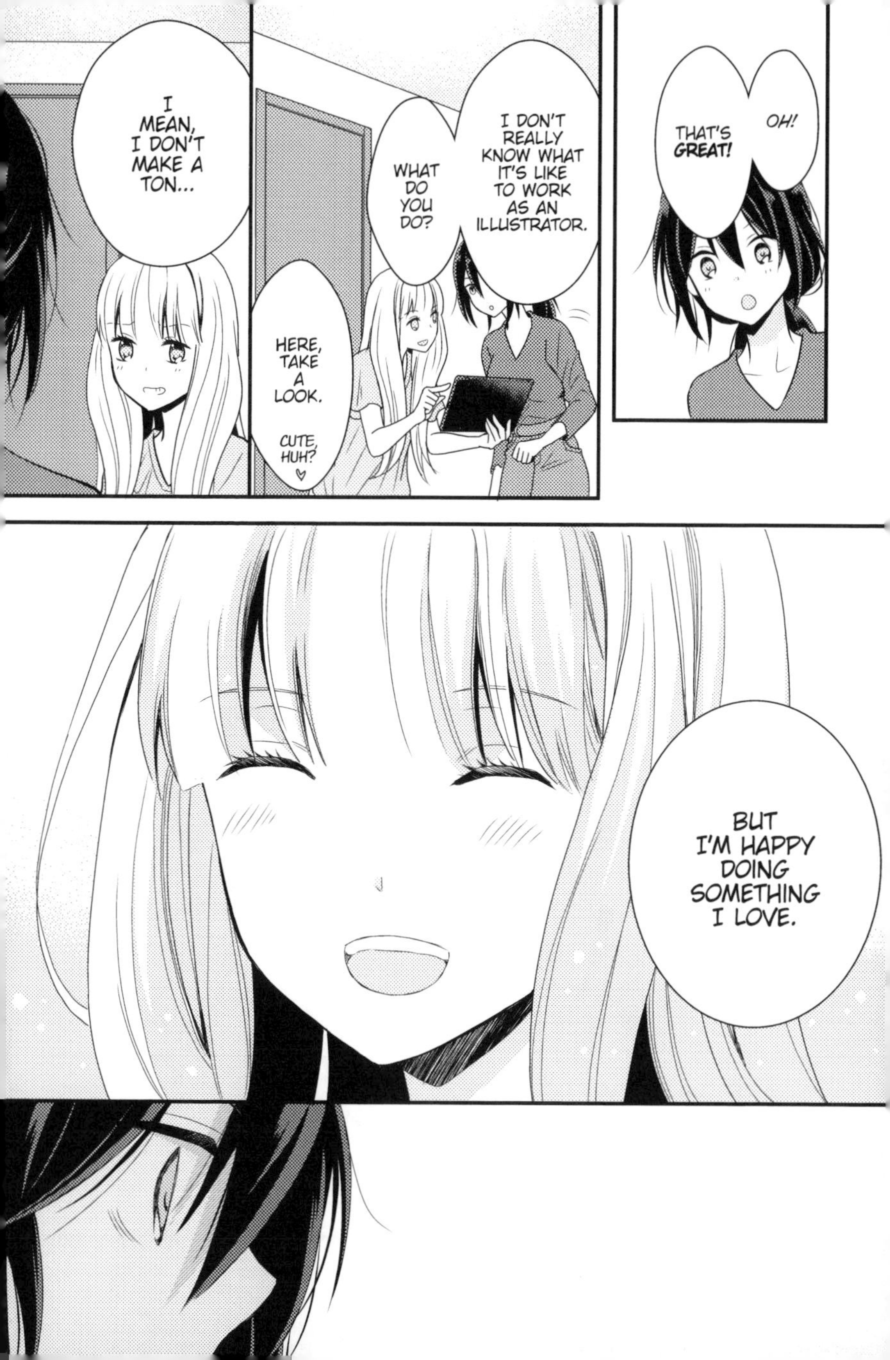
OH!
THAT'S **GREAT!**
I DON'T REALLY KNOW WHAT IT'S LIKE TO WORK AS AN ILLUSTRATOR.
WHAT DO YOU DO?
HERE, TAKE A LOOK.
CUTE, HUH? ♡
I MEAN, I DON'T MAKE A TON...
BUT I'M HAPPY DOING SOMETHING I LOVE.

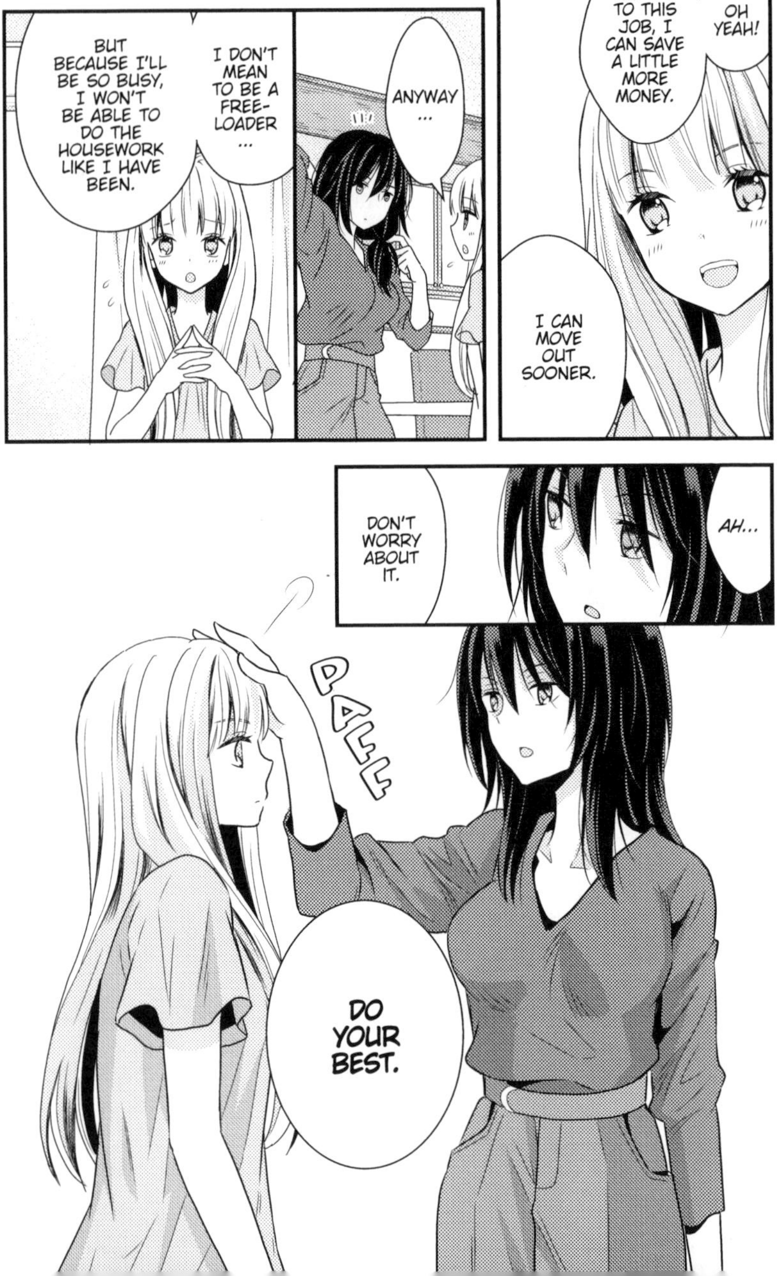
OH YEAH!
THANKS TO THIS JOB, I CAN SAVE A LITTLE MORE MONEY.
I CAN MOVE OUT SOONER.
ANYWAY ...
I DON'T MEAN TO BE A FREE-LOADER ...
BUT BECAUSE I'LL BE SO BUSY, I WON'T BE ABLE TO DO THE HOUSEWORK LIKE I HAVE BEEN.
AH...
DON'T WORRY ABOUT IT.
PAFF
DO YOUR BEST.

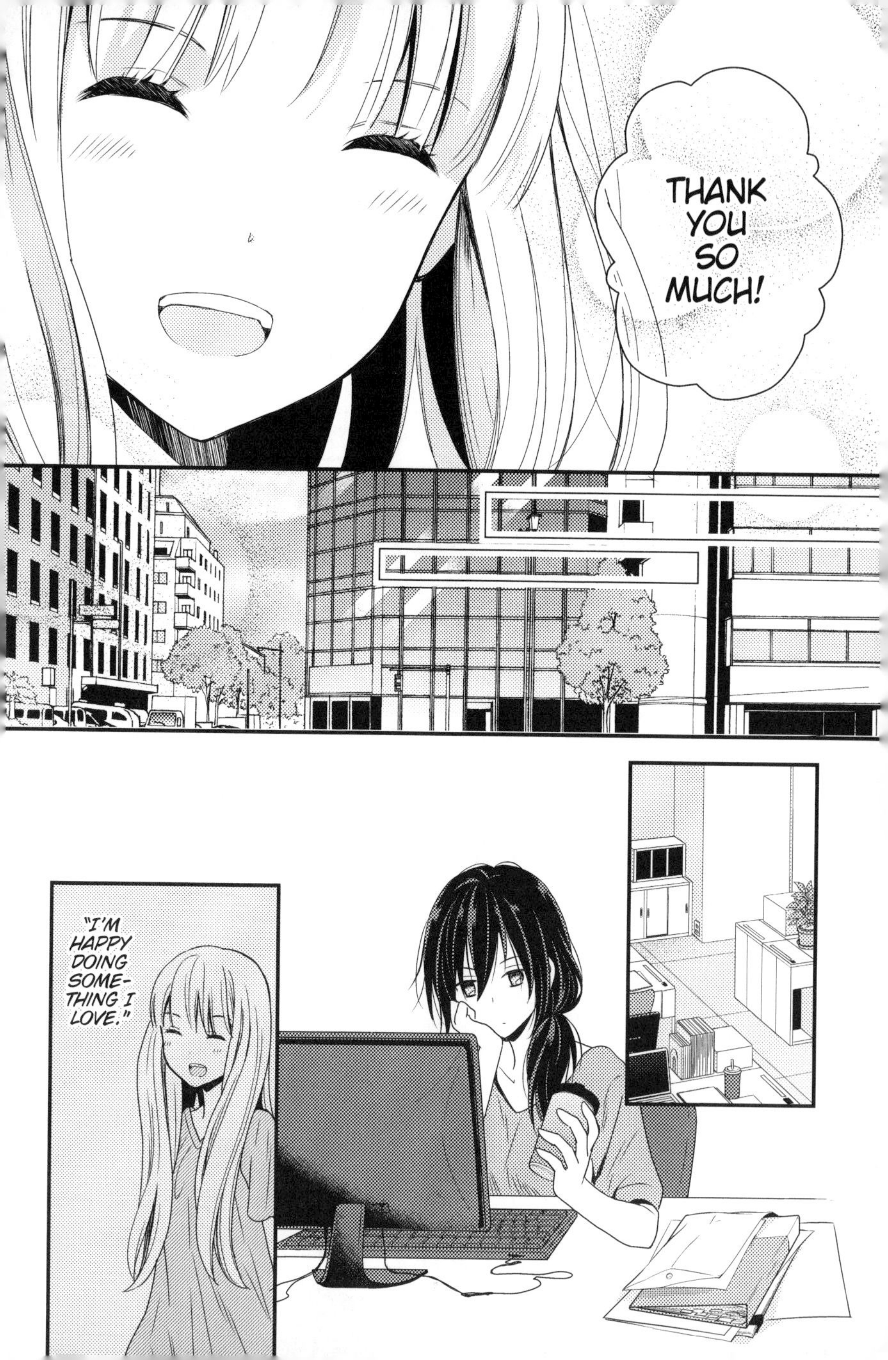
THANK YOU SO MUCH!
"I'M HAPPY DOING SOME-THING I LOVE."

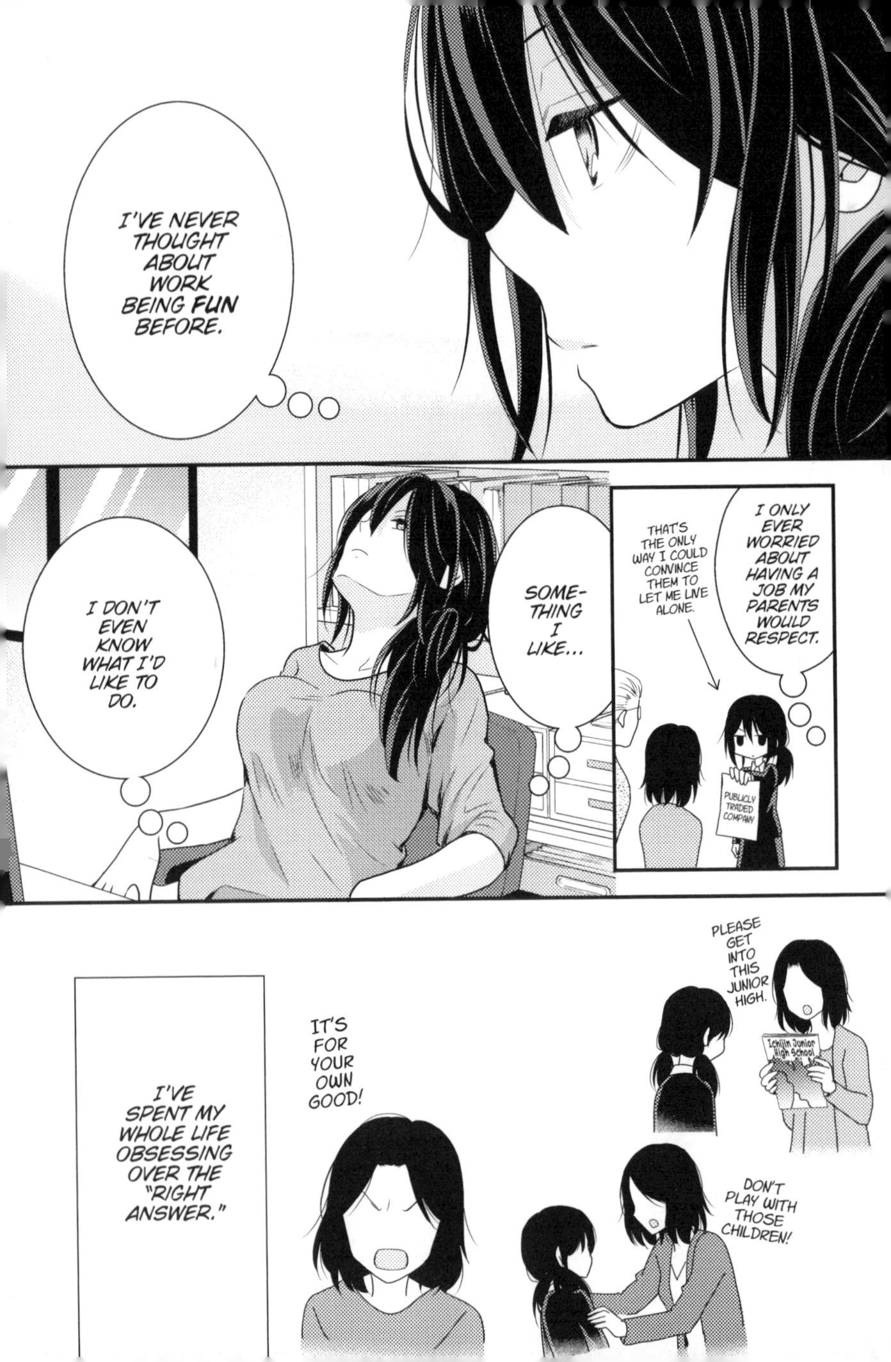
I'VE NEVER THOUGHT ABOUT WORK BEING FUN BEFORE.
I ONLY EVER WORRIED ABOUT HAVING A JOB MY PARENTS WOULD RESPECT.
THAT'S THE ONLY WAY I COULD CONVINCE THEM TO LET ME LIVE ALONE.
PUBLICLY TRADED COMPANY
SOME-THING I LIKE...
I DON'T EVEN KNOW WHAT I'D LIKE TO DO.
PLEASE GET INTO THIS JUNIOR HIGH.
Ichijin Junior High School
DON'T PLAY WITH THOSE CHILDREN!
IT'S FOR YOUR OWN GOOD!
I'VE SPENT MY WHOLE LIFE OBSESSING OVER THE "RIGHT ANSWER."

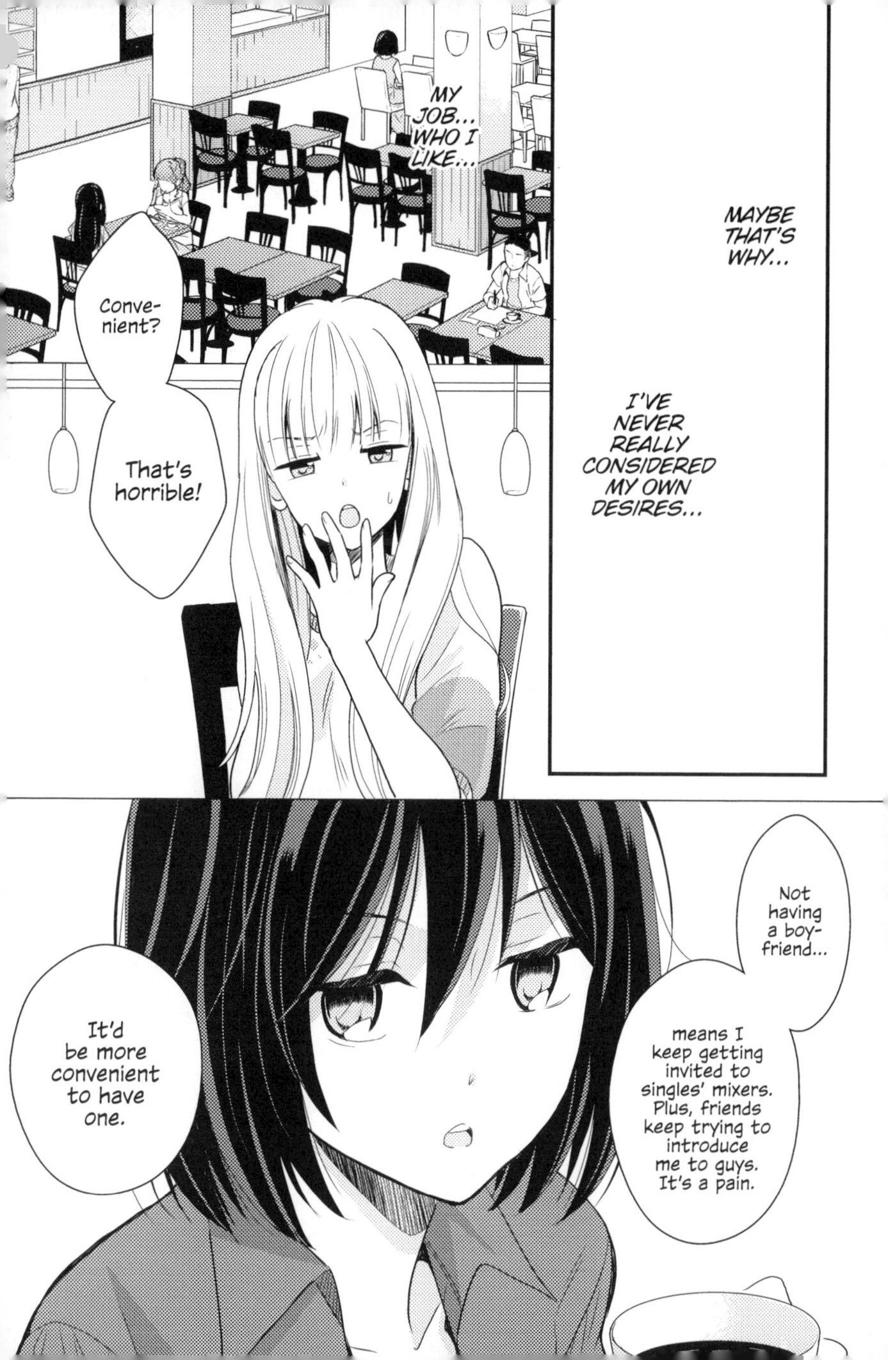

MAYBE THAT'S WHY...
I'VE NEVER REALLY CONSIDERED MY OWN DESIRES...
MY JOB... WHO I LIKE...
Convenient?
That's horrible!
Not having a boyfriend...
means I keep getting invited to singles' mixers. Plus, friends keep trying to introduce me to guys. It's a pain.
It'd be more convenient to have one.

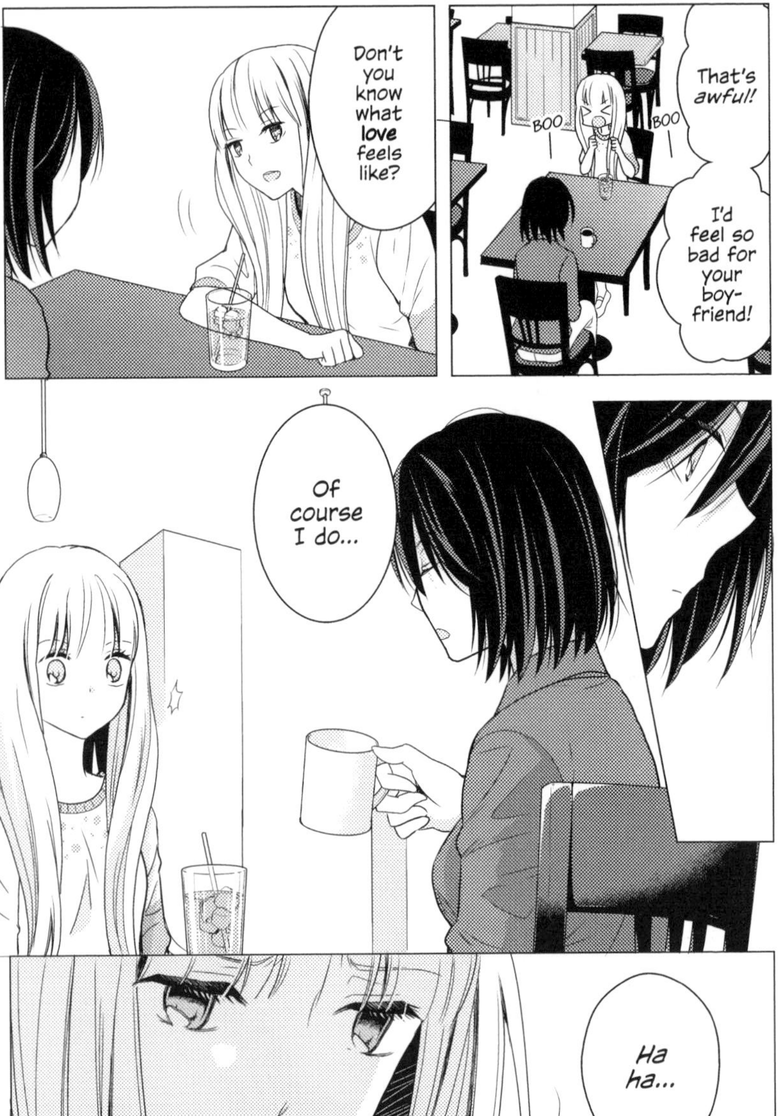
That's *awful!*
BOO
BOO
I'd feel so bad for your boy-friend!
Don't you know what **love** feels like?
Of course I do...
Ha ha...

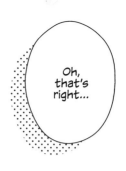

Oh, that's right...

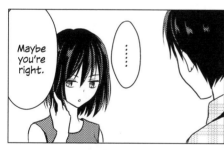

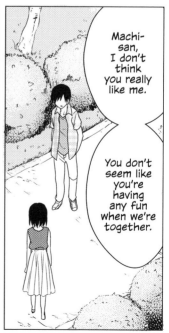

Machi-san, I don't think you really like me.
You don't seem like you're having any fun when we're together.
......
Maybe you're right.
There's this other girl who says she's into me...

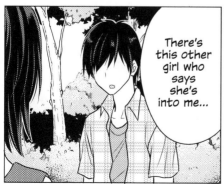

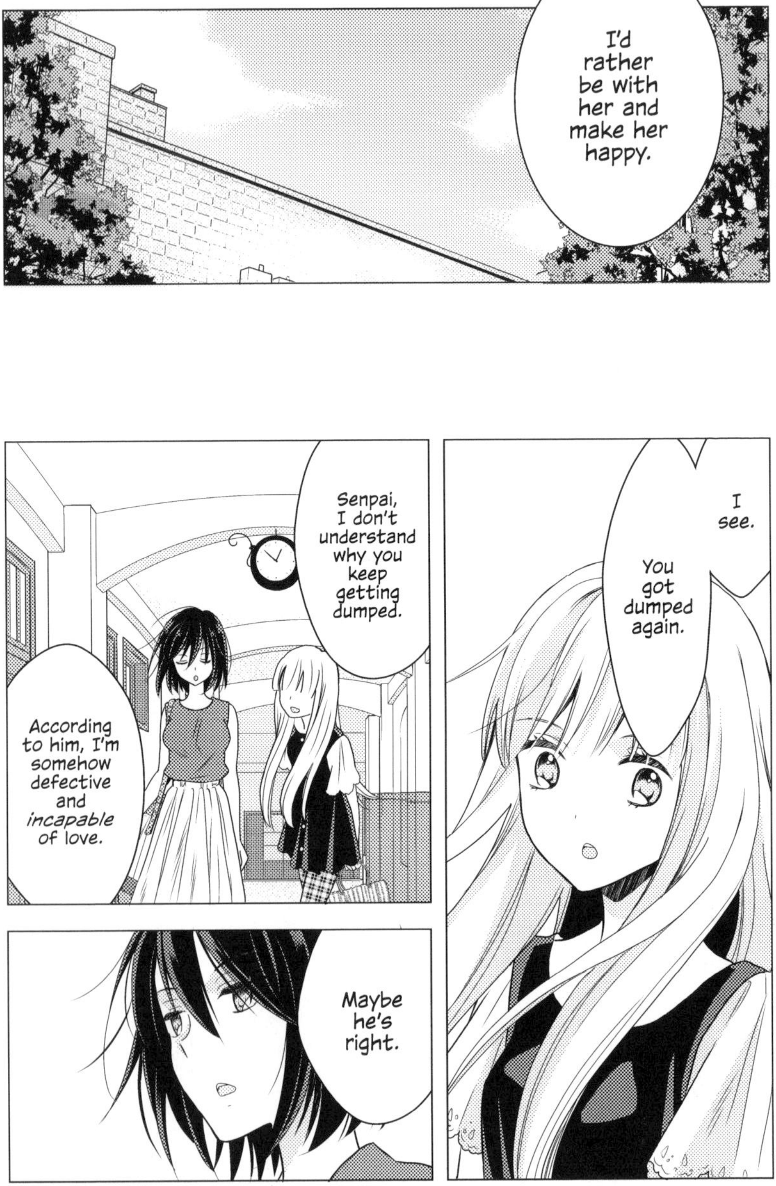
I'd rather be with her and make her happy.
I see.
You got dumped again.
Senpai, I don't understand why you keep getting dumped.
According to him, I'm somehow defective and *incapable* of love.
Maybe he's right.

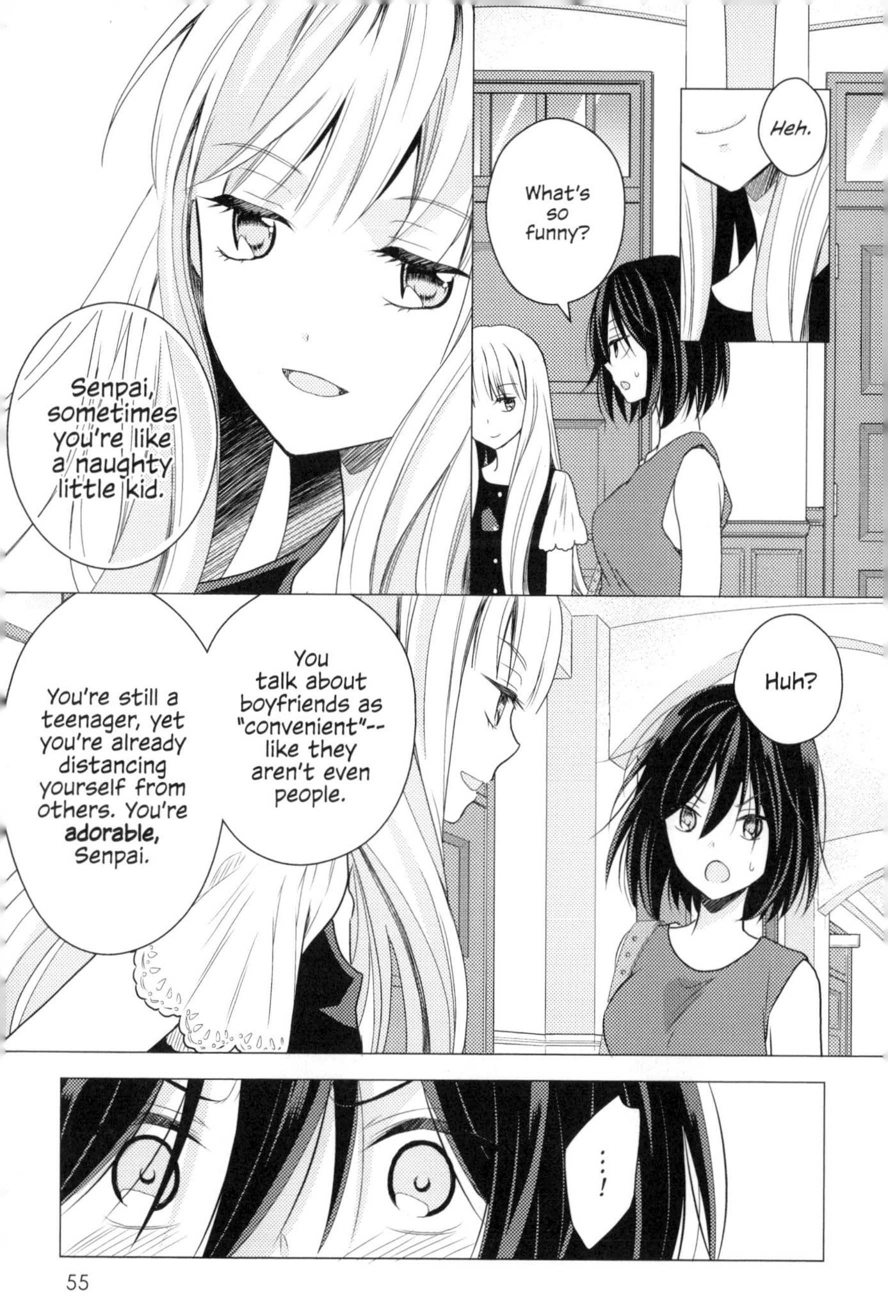
Heh.
What's so funny?
Senpai, sometimes you're like a naughty little kid.
Huh?
You talk about boyfriends as "convenient"-- like they aren't even people.
You're still a teenager, yet you're already distancing yourself from others. You're **adorable,** Senpai.
...!

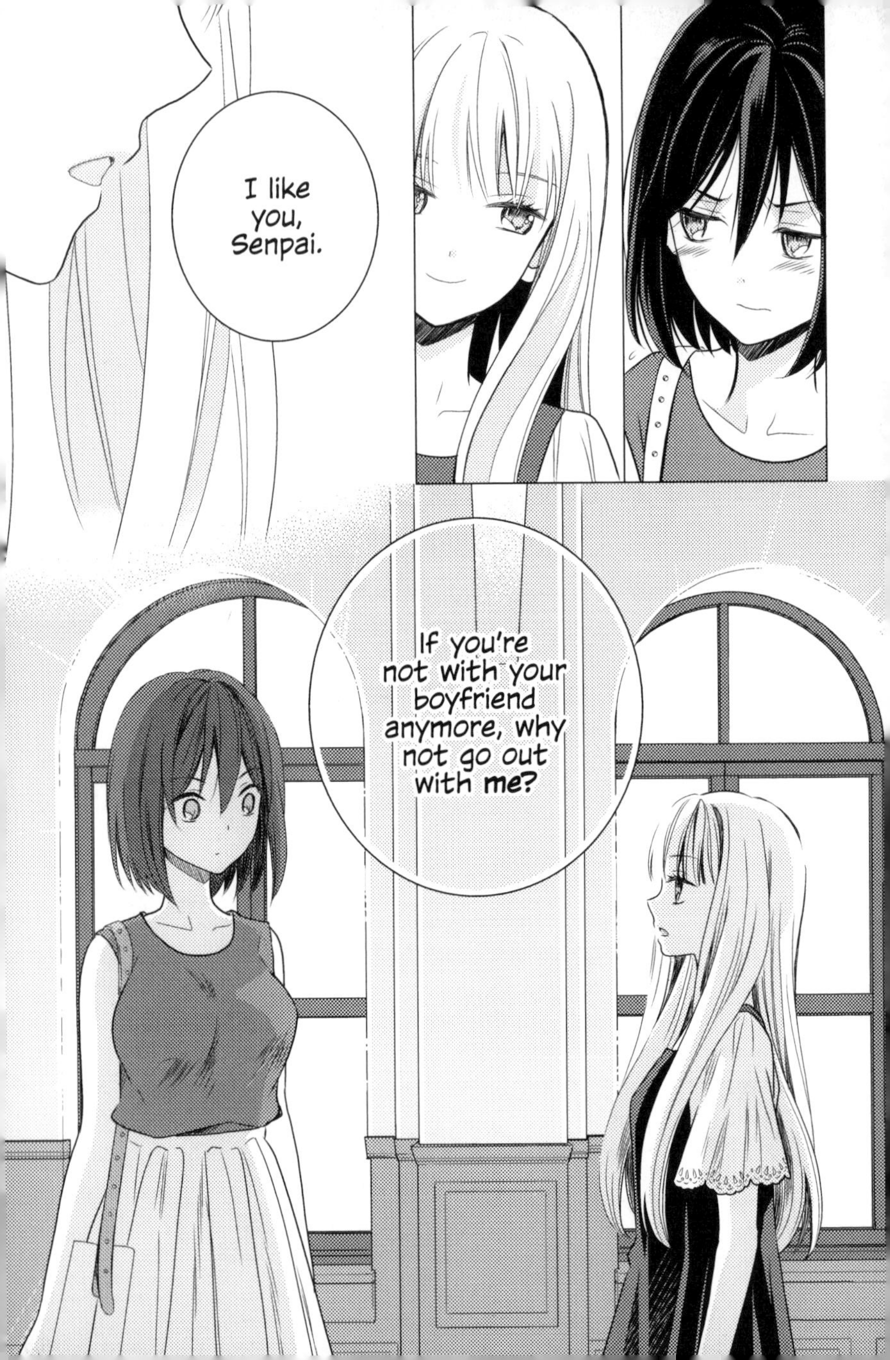
I like you, Senpai.
If you're not with your boyfriend anymore, why not go out with me?

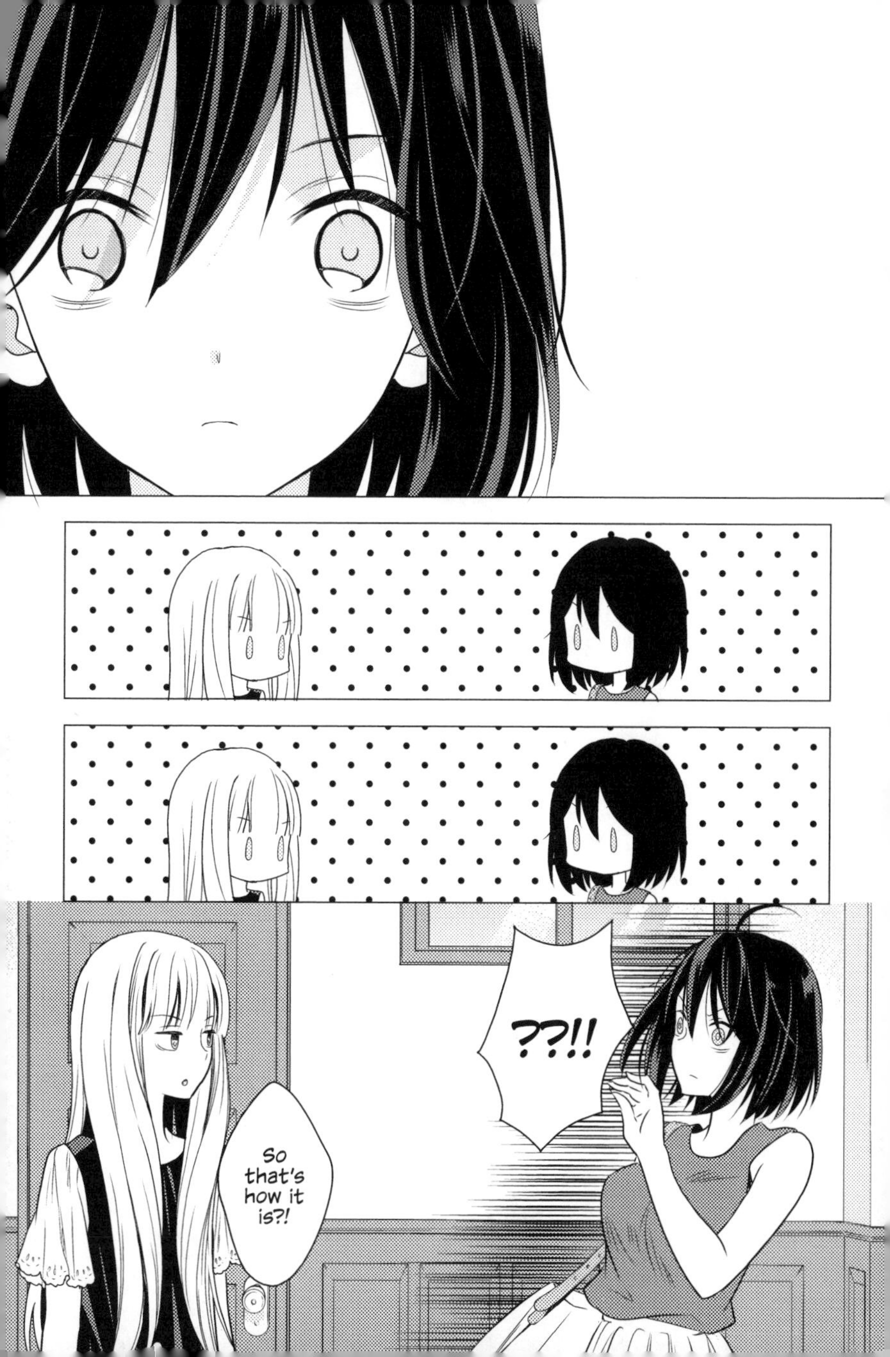
??!!
So that's how it is?!

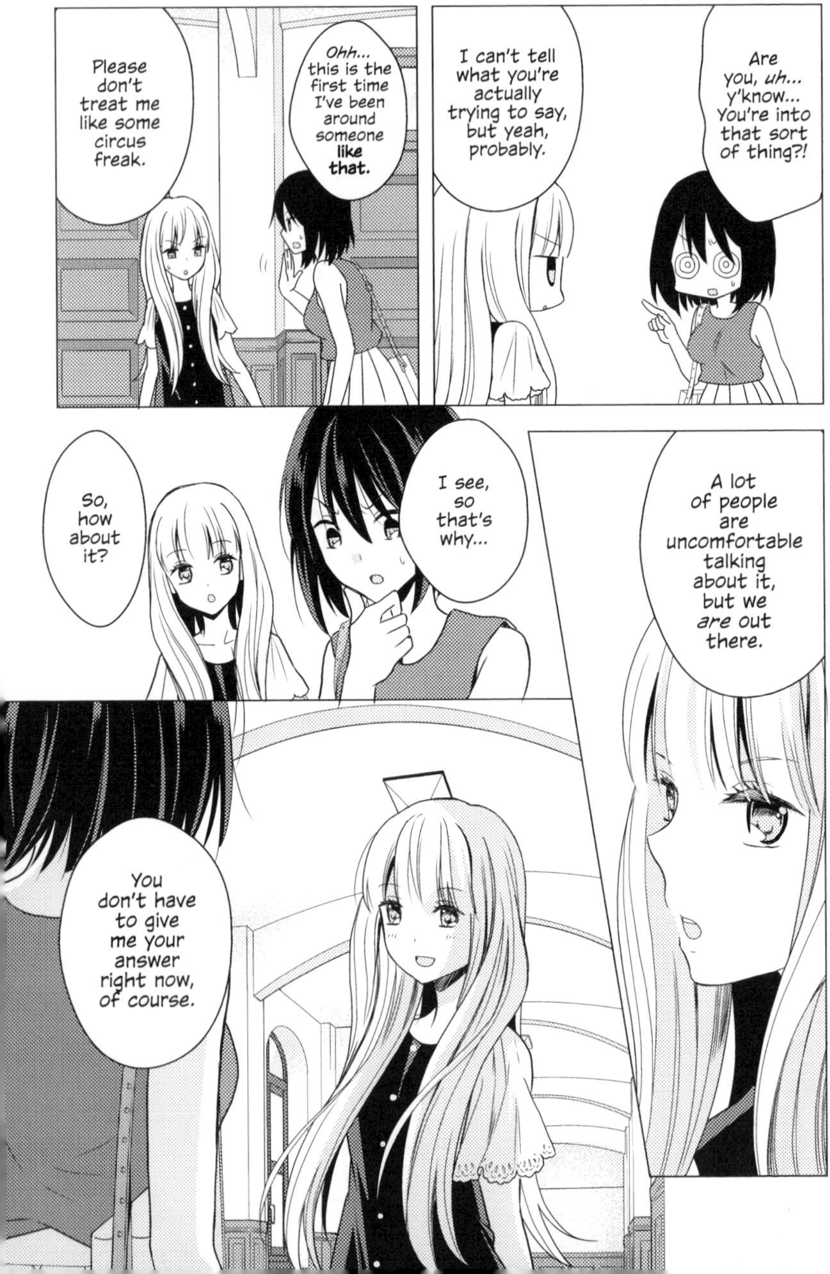
Are you, *uh*... y'know... You're into that sort of thing?!
I can't tell what you're actually trying to say, but yeah, probably.
Ohh... this is the first time I've been around someone **like that.**
Please don't treat me like some circus freak.
A lot of people are uncomfortable talking about it, but we *are* out there.
I see, so that's why...
So, how about it?
You don't have to give me your answer right now, of course.

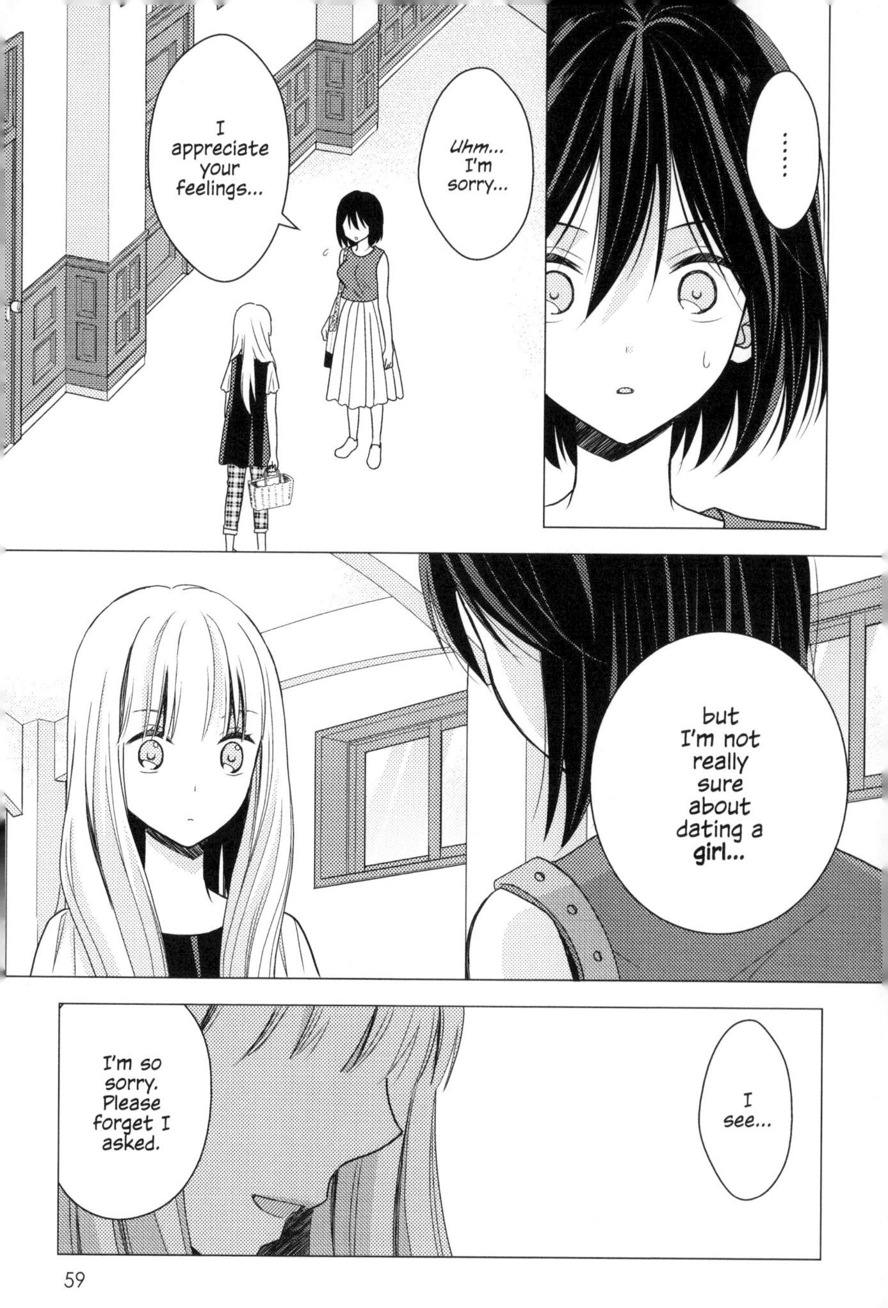
......
Uhm... I'm sorry...
I appreciate your feelings...
but I'm not really sure about dating a **girl...**
I see...
I'm so sorry. Please forget I asked.

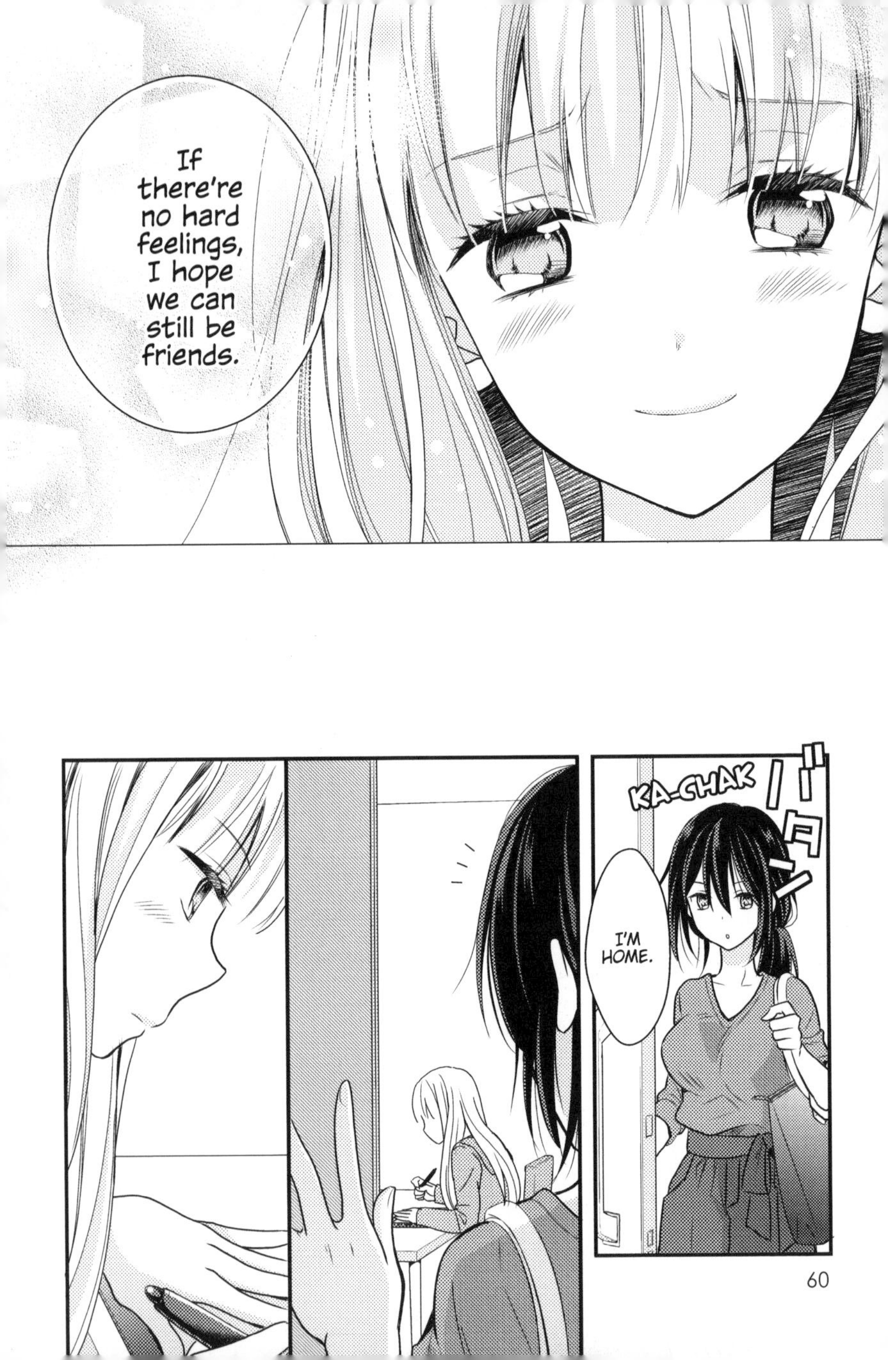
If there're no hard feelings, I hope we can still be friends.
KA-CHAK
I'M HOME.

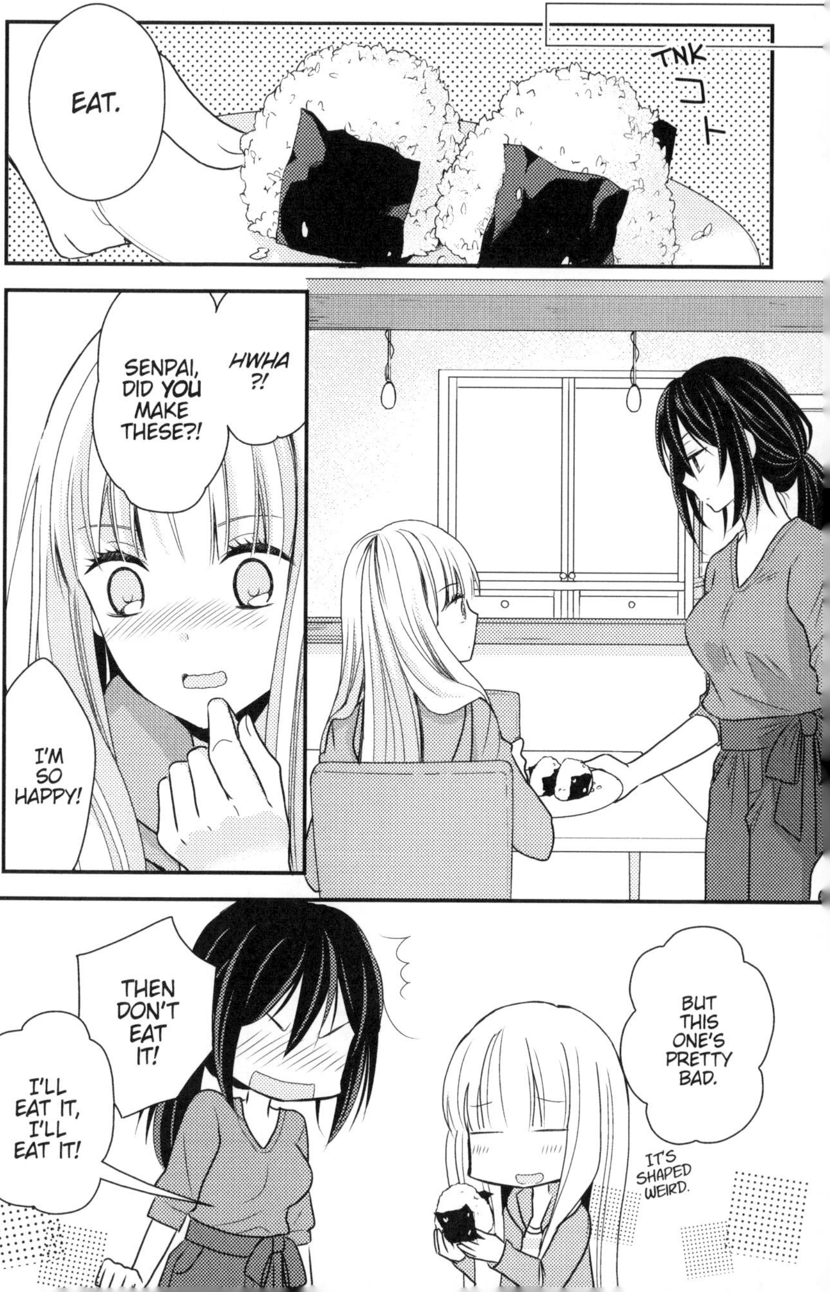
TNK
コト
EAT.
HWHA ?!
SENPAI, DID YOU MAKE THESE?!
I'M SO HAPPY!
BUT THIS ONE'S PRETTY BAD.
IT'S SHAPED WEIRD.
THEN DON'T EAT IT!
I'LL EAT IT, I'LL EAT IT!

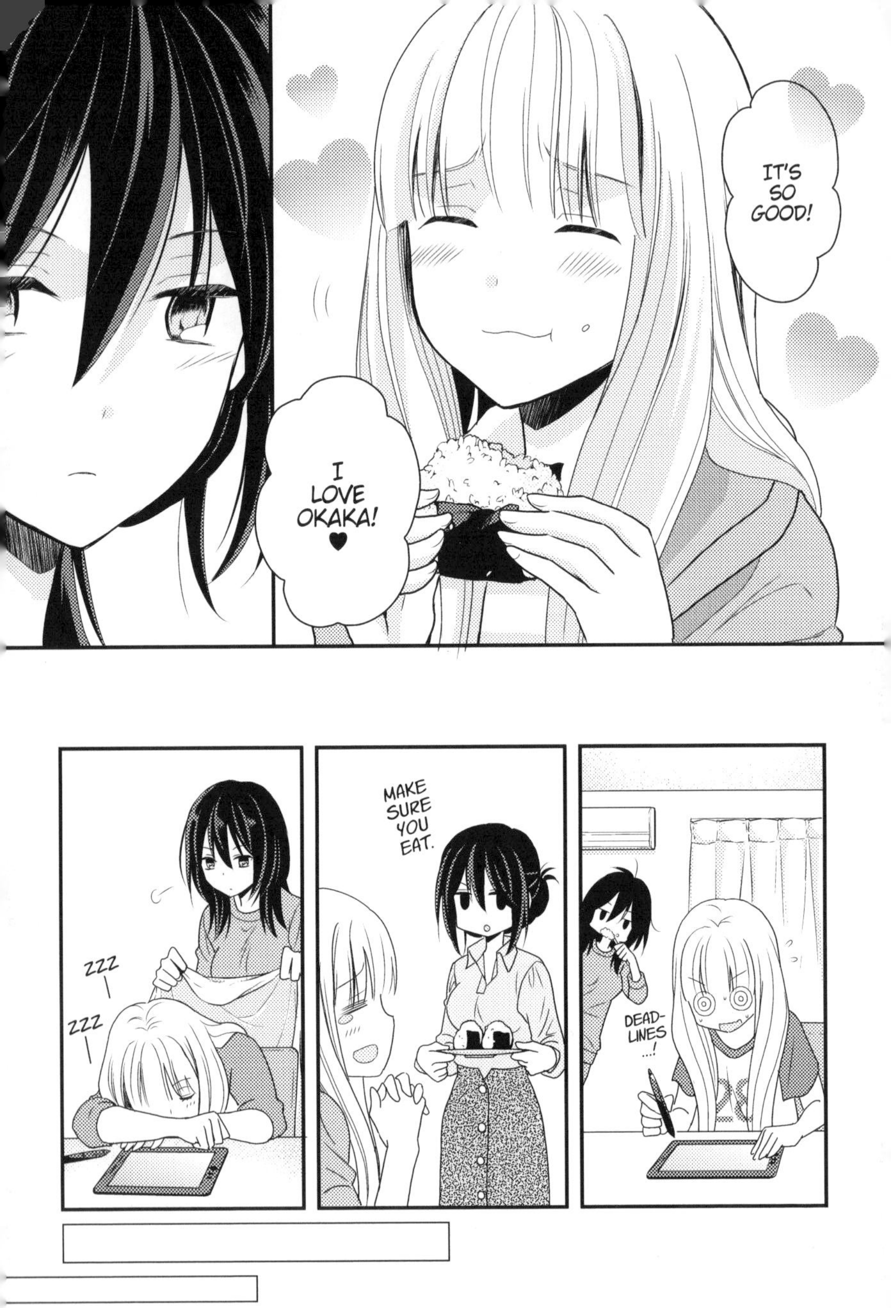
IT'S SO GOOD!
I LOVE OKAKA! ♥
DEAD-LINES ...!
MAKE SURE YOU EAT.
ZZZ
ZZZ

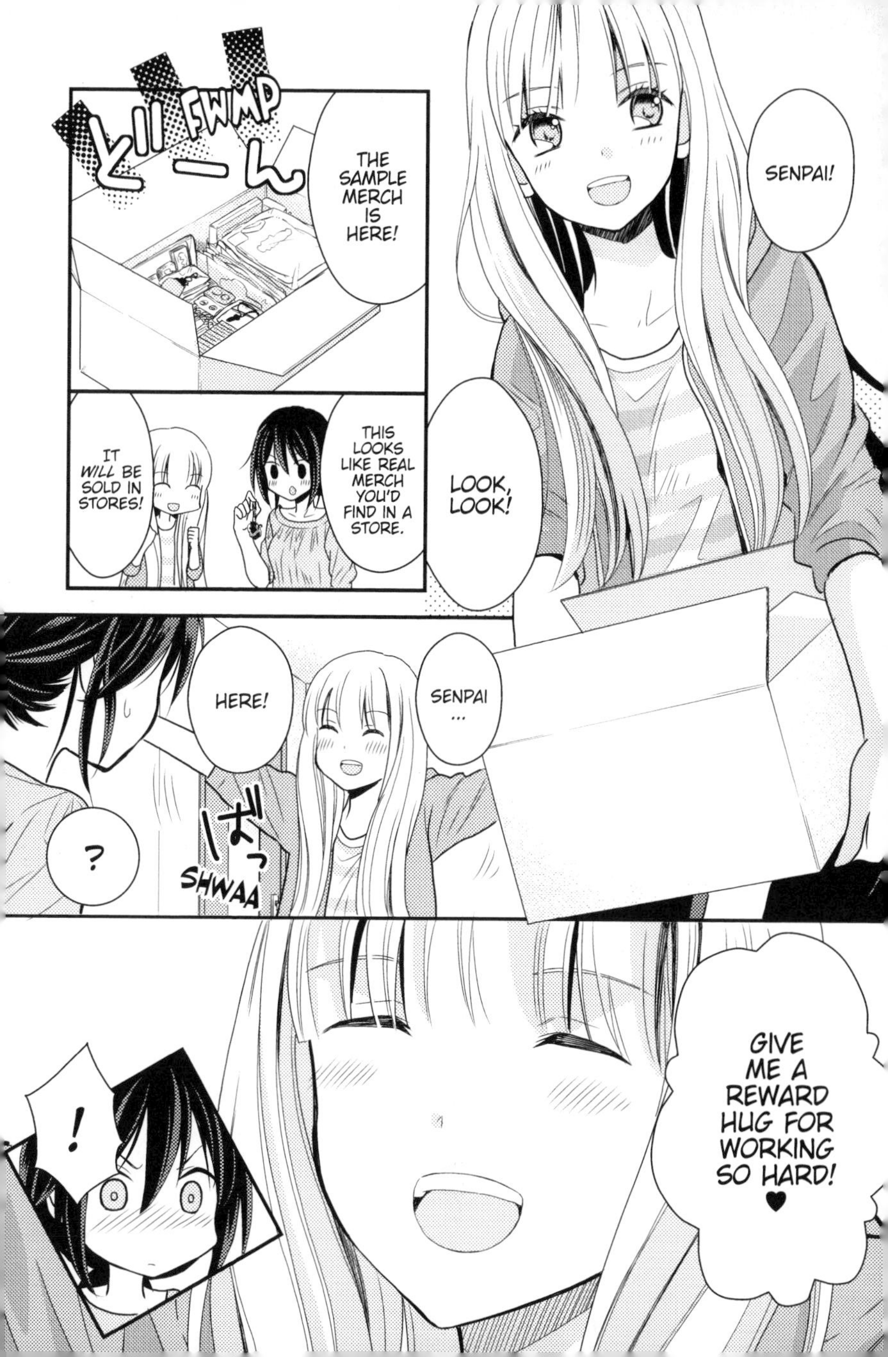
SENPAI!
LOOK, LOOK!
どーん FWMP
THE SAMPLE MERCH IS HERE!
THIS LOOKS LIKE REAL MERCH YOU'D FIND IN A STORE.
IT WILL BE SOLD IN STORES!
SENPAI ...
HERE!
ぱっ SHWAA
?
GIVE ME A REWARD HUG FOR WORKING SO HARD! ♥
!

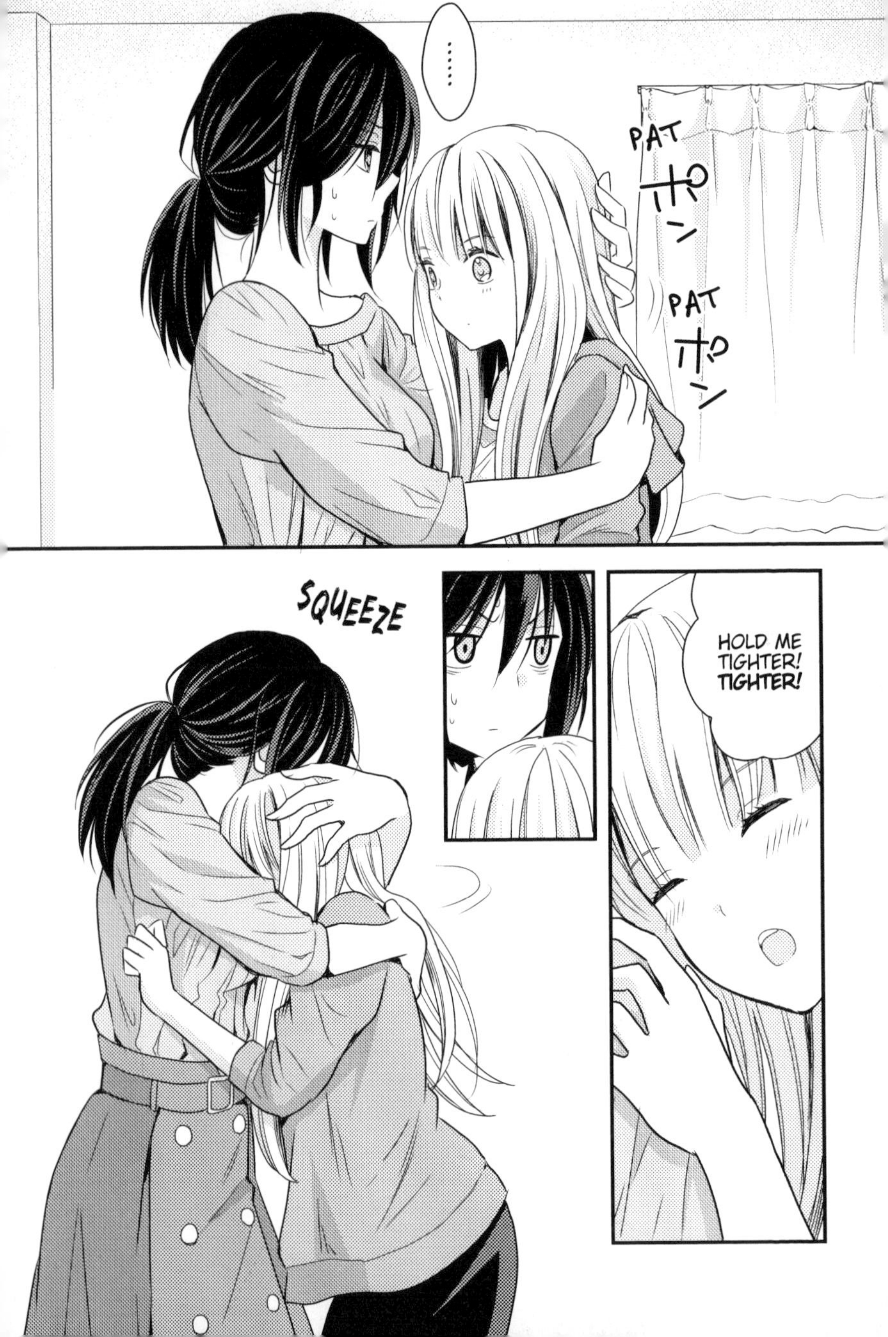
......
PAT
ポン
PAT
ポン
HOLD ME TIGHTER! TIGHTER!
SQUEEZE

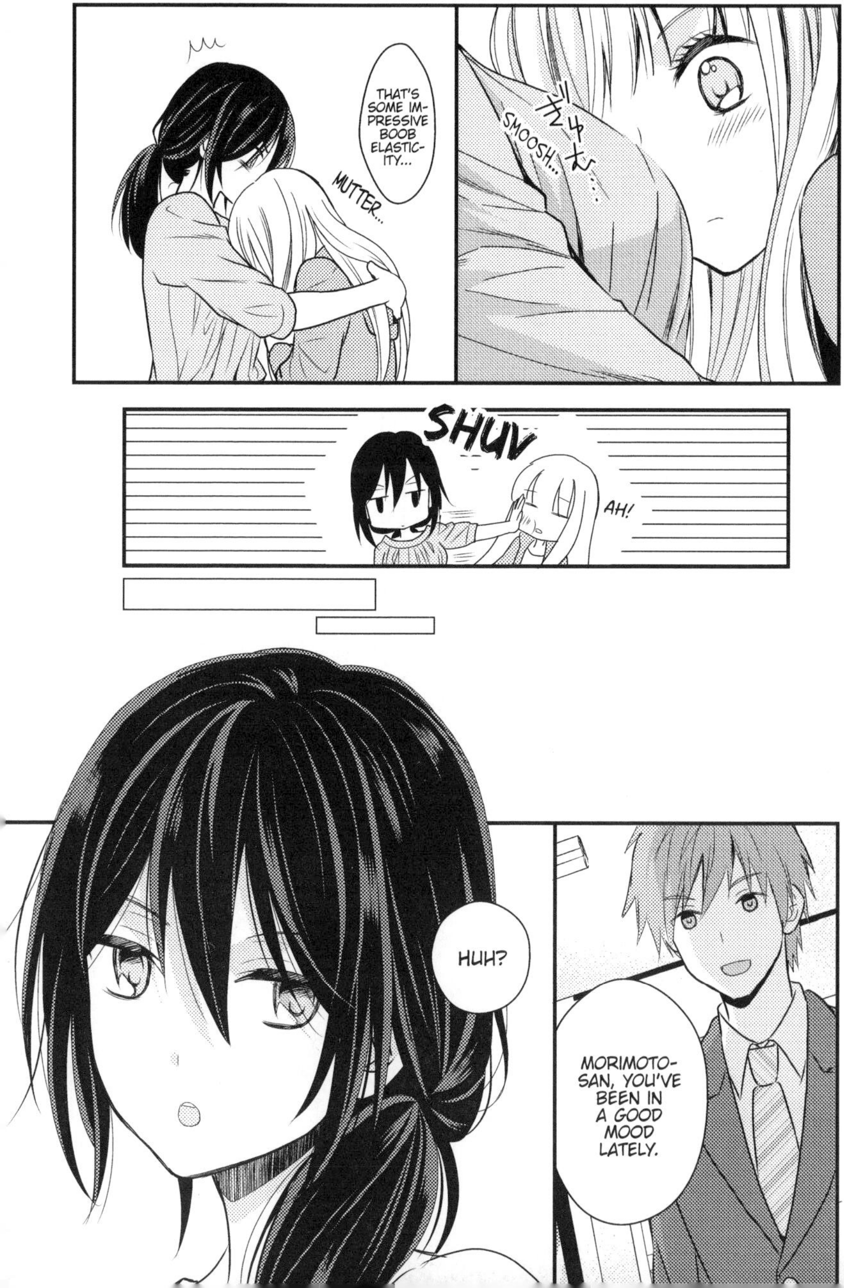
ぎゅむ…
SMOOSH...
THAT'S SOME IM-PRESSIVE BOOB ELASTIC-ITY...
MUTTER...
SHUV
AH!
MORIMOTO-SAN, YOU'VE BEEN IN A GOOD MOOD LATELY.
HUH?

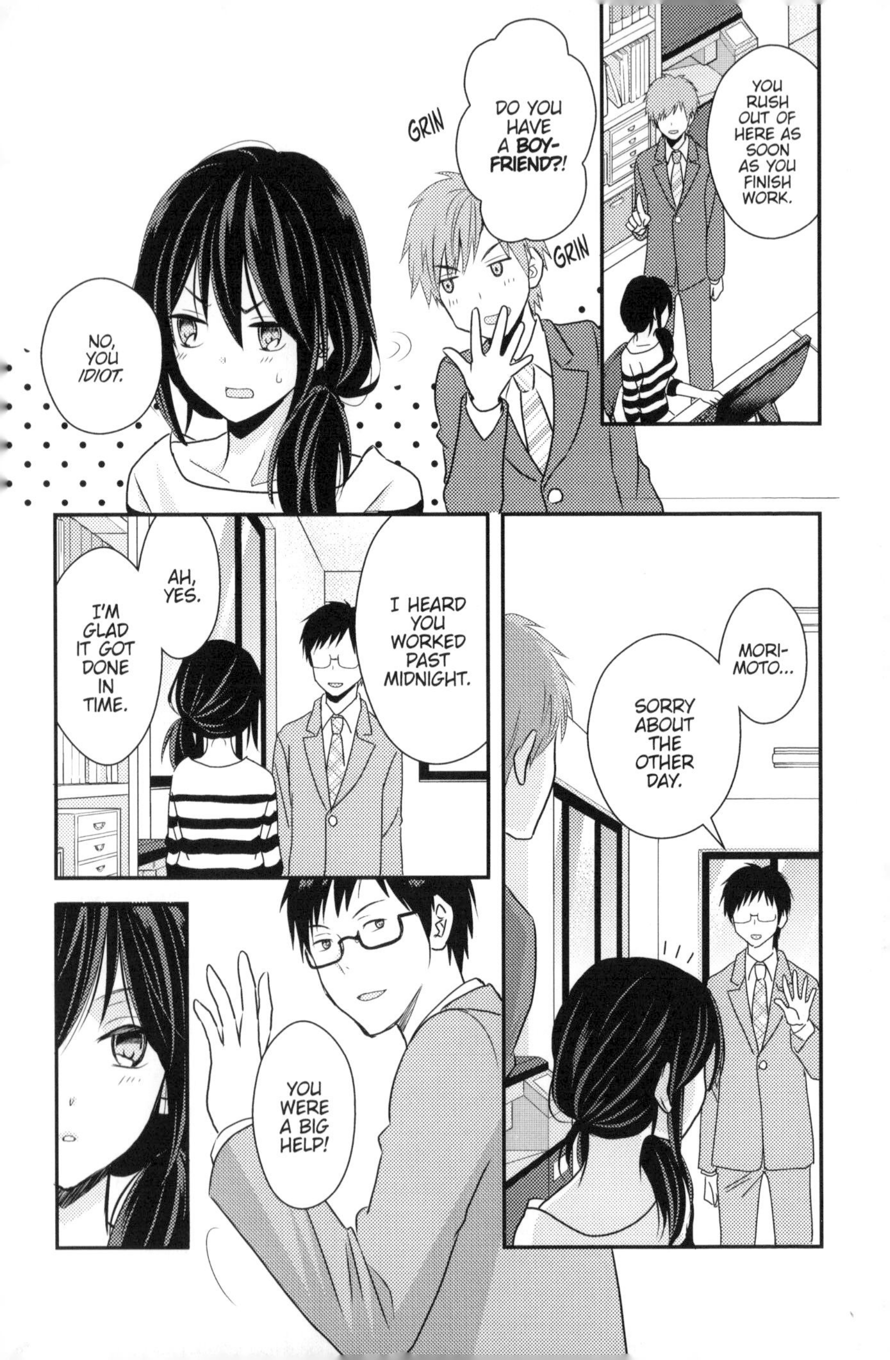
YOU RUSH OUT OF HERE AS SOON AS YOU FINISH WORK.
GRIN
DO YOU HAVE A **BOY-FRIEND?!**
GRIN
NO, YOU IDIOT.
MORI-MOTO...
SORRY ABOUT THE OTHER DAY.
I HEARD YOU WORKED PAST MIDNIGHT.
AH, YES.
I'M GLAD IT GOT DONE IN TIME.
YOU WERE A BIG HELP!

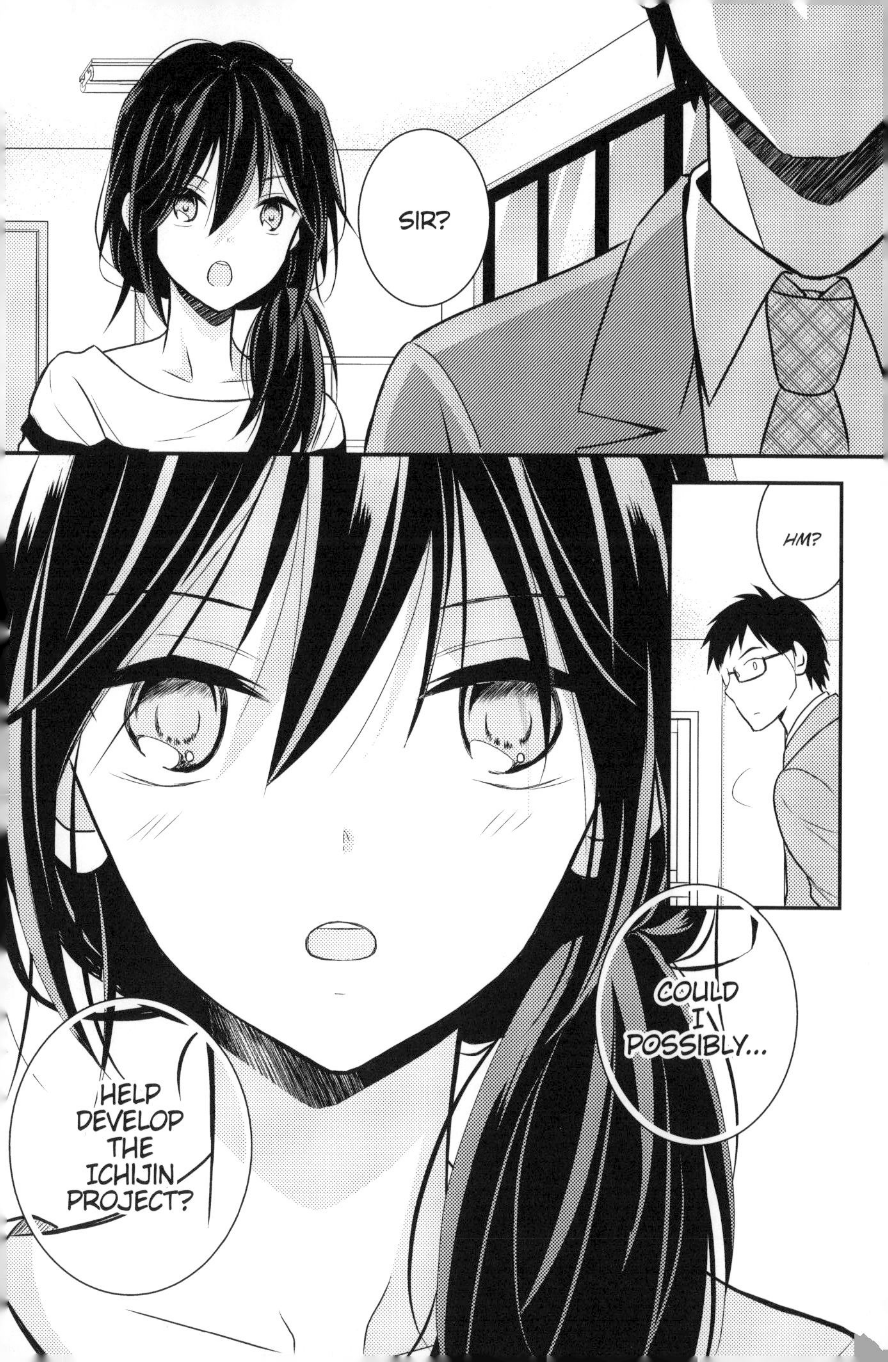
SIR?
HM?
COULD I POSSIBLY...
HELP DEVELOP THE ICHIJIN PROJECT?

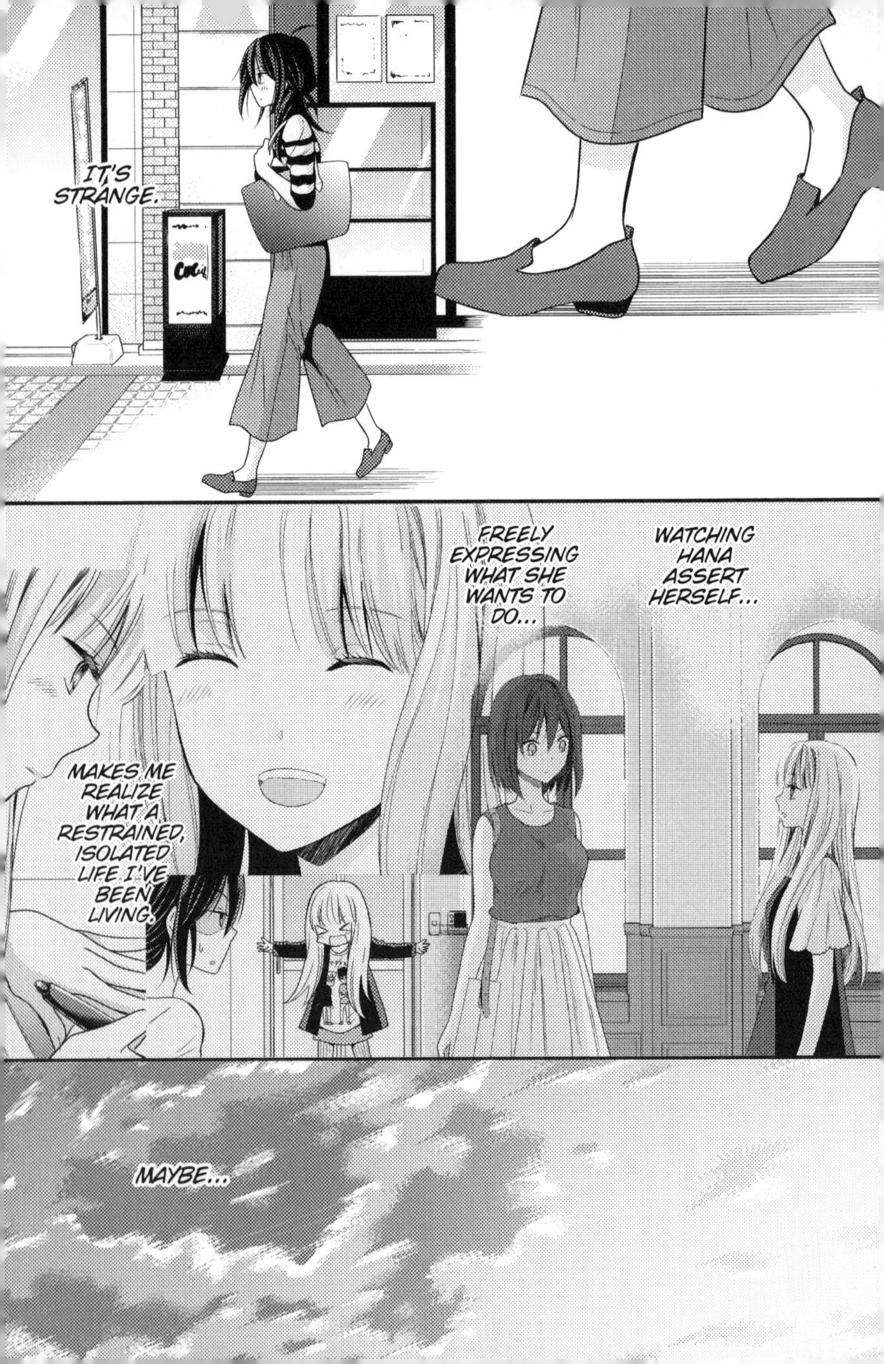
IT'S STRANGE.
WATCHING HANA ASSERT HERSELF...
FREELY EXPRESSING WHAT SHE WANTS TO DO...
MAKES ME REALIZE WHAT A RESTRAINED, ISOLATED LIFE I'VE BEEN LIVING.
MAYBE...

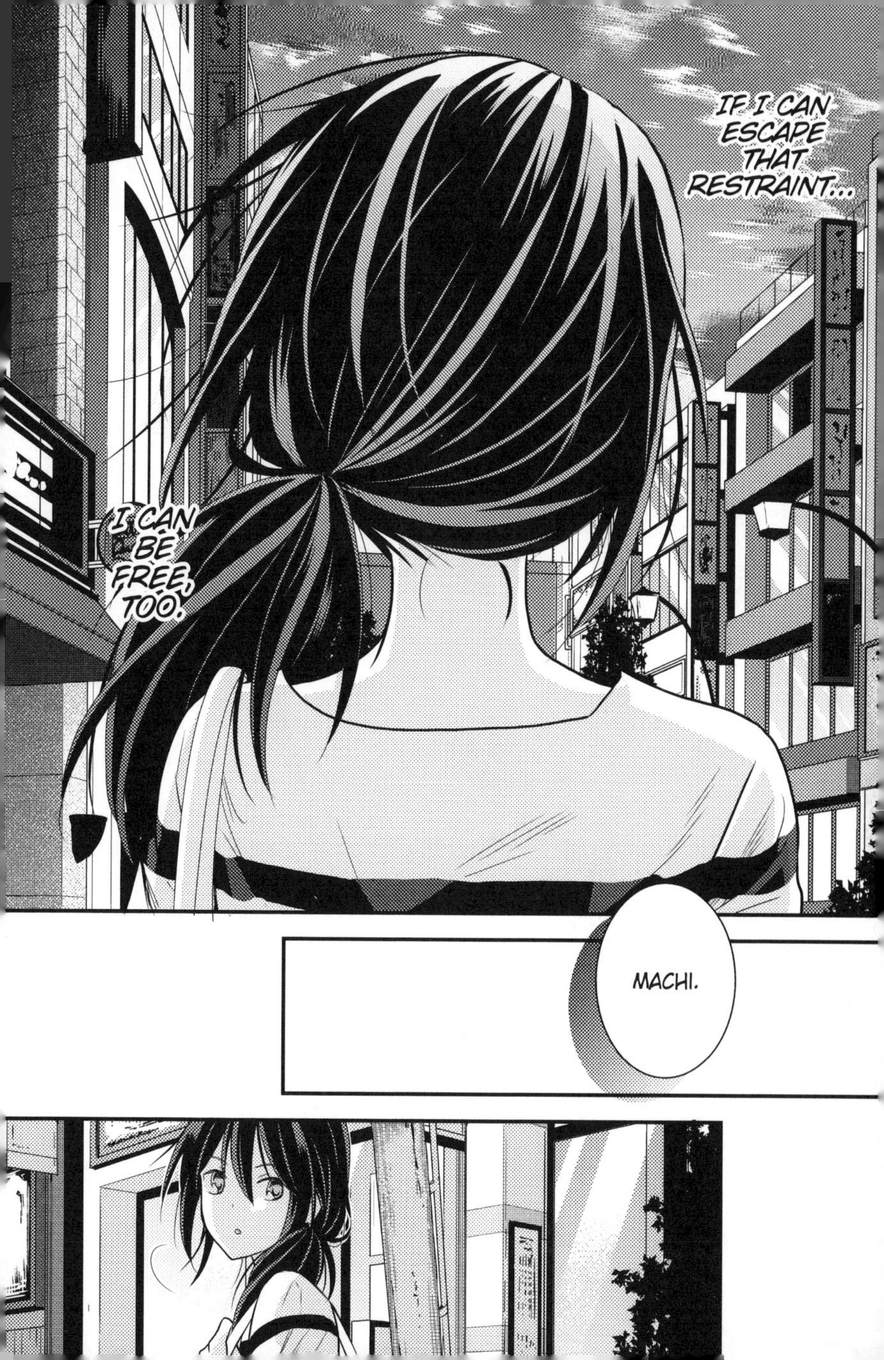
IF I CAN ESCAPE THAT RESTRAINT...
I CAN BE FREE, TOO.
MACHI.

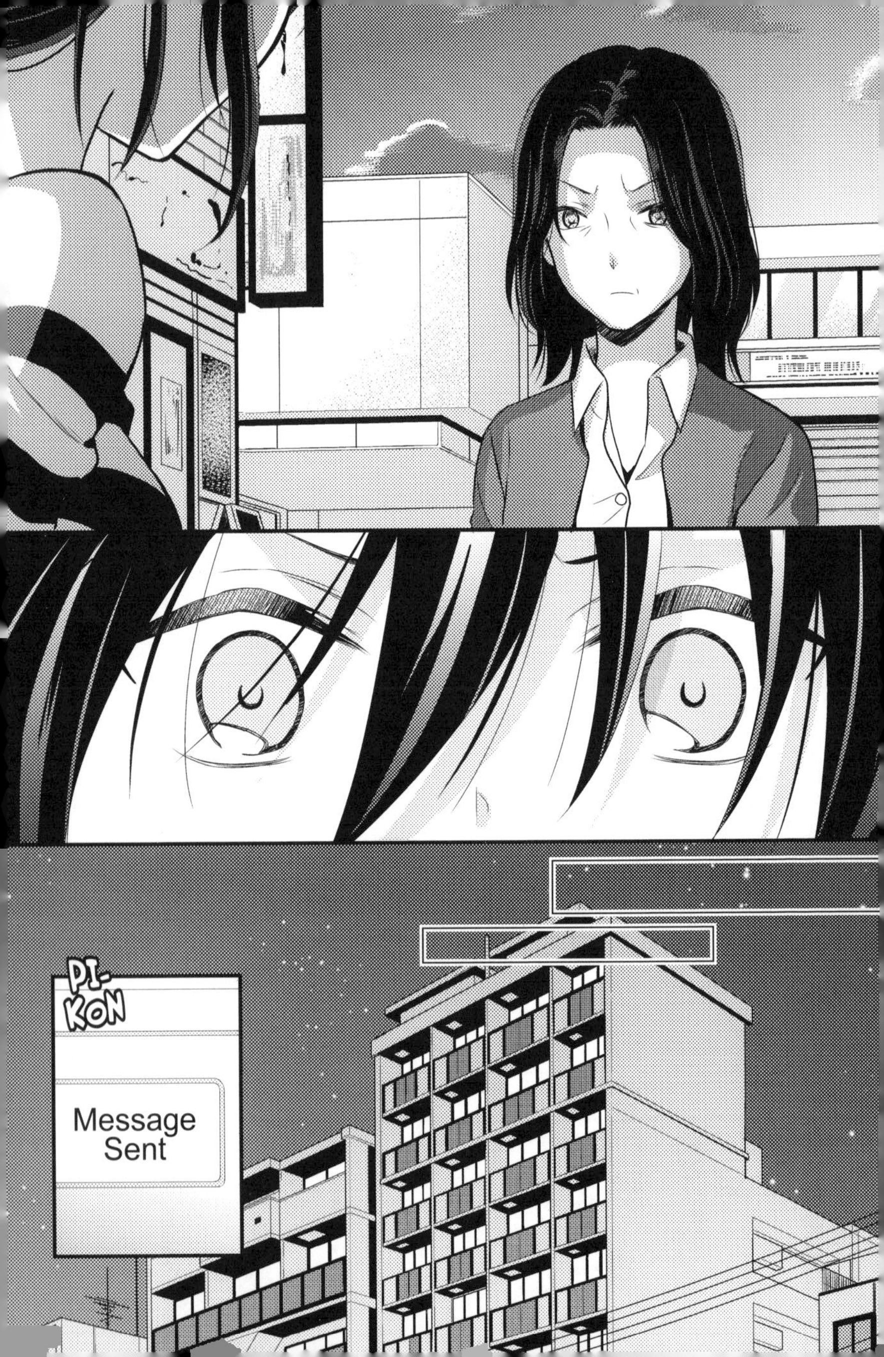
PI-KON
Message Sent

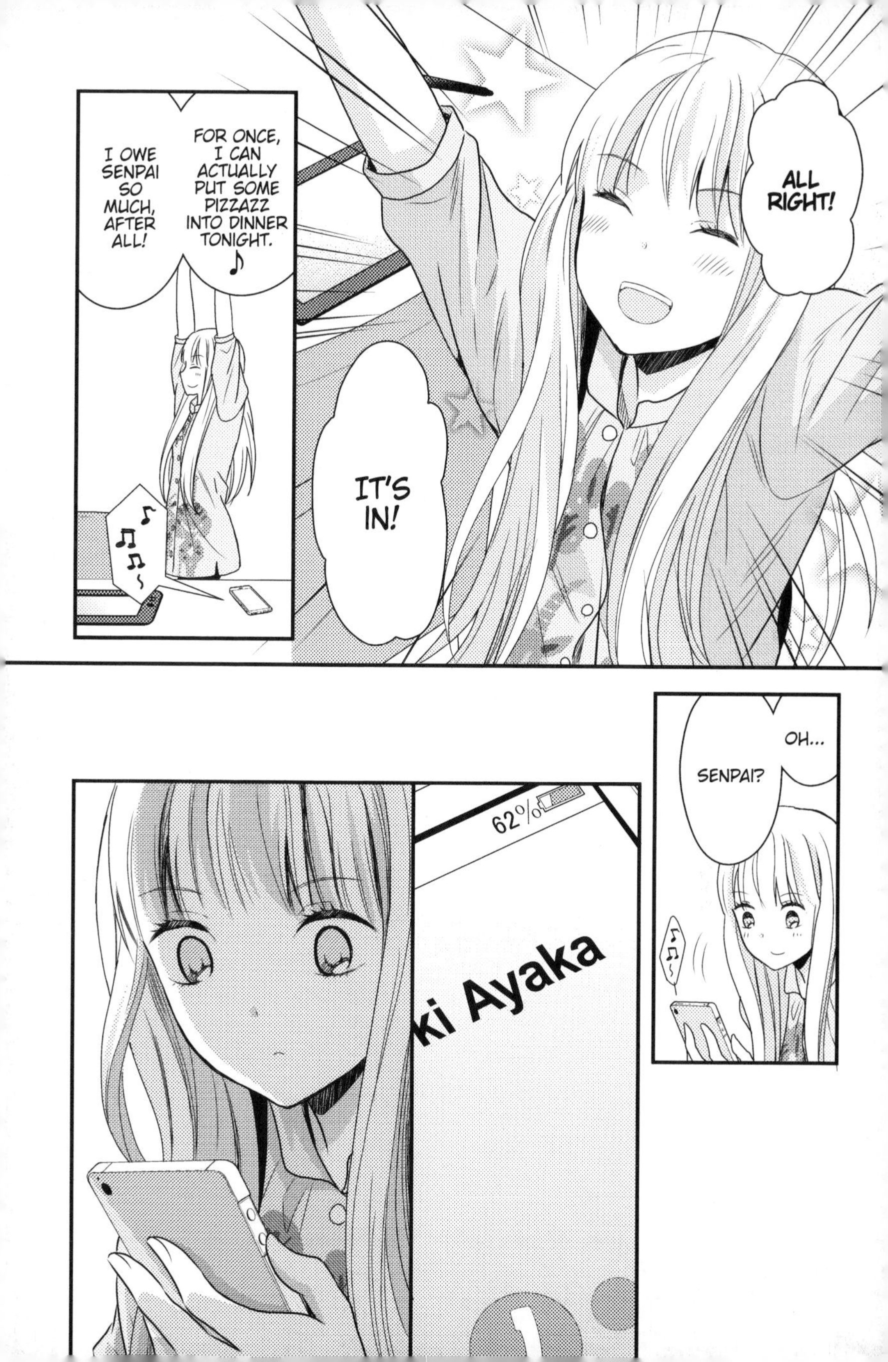
ALL RIGHT!
IT'S IN!
FOR ONCE, I CAN ACTUALLY PUT SOME PIZZAZZ INTO DINNER TONIGHT. ♪
I OWE SENPAI SO MUCH, AFTER ALL!
OH...
SENPAI?
62%
ki Ayaka

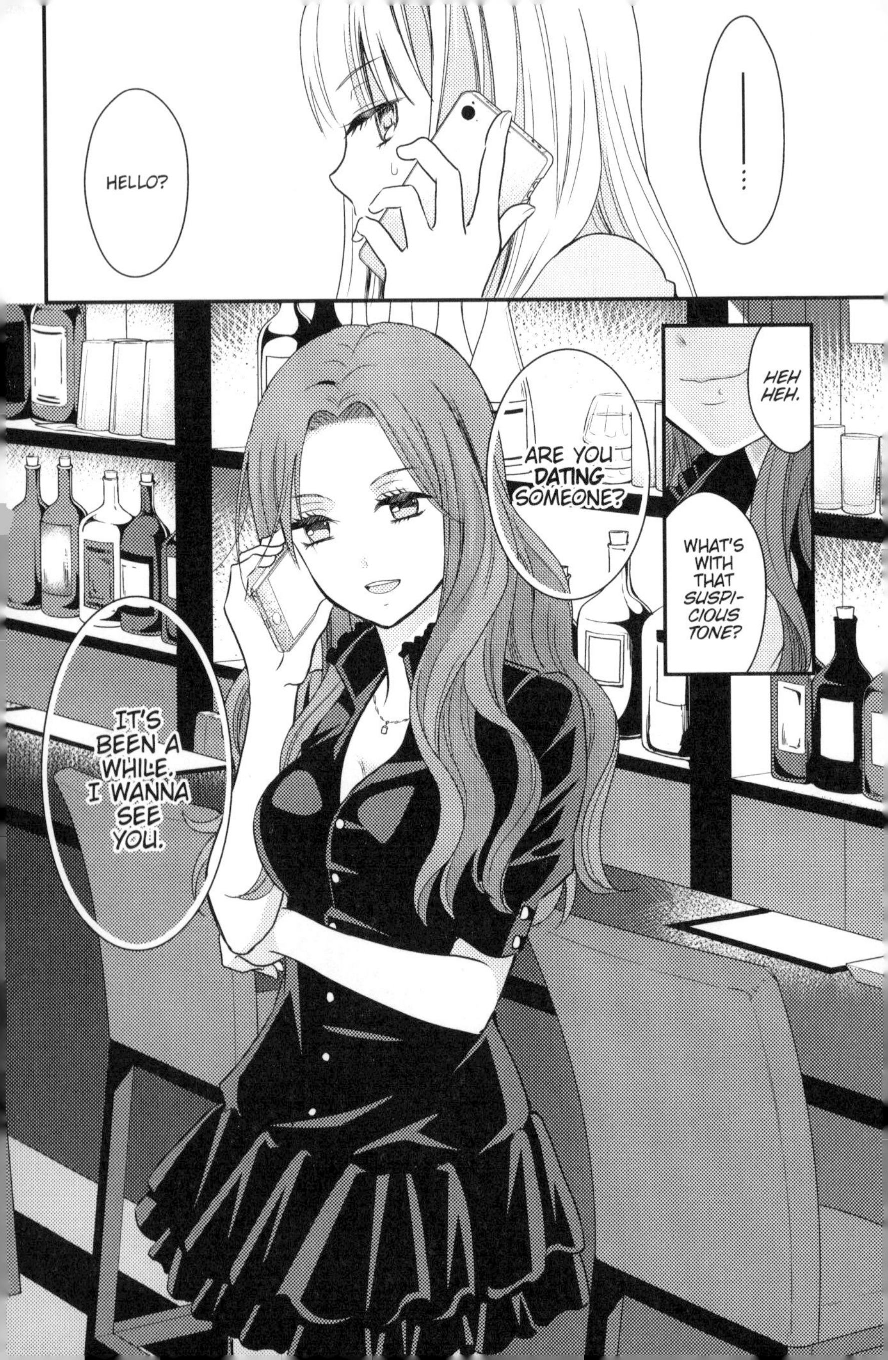
—...
HELLO?
HEH HEH.
WHAT'S WITH THAT SUSPICIOUS TONE?
ARE YOU DATING SOMEONE?
IT'S BEEN A WHILE. I WANNA SEE YOU.

3. marriage

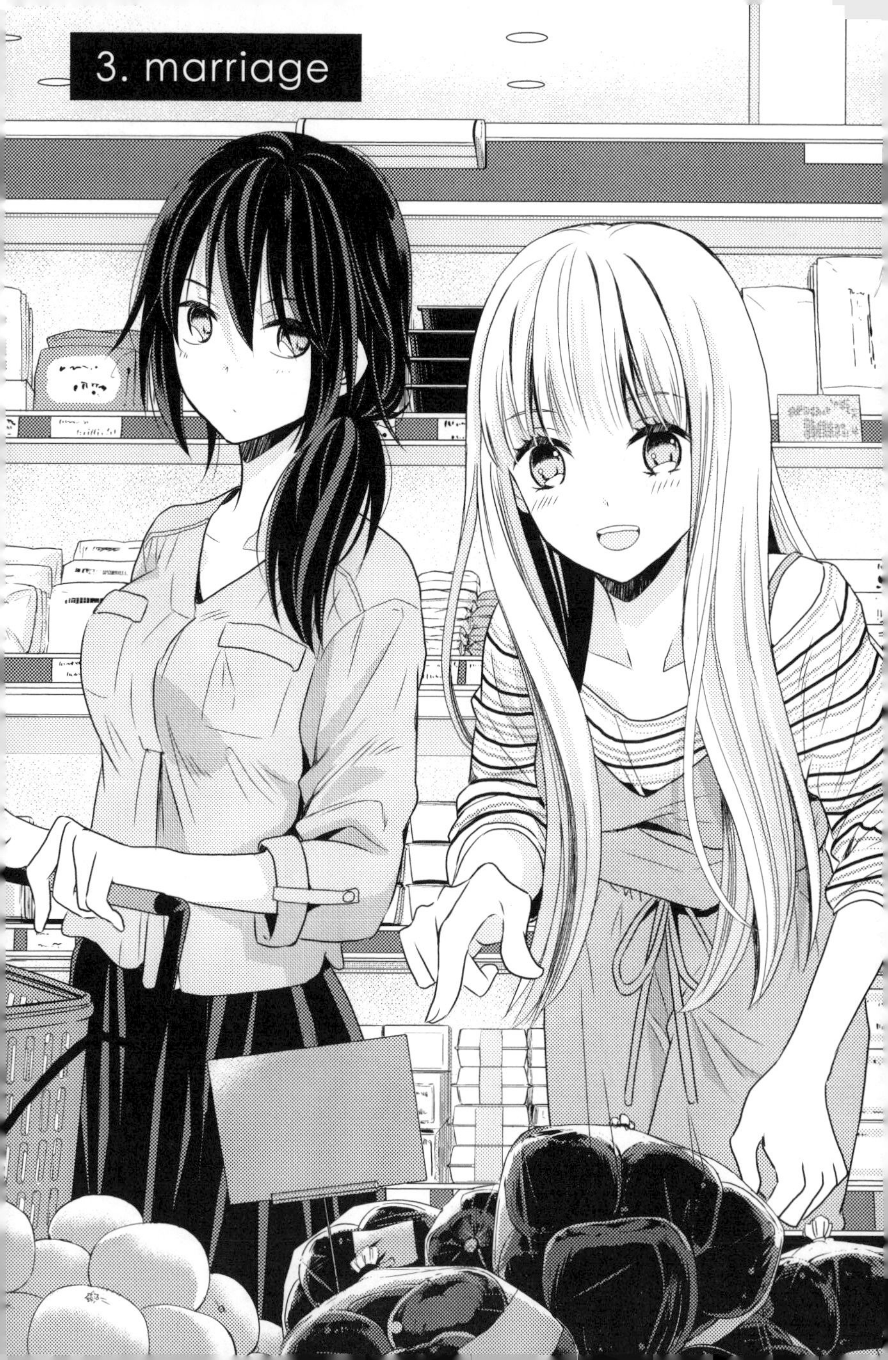

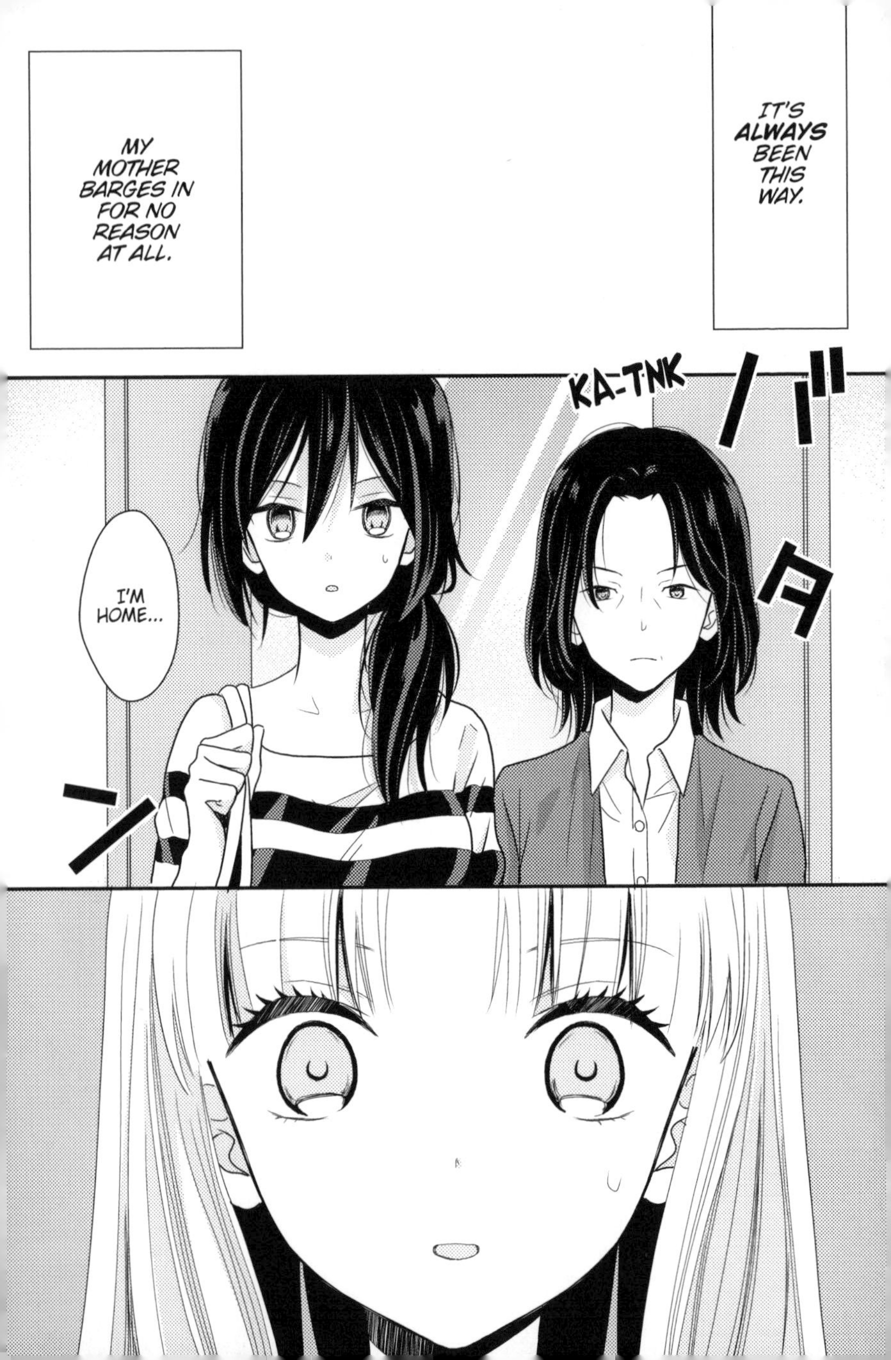
IT'S **ALWAYS** BEEN THIS WAY.
MY MOTHER BARGES IN FOR NO REASON AT ALL.
KA-TNK
バタン
I'M HOME...

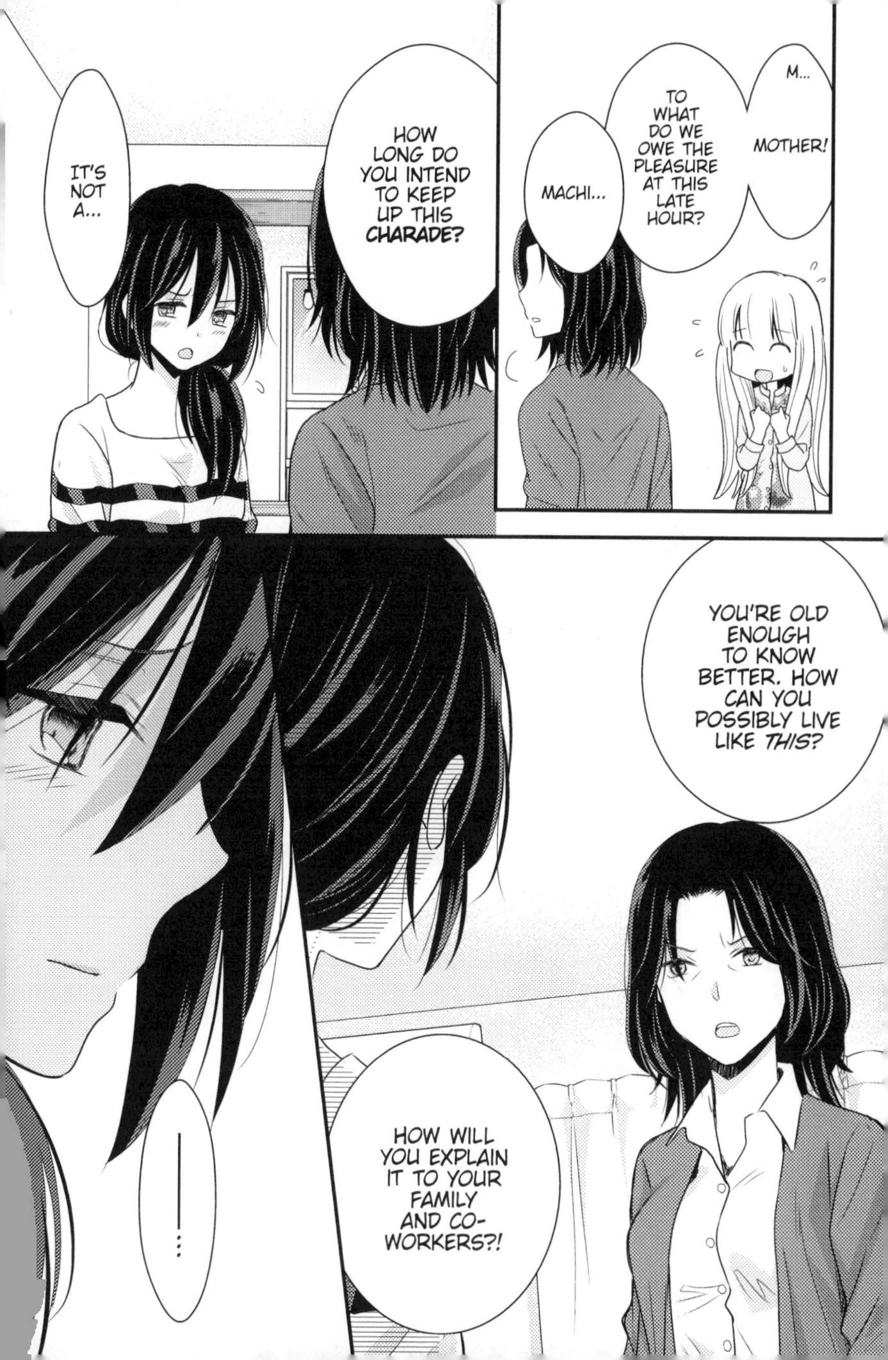
M... MOTHER!
TO WHAT DO WE OWE THE PLEASURE AT THIS LATE HOUR?
MACHI...
HOW LONG DO YOU INTEND TO KEEP UP THIS CHARADE?
IT'S NOT A...
YOU'RE OLD ENOUGH TO KNOW BETTER. HOW CAN YOU POSSIBLY LIVE LIKE THIS?
HOW WILL YOU EXPLAIN IT TO YOUR FAMILY AND CO-WORKERS?!
—...

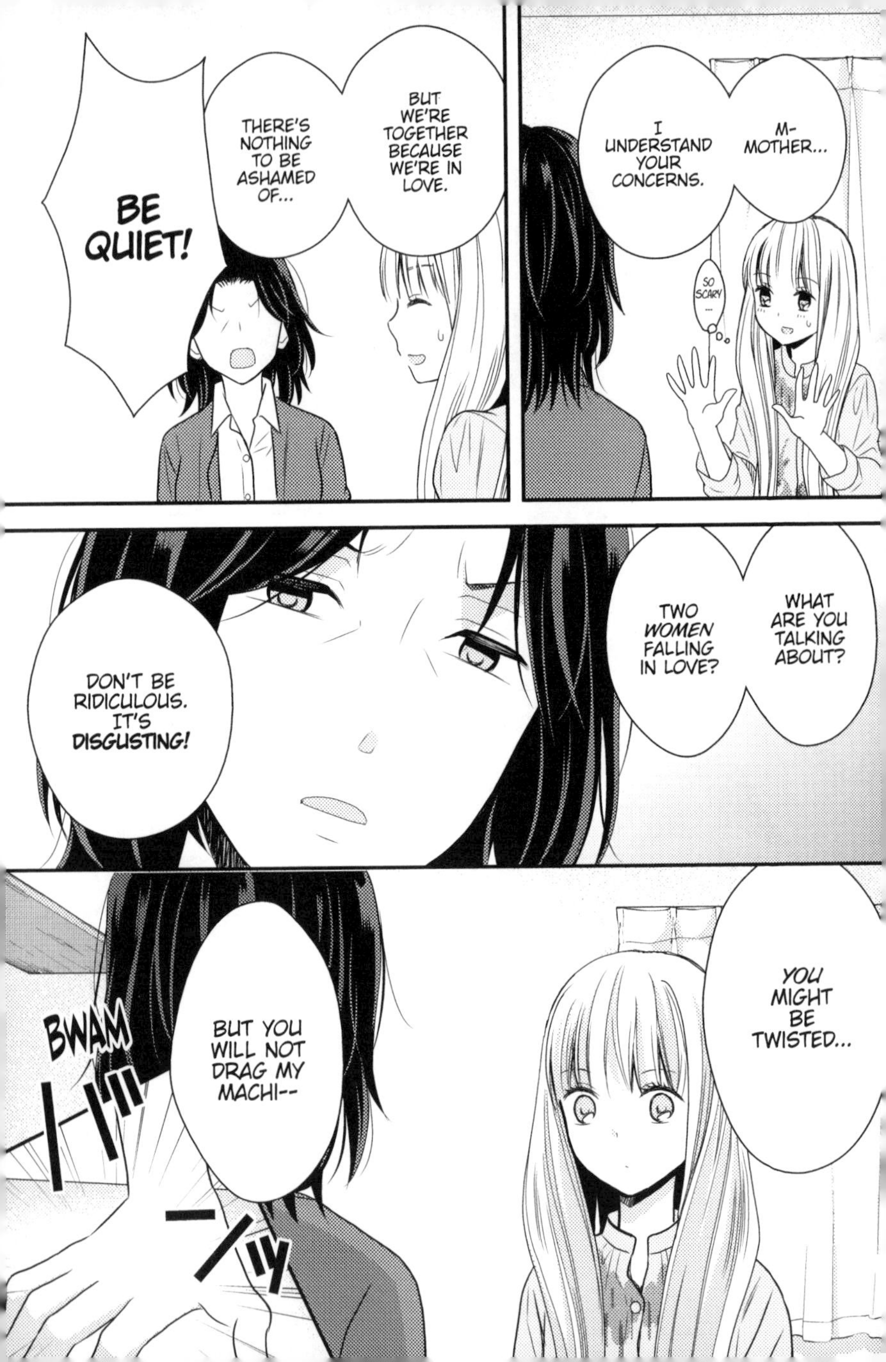
M-MOTHER...
I UNDERSTAND YOUR CONCERNS.
SO SCARY...
BUT WE'RE TOGETHER BECAUSE WE'RE IN LOVE.
THERE'S NOTHING TO BE ASHAMED OF...
BE QUIET!
WHAT ARE YOU TALKING ABOUT?
TWO *WOMEN* FALLING IN LOVE?
DON'T BE RIDICULOUS. IT'S **DISGUSTING!**
YOU MIGHT BE TWISTED...
BUT YOU WILL NOT DRAG MY MACHI--
BWAM

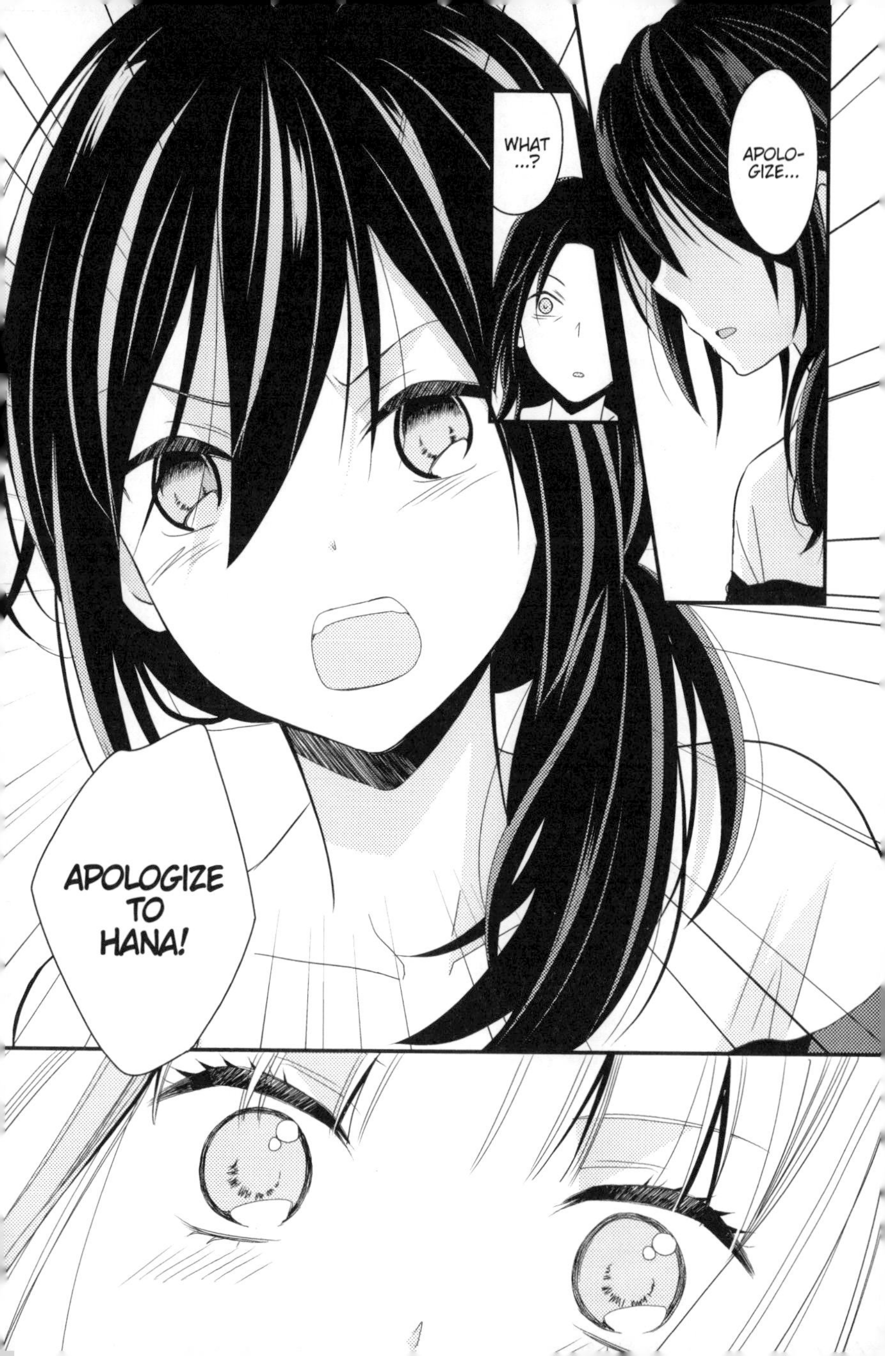
APOLO-
GIZE...
WHAT
...?
APOLOGIZE TO HANA!

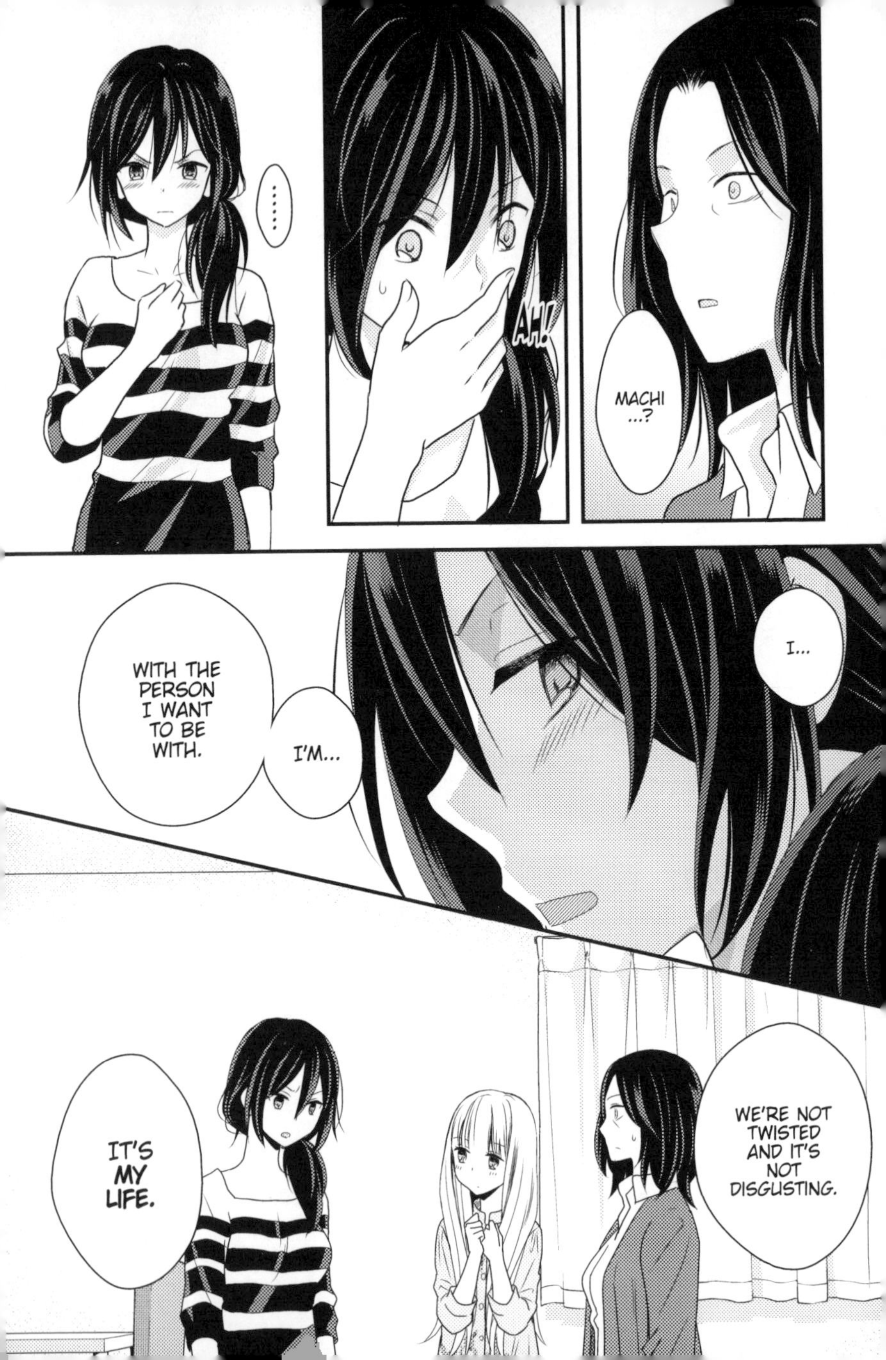
MACHI ...?
AH!
......
I...
I'M...
WITH THE PERSON I WANT TO BE WITH.
WE'RE NOT TWISTED AND IT'S NOT DISGUSTING.
IT'S MY LIFE.

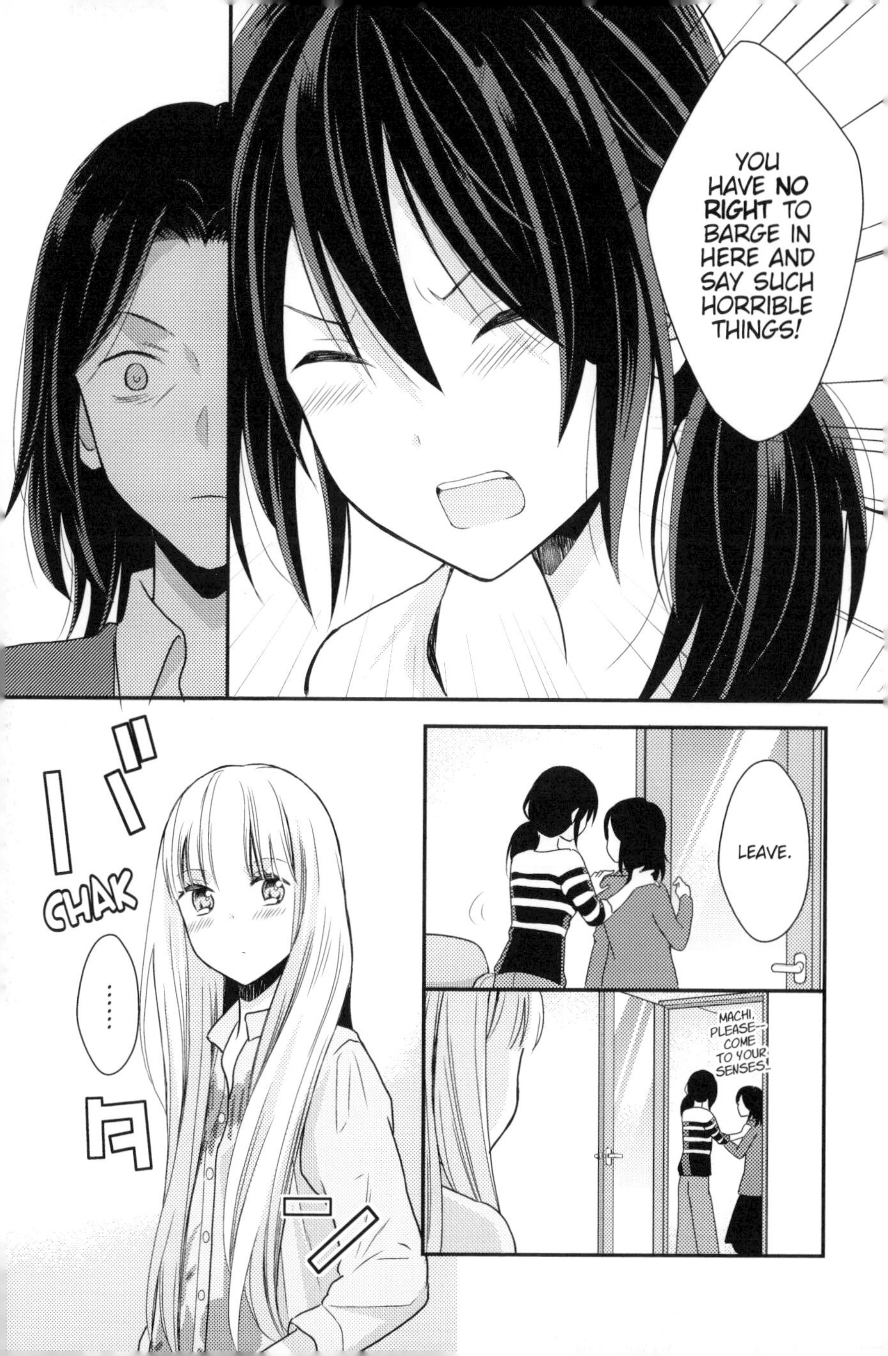
YOU HAVE NO RIGHT TO BARGE IN HERE AND SAY SUCH HORRIBLE THINGS!
LEAVE.
MACHI, PLEASE— COME TO YOUR SENSES!
CHAK
......

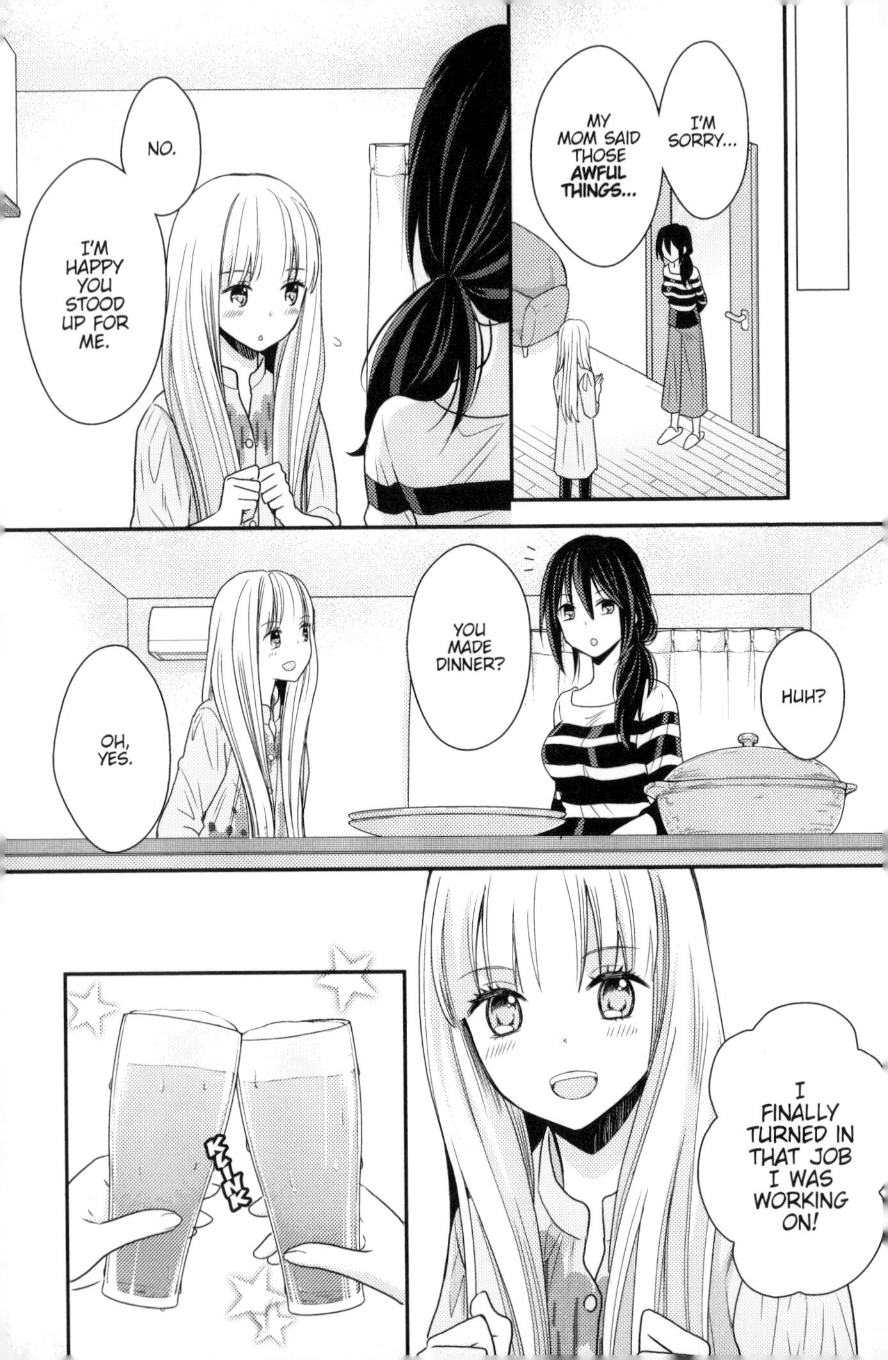
I'M SORRY...
MY MOM SAID THOSE AWFUL THINGS...
NO.
I'M HAPPY YOU STOOD UP FOR ME.
HUH?
YOU MADE DINNER?
OH, YES.
I FINALLY TURNED IN THAT JOB I WAS WORKING ON!
KLINK

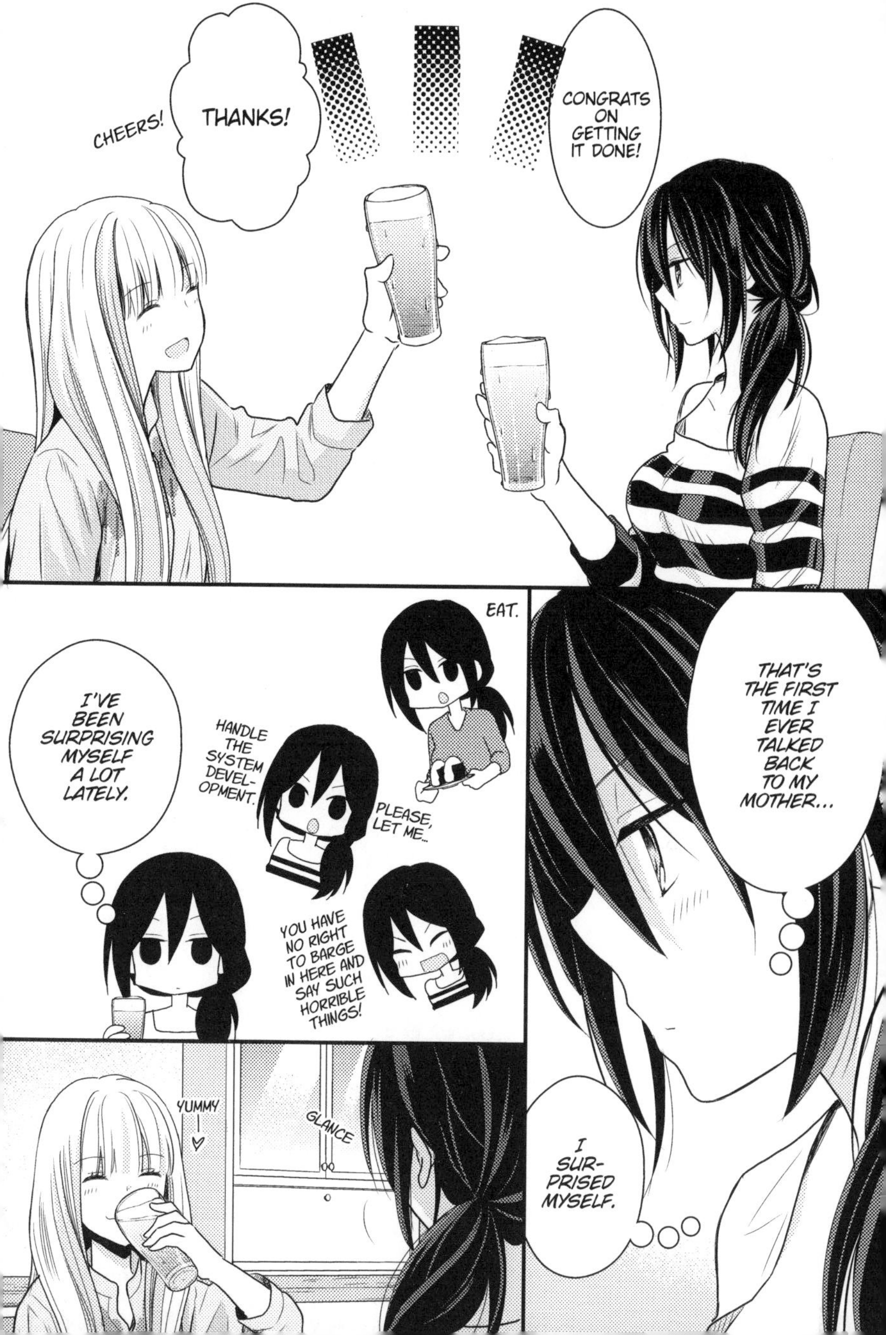

CONGRATS ON GETTING IT DONE!
THANKS!
CHEERS!
THAT'S THE FIRST TIME I EVER TALKED BACK TO MY MOTHER...
I SURPRISED MYSELF.
EAT.
HANDLE THE SYSTEM DEVELOPMENT.
PLEASE, LET ME...
I'VE BEEN SURPRISING MYSELF A LOT LATELY.
YOU HAVE NO RIGHT TO BARGE IN HERE AND SAY SUCH HORRIBLE THINGS!
GLANCE
YUMMY ♥

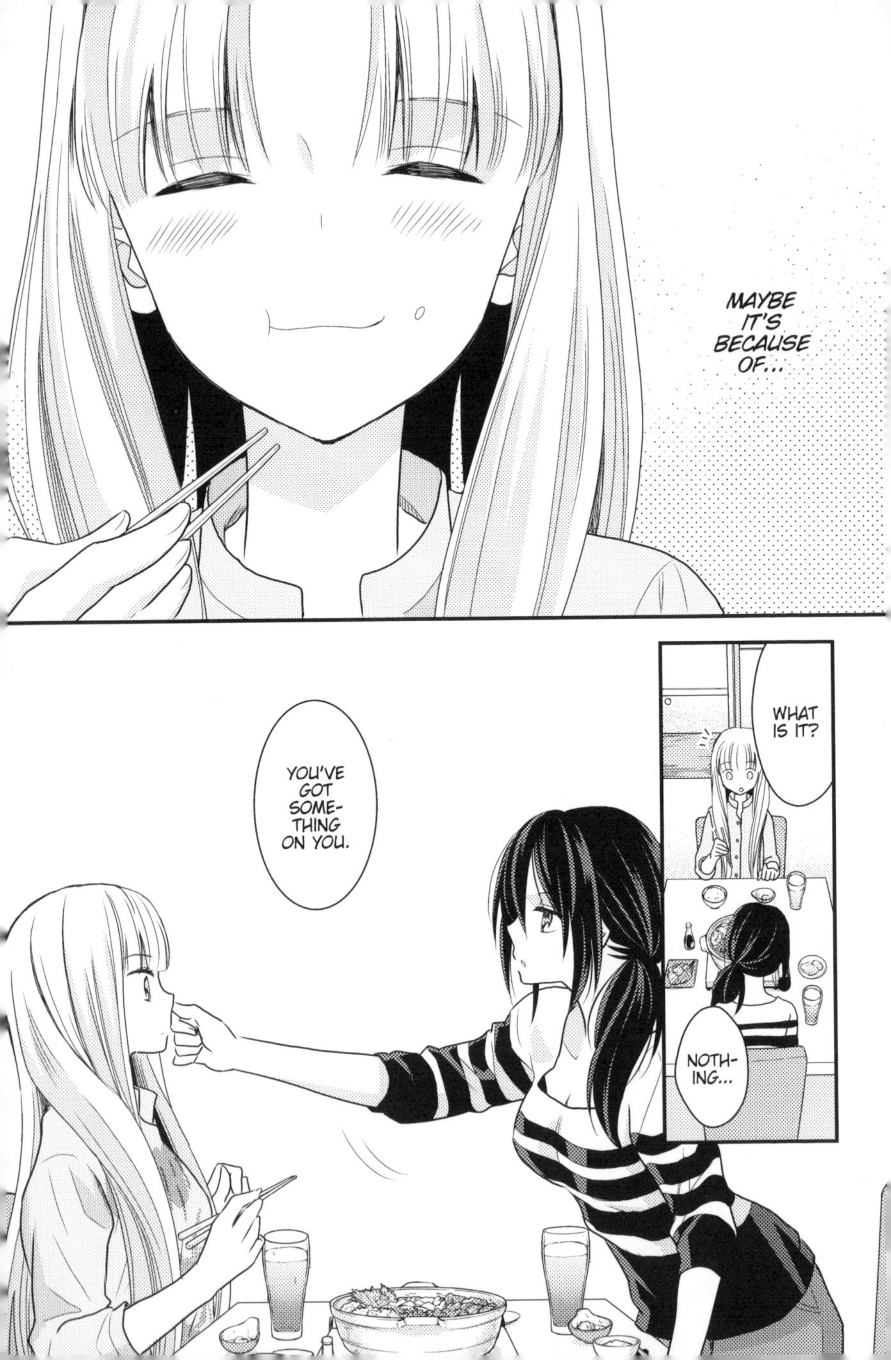
MAYBE IT'S BECAUSE OF...
WHAT IS IT?
NOTHING...
YOU'VE GOT SOMETHING ON YOU.

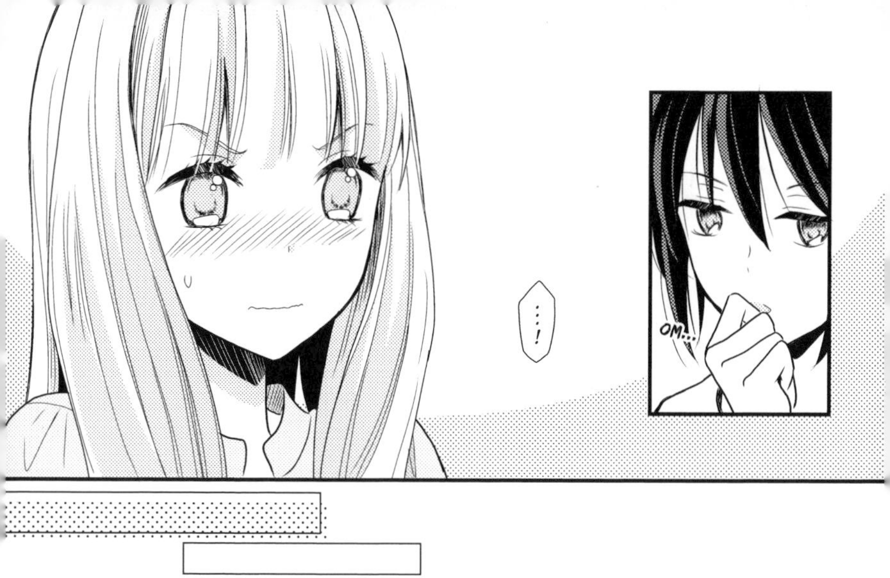
OM...
...!

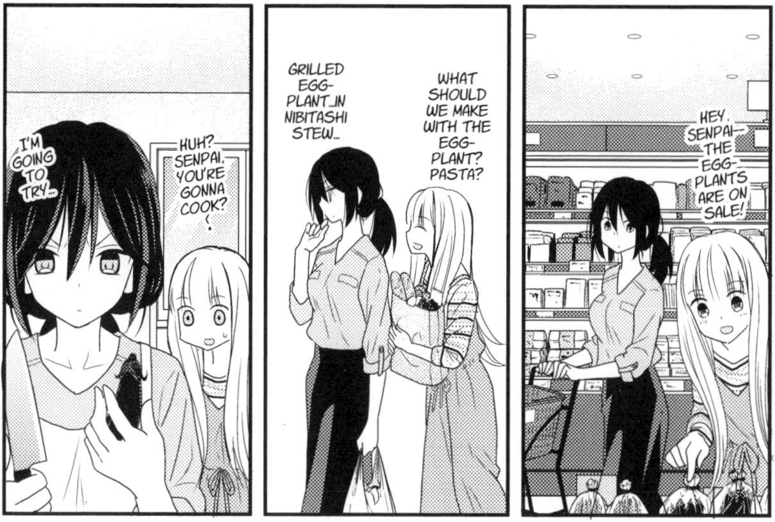
HEY, SENPAI—THE EGG-PLANTS ARE ON SALE!
WHAT SHOULD WE MAKE WITH THE EGG-PLANT? PASTA?
GRILLED EGG-PLANT...IN NIBITASHI STEW...
HUH? SENPAI, YOU'RE GONNA COOK?
I'M GOING TO TRY...

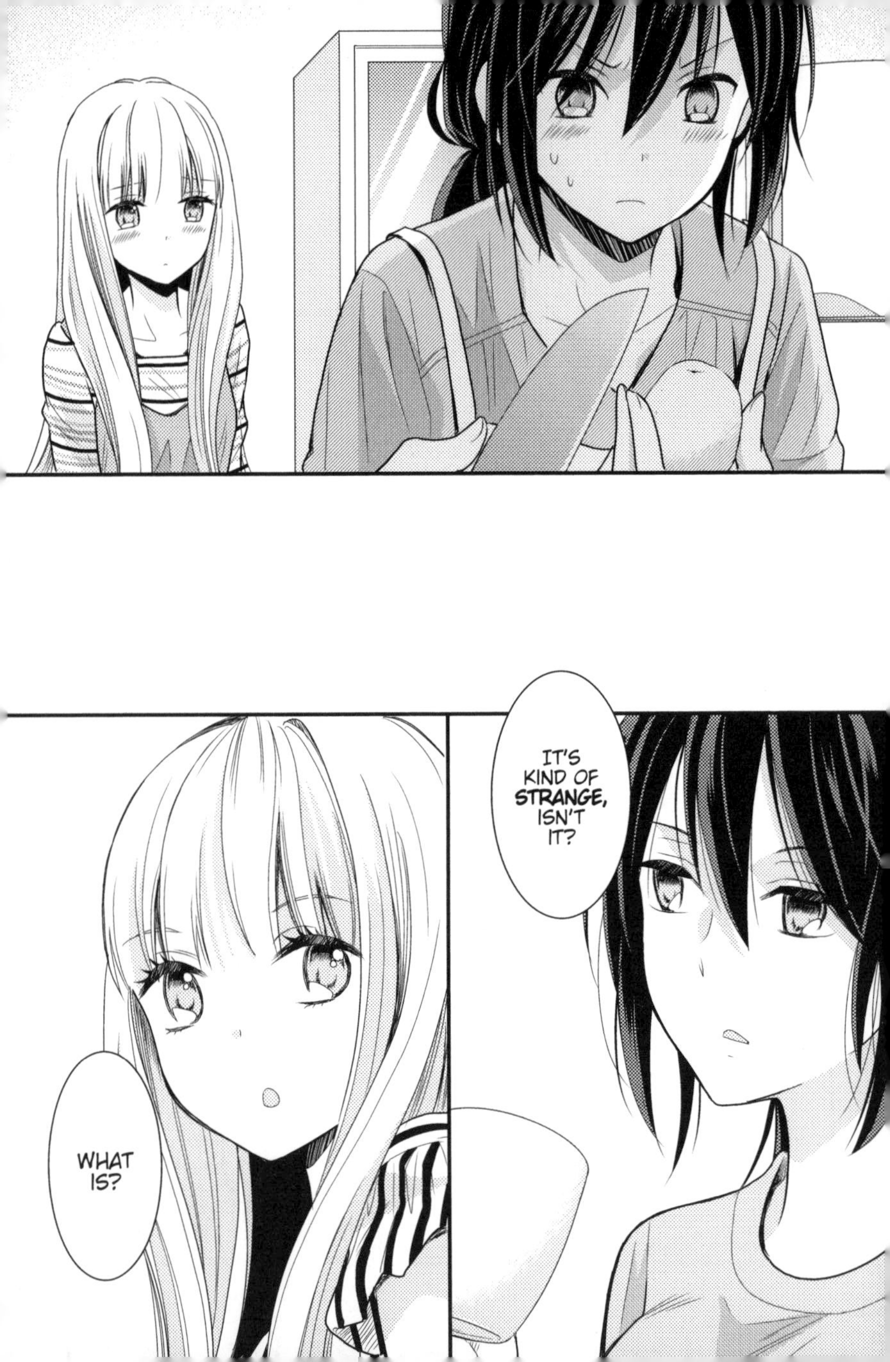
IT'S KIND OF STRANGE, ISN'T IT?
WHAT IS?

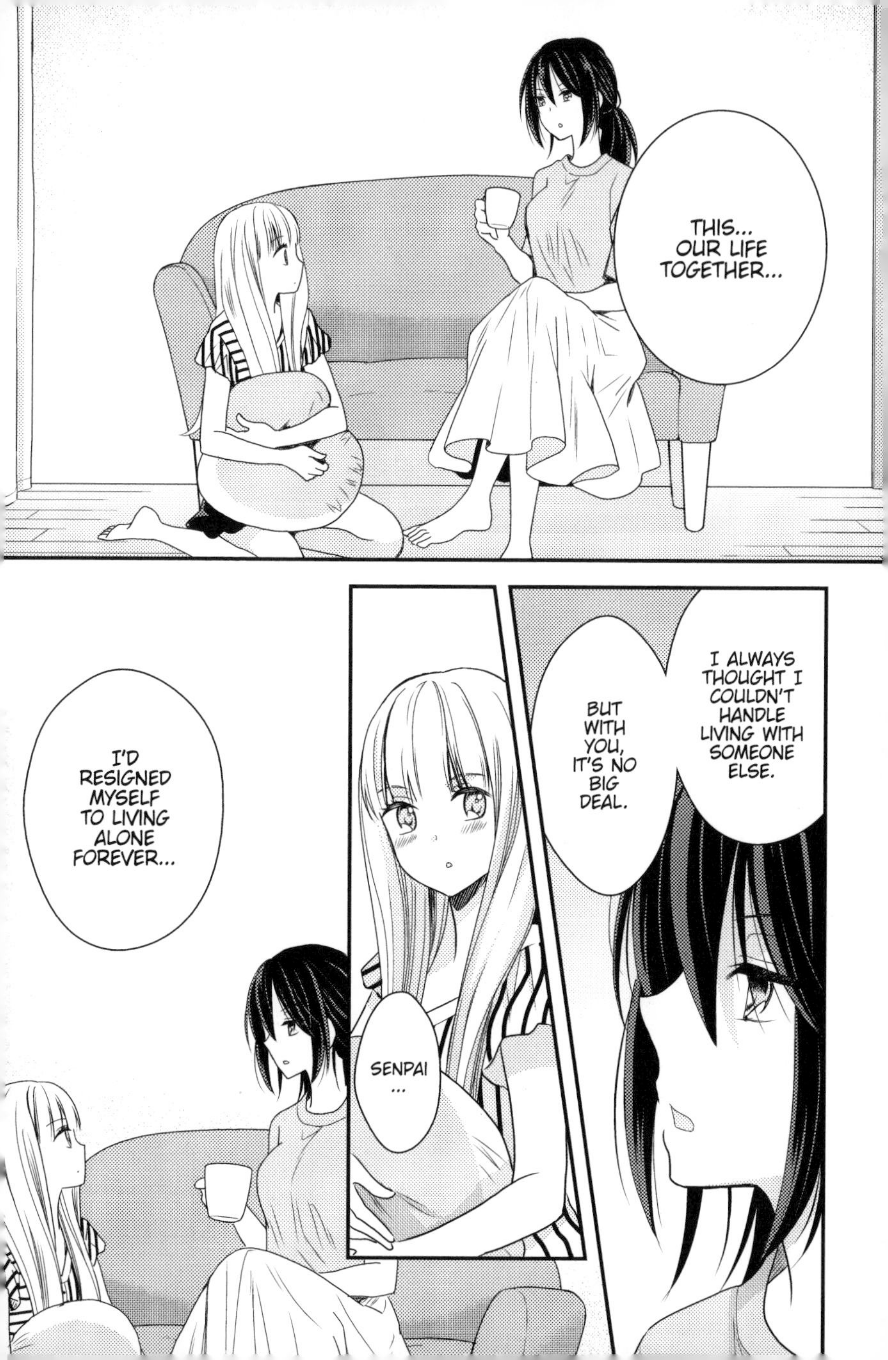
THIS... OUR LIFE TOGETHER...
I ALWAYS THOUGHT I COULDN'T HANDLE LIVING WITH SOMEONE ELSE.
BUT WITH YOU, IT'S NO BIG DEAL.
SENPAI ...
I'D RESIGNED MYSELF TO LIVING ALONE FOREVER...

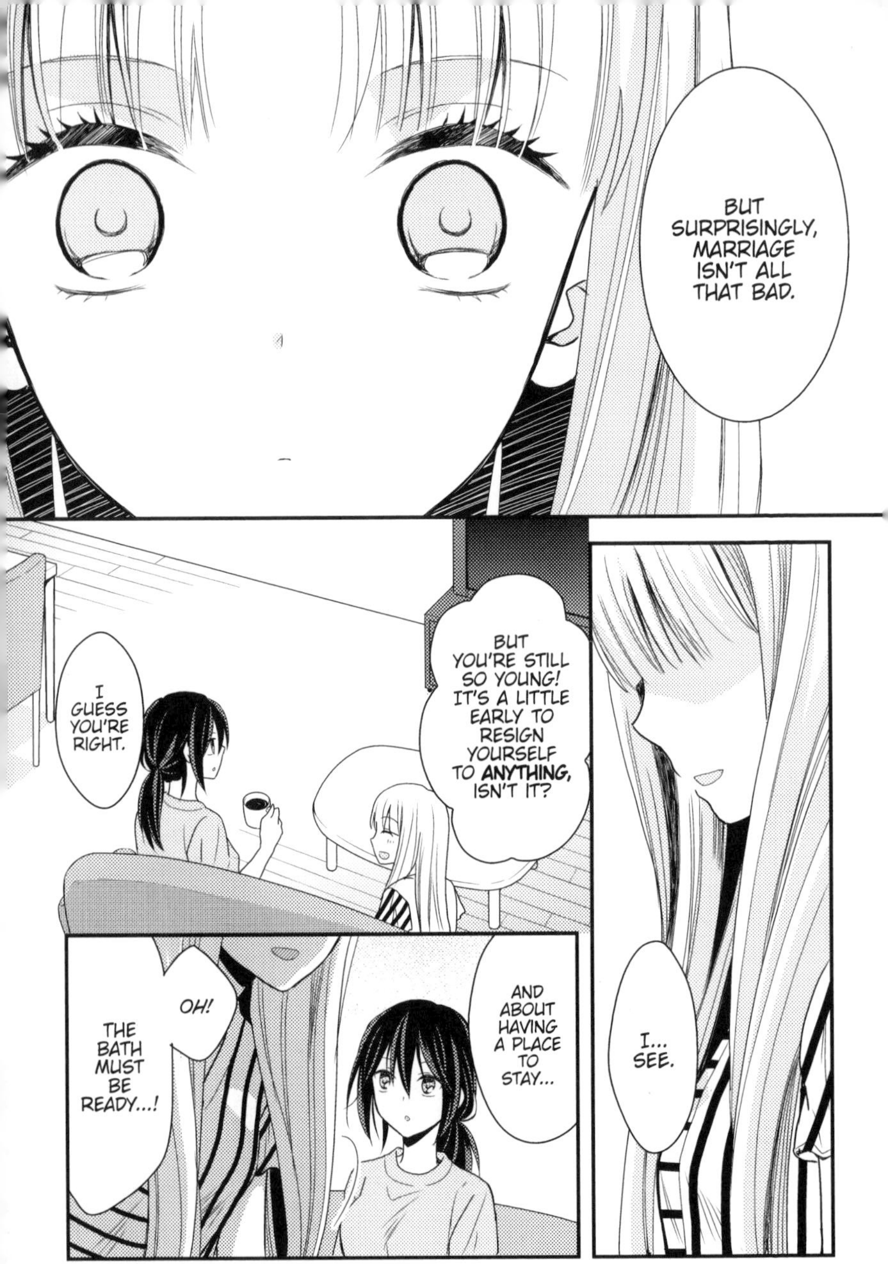
BUT SURPRISINGLY, MARRIAGE ISN'T ALL THAT BAD.
BUT YOU'RE STILL SO YOUNG! IT'S A LITTLE EARLY TO RESIGN YOURSELF TO **ANYTHING**, ISN'T IT?
I GUESS YOU'RE RIGHT.
I... SEE.
AND ABOUT HAVING A PLACE TO STAY...
OH!
THE BATH MUST BE READY...!

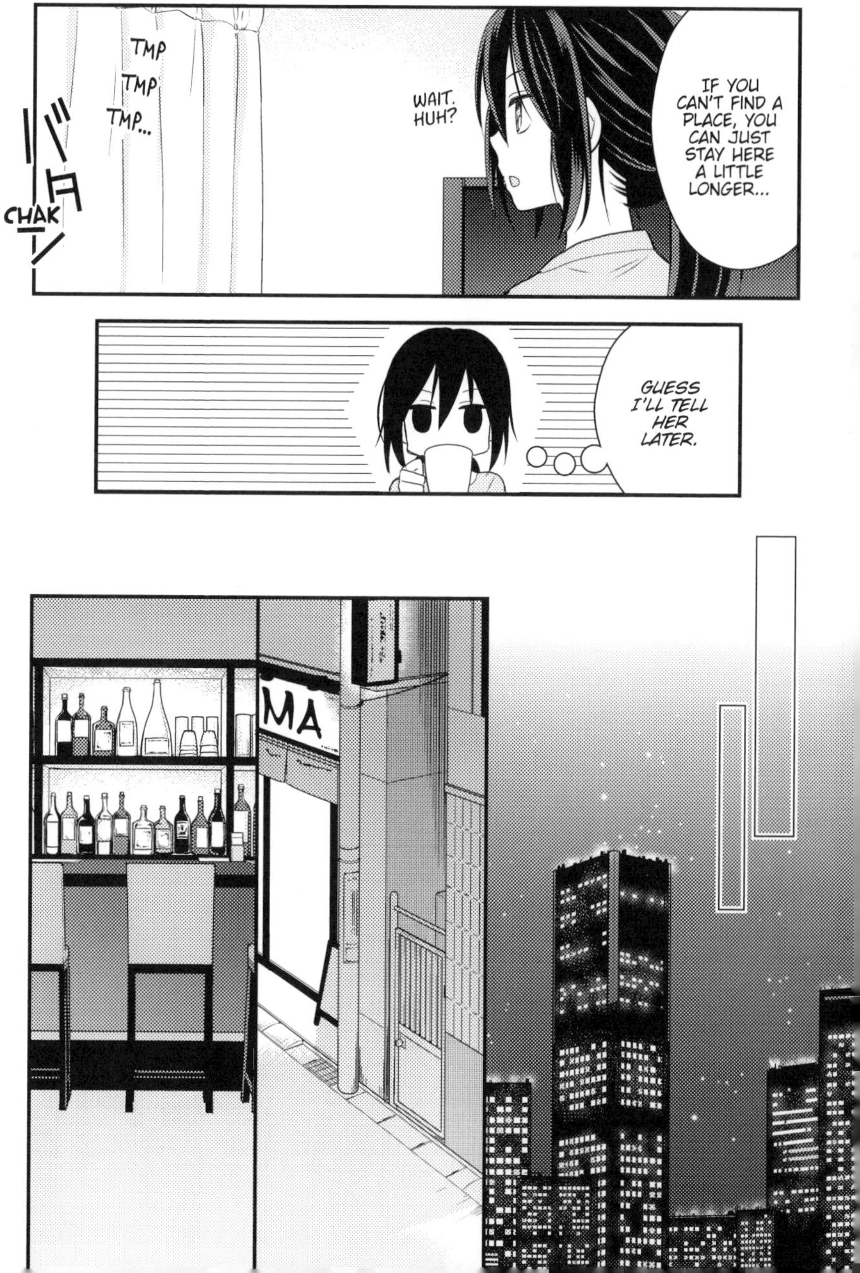
IF YOU CAN'T FIND A PLACE, YOU CAN JUST STAY HERE A LITTLE LONGER...
WAIT. HUH?
TMP
TMP
TMP...
CHAK
GUESS I'LL TELL HER LATER.

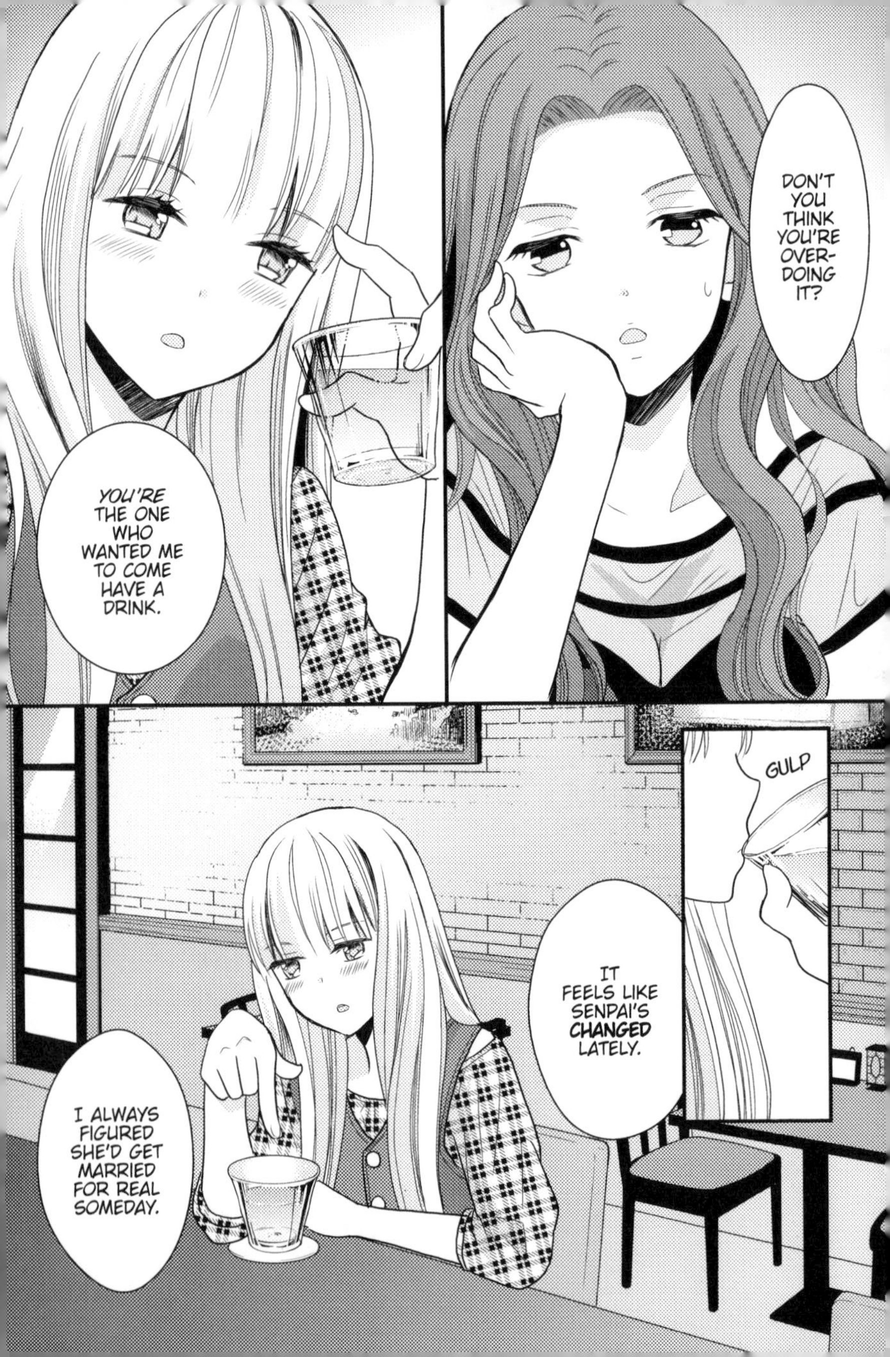
DON'T YOU THINK YOU'RE OVER-DOING IT?
YOU'RE THE ONE WHO WANTED ME TO COME HAVE A DRINK.
GULP
IT FEELS LIKE SENPAI'S **CHANGED** LATELY.
I ALWAYS FIGURED SHE'D GET MARRIED FOR REAL SOMEDAY.

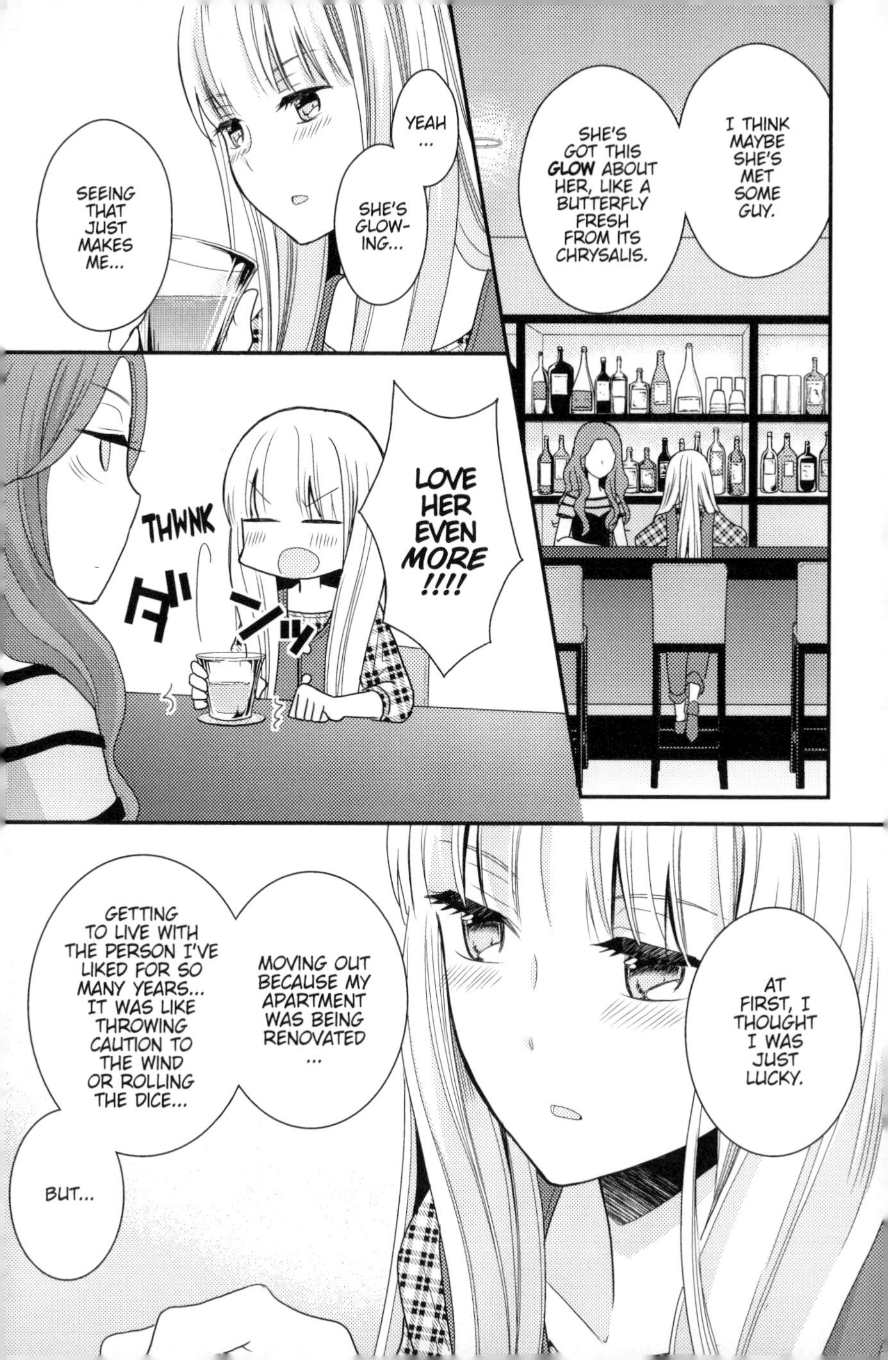
I THINK MAYBE SHE'S MET SOME GUY.
SHE'S GOT THIS **GLOW** ABOUT HER, LIKE A BUTTERFLY FRESH FROM ITS CHRYSALIS.
YEAH...
SHE'S GLOWING...
SEEING THAT JUST MAKES ME...
LOVE HER EVEN MORE!!!!
THWNK
AT FIRST, I THOUGHT I WAS JUST LUCKY.
MOVING OUT BECAUSE MY APARTMENT WAS BEING RENOVATED...
GETTING TO LIVE WITH THE PERSON I'VE LIKED FOR SO MANY YEARS... IT WAS LIKE THROWING CAUTION TO THE WIND OR ROLLING THE DICE...
BUT...

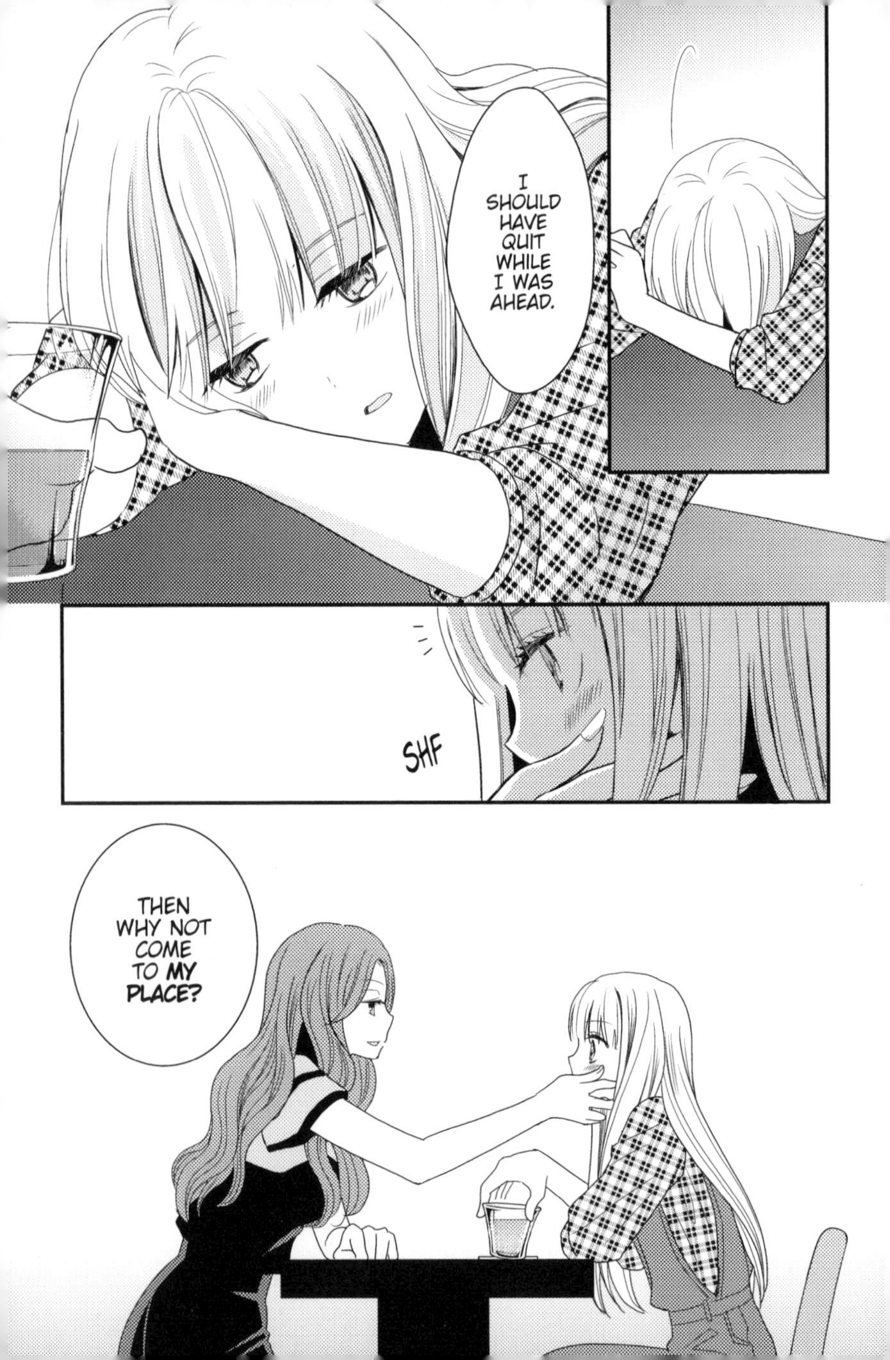
I SHOULD HAVE QUIT WHILE I WAS AHEAD.
SHF
THEN WHY NOT COME TO MY PLACE?

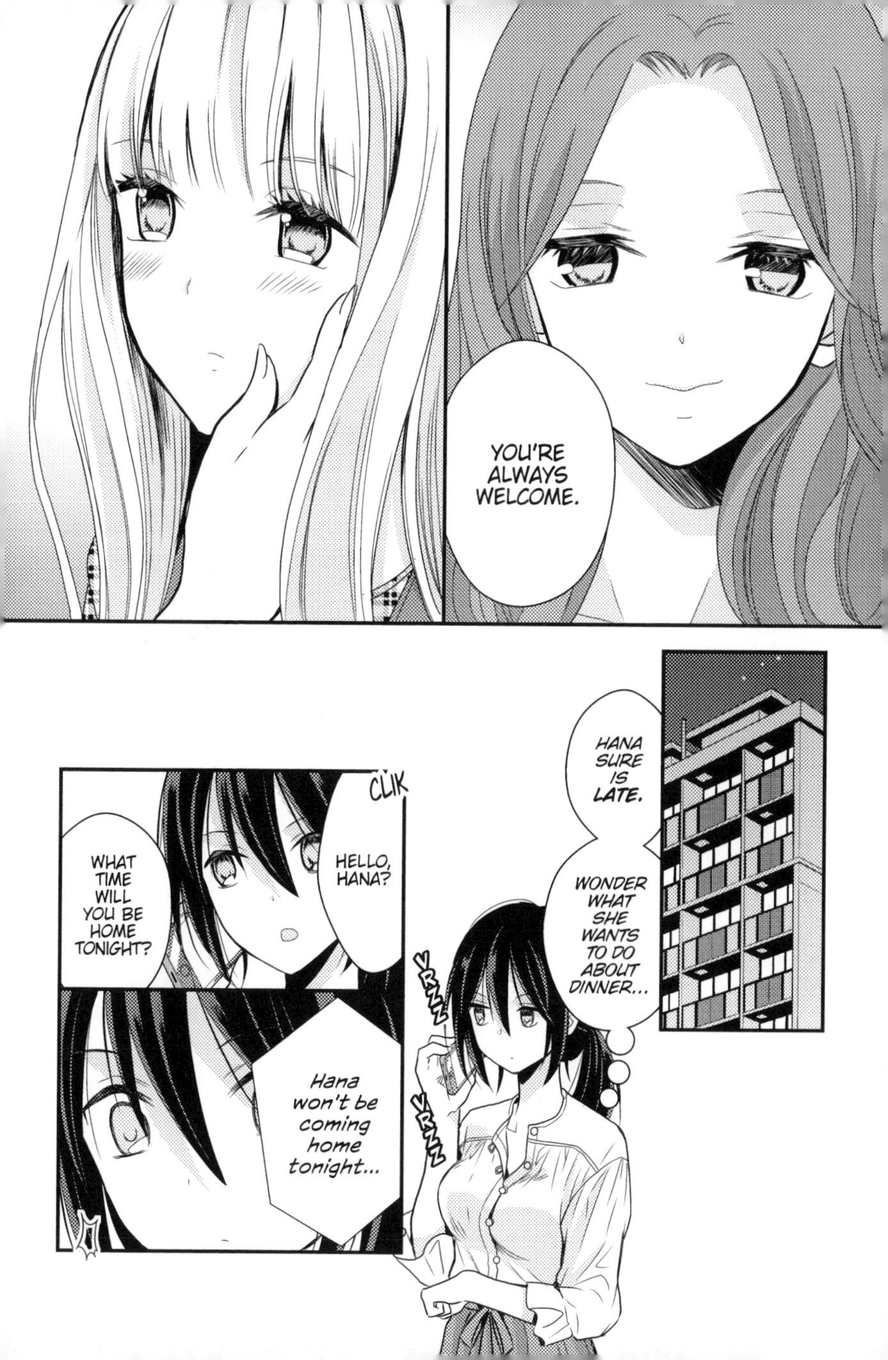
YOU'RE ALWAYS WELCOME.
HANA SURE IS LATE.
WONDER WHAT SHE WANTS TO DO ABOUT DINNER...
VRZZ
VRZZ
CLIK
HELLO, HANA?
WHAT TIME WILL YOU BE HOME TONIGHT?
Hana won't be coming home tonight...

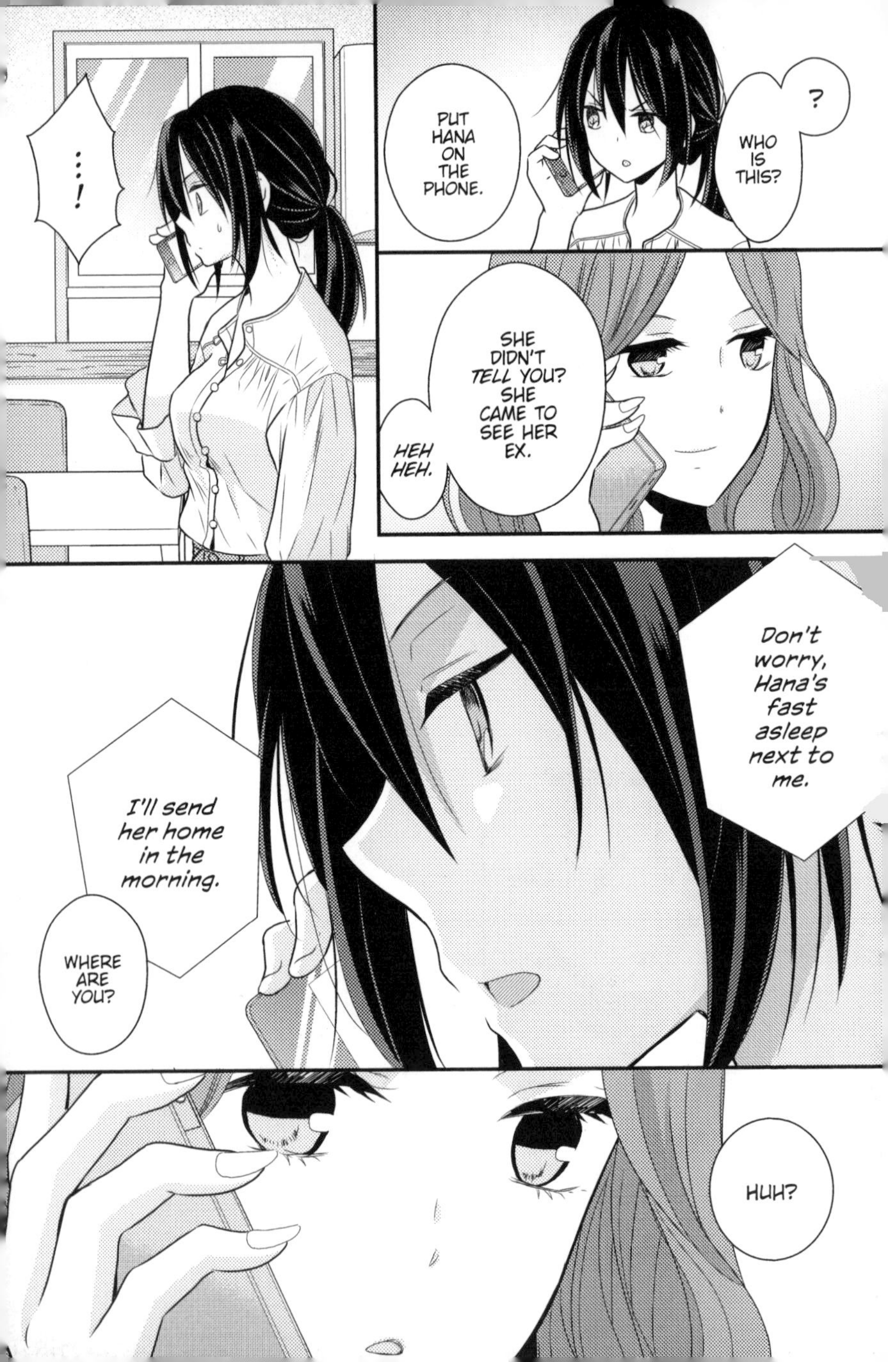
?
WHO IS THIS?
PUT HANA ON THE PHONE.
SHE DIDN'T *TELL* YOU? SHE CAME TO SEE HER EX.
HEH HEH.
...!
Don't worry, Hana's fast asleep next to me.
I'll send her home in the morning.
WHERE ARE YOU?
HUH?

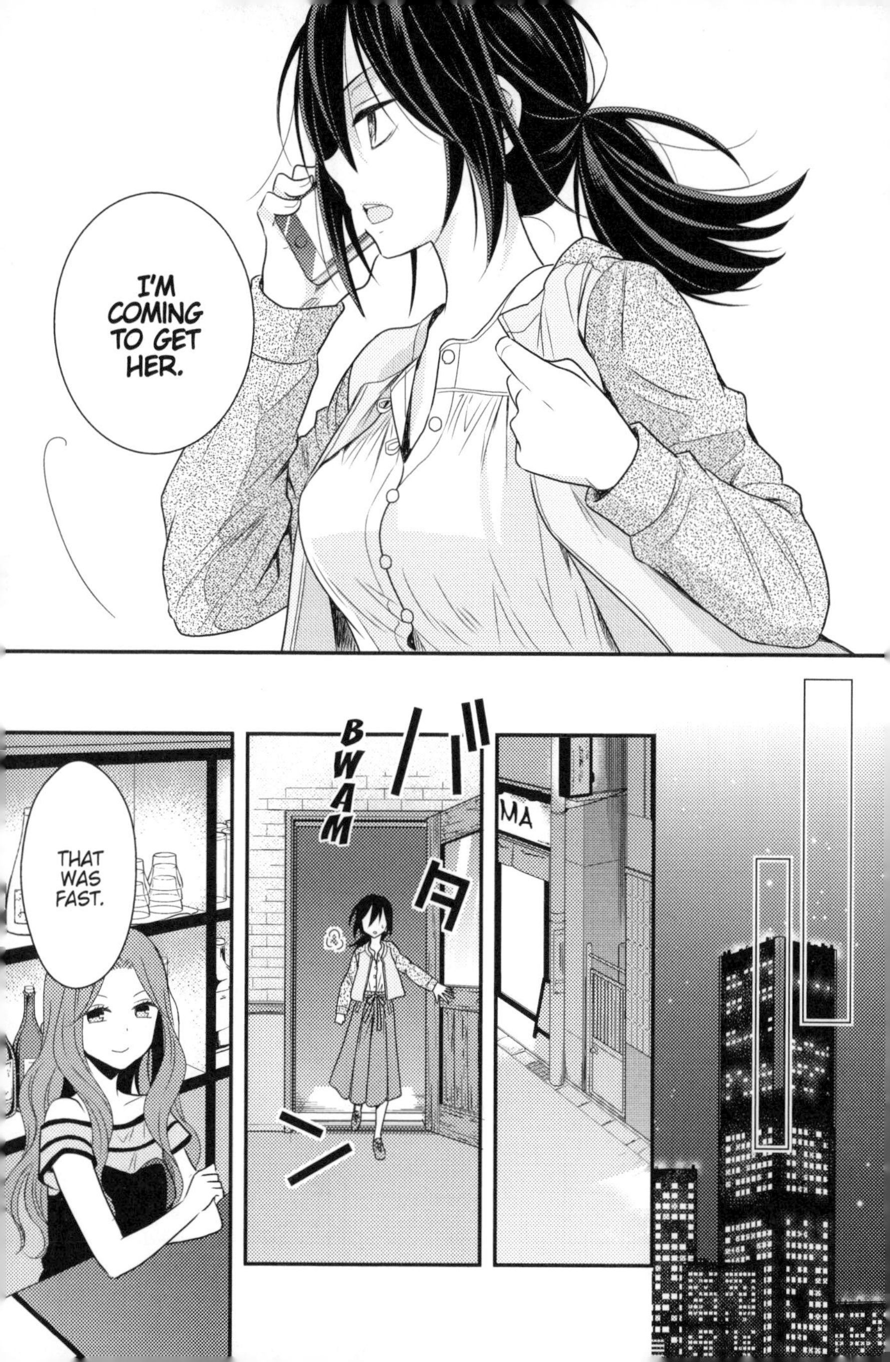
I'M COMING TO GET HER.
MA
BWAM
THAT WAS FAST.

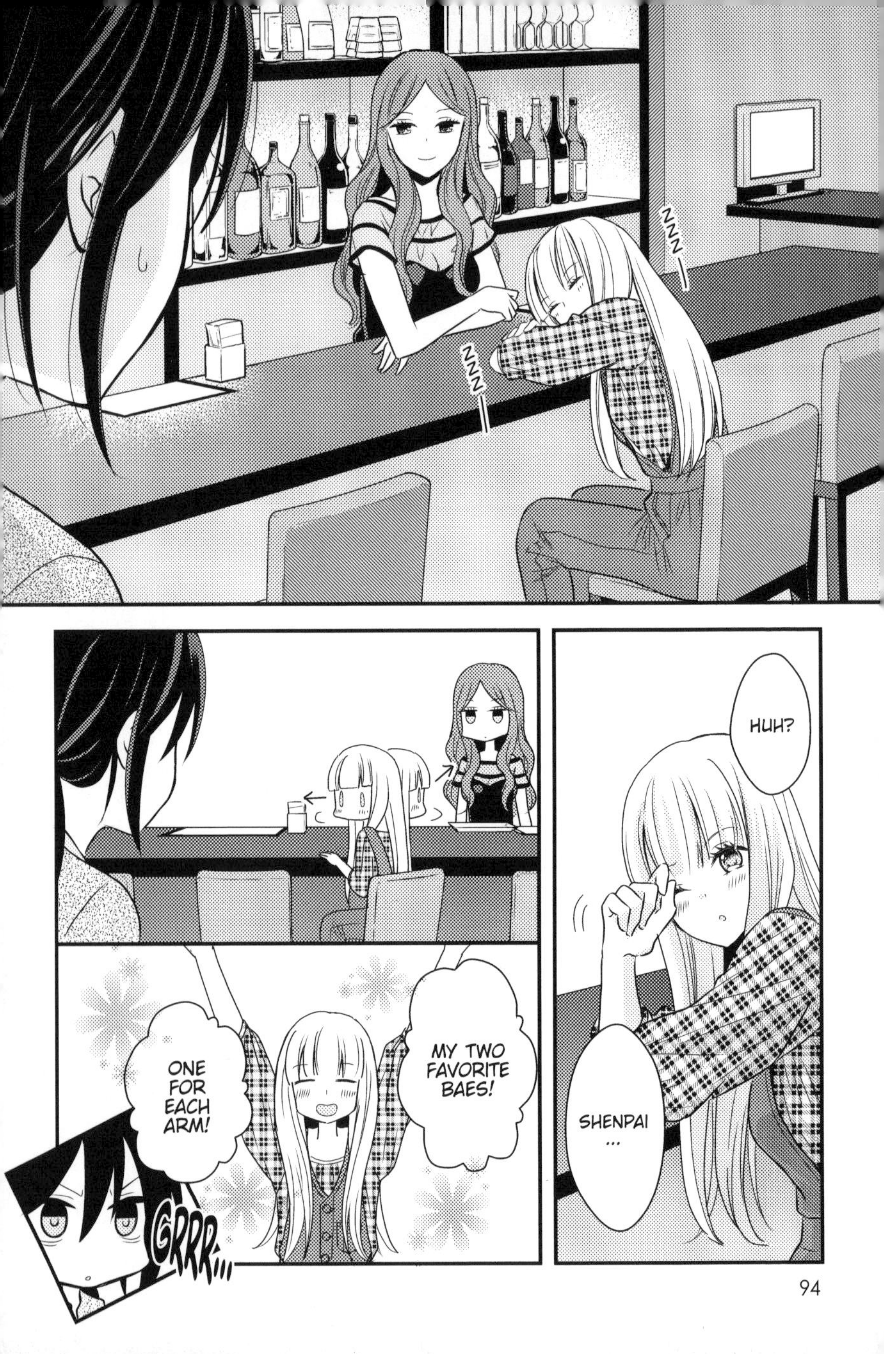
NNN—
NNN—
HUH?
SHENPAI...
MY TWO FAVORITE BAES!
ONE FOR EACH ARM!
GRRR...

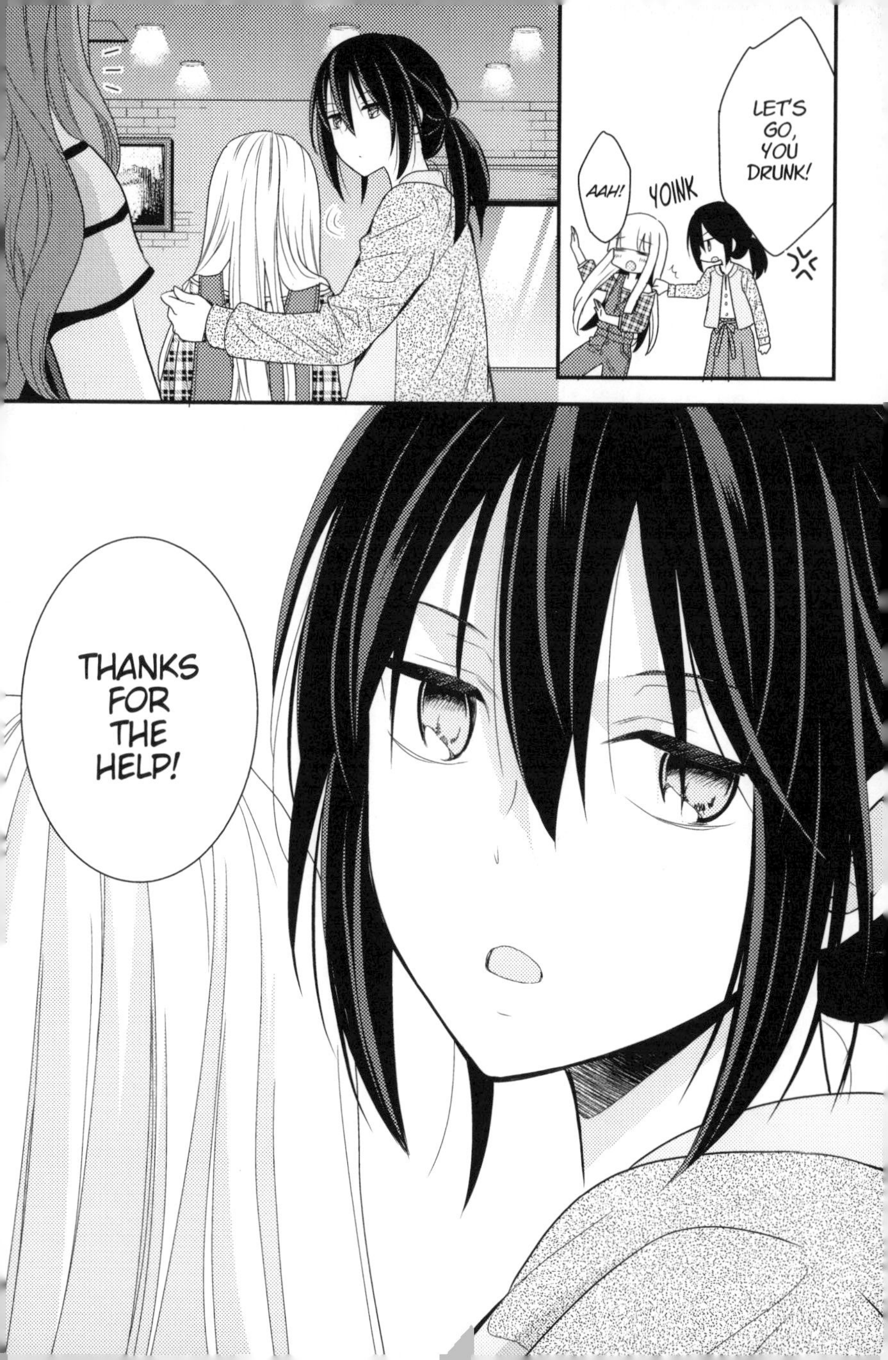
LET'S GO, YOU DRUNK!
YOINK
AAH!
THANKS FOR THE HELP!

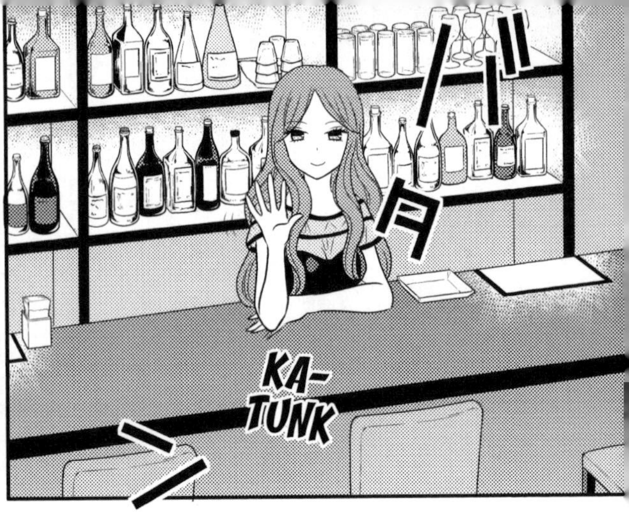
KA-TUNK

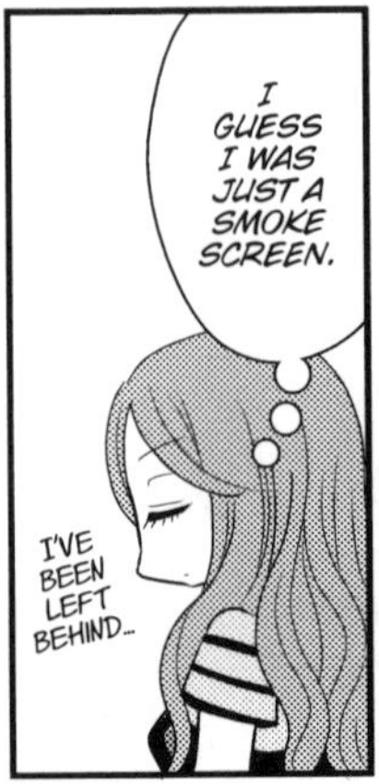
I GUESS I WAS JUST A SMOKE SCREEN.
I'VE BEEN LEFT BEHIND...

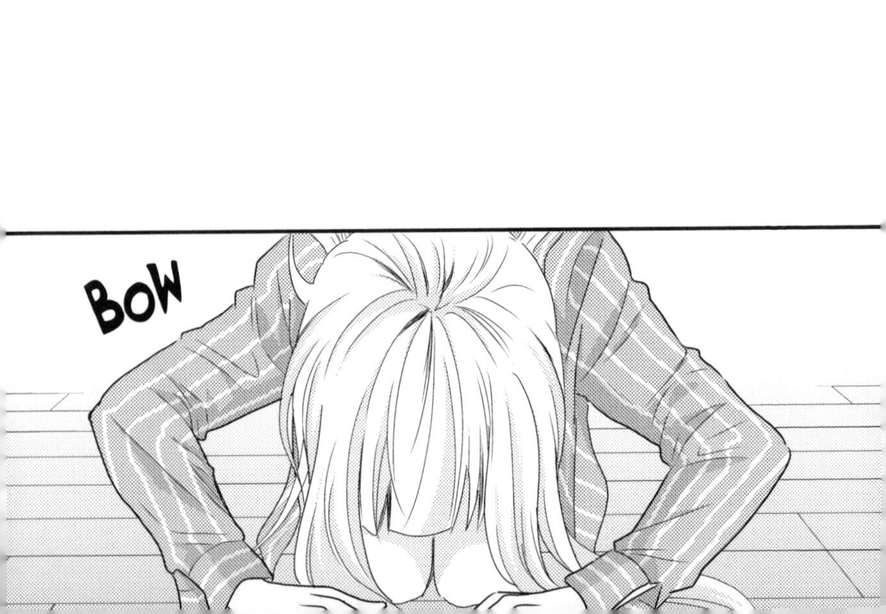
BOW

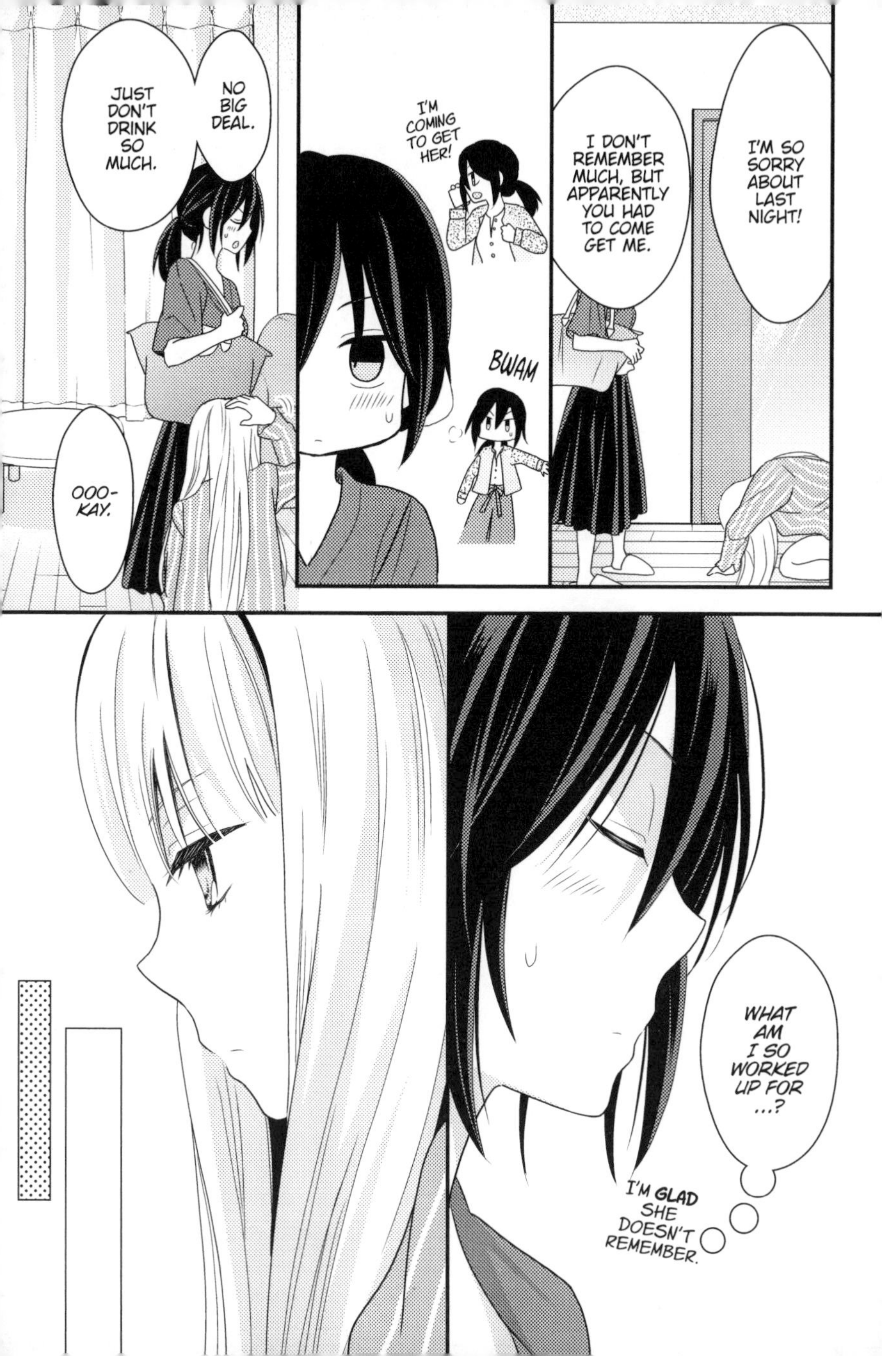
I'M SO SORRY ABOUT LAST NIGHT!
I DON'T REMEMBER MUCH, BUT APPARENTLY YOU HAD TO COME GET ME.
I'M COMING TO GET HER!
BWAM
NO BIG DEAL.
JUST DON'T DRINK SO MUCH.
OOO-KAY.
WHAT AM I SO WORKED UP FOR ...?
I'M GLAD SHE DOESN'T REMEMBER.

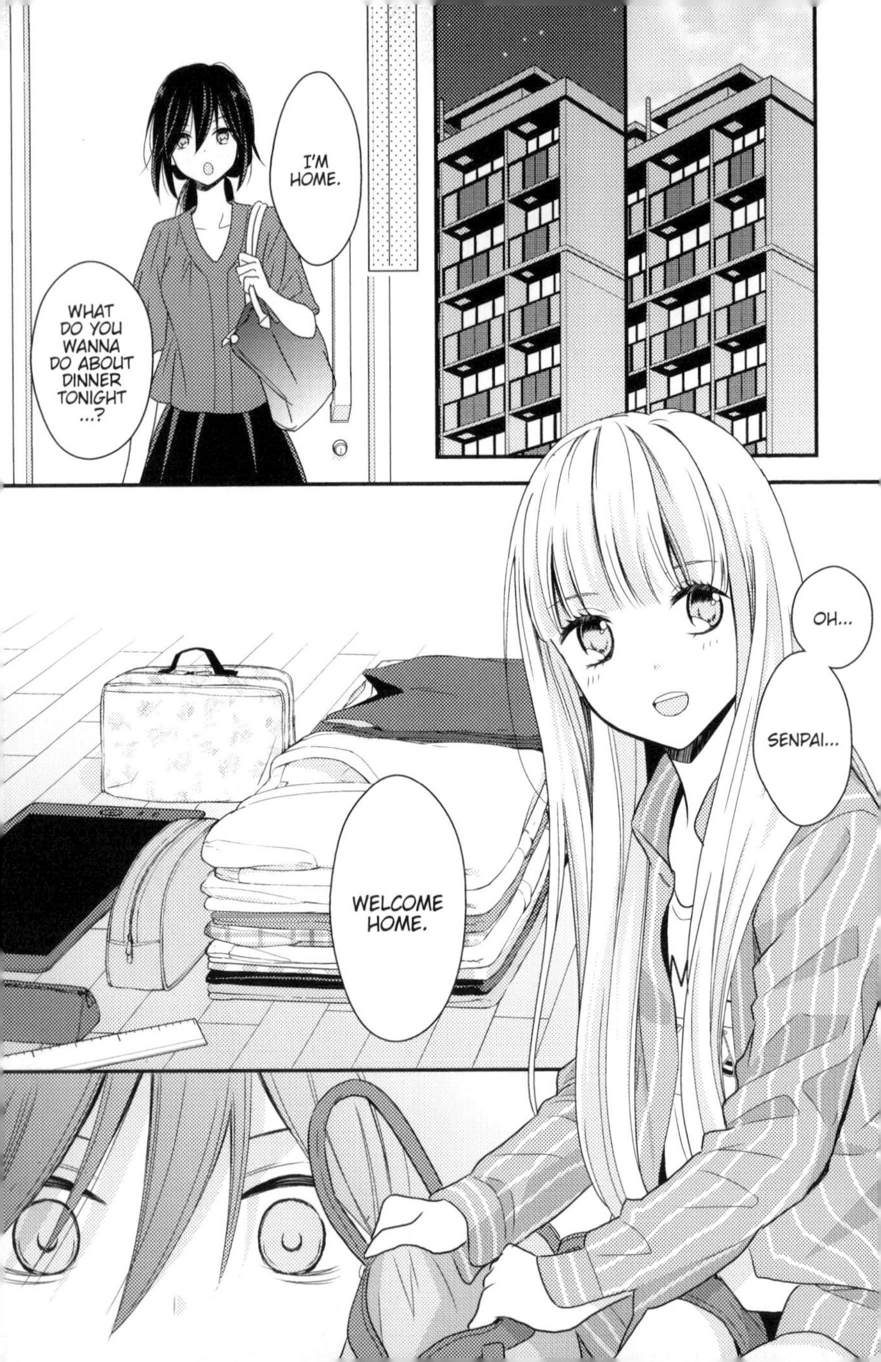
I'M HOME.
WHAT DO YOU WANNA DO ABOUT DINNER TONIGHT ...?
OH...
SENPAI...
WELCOME HOME.

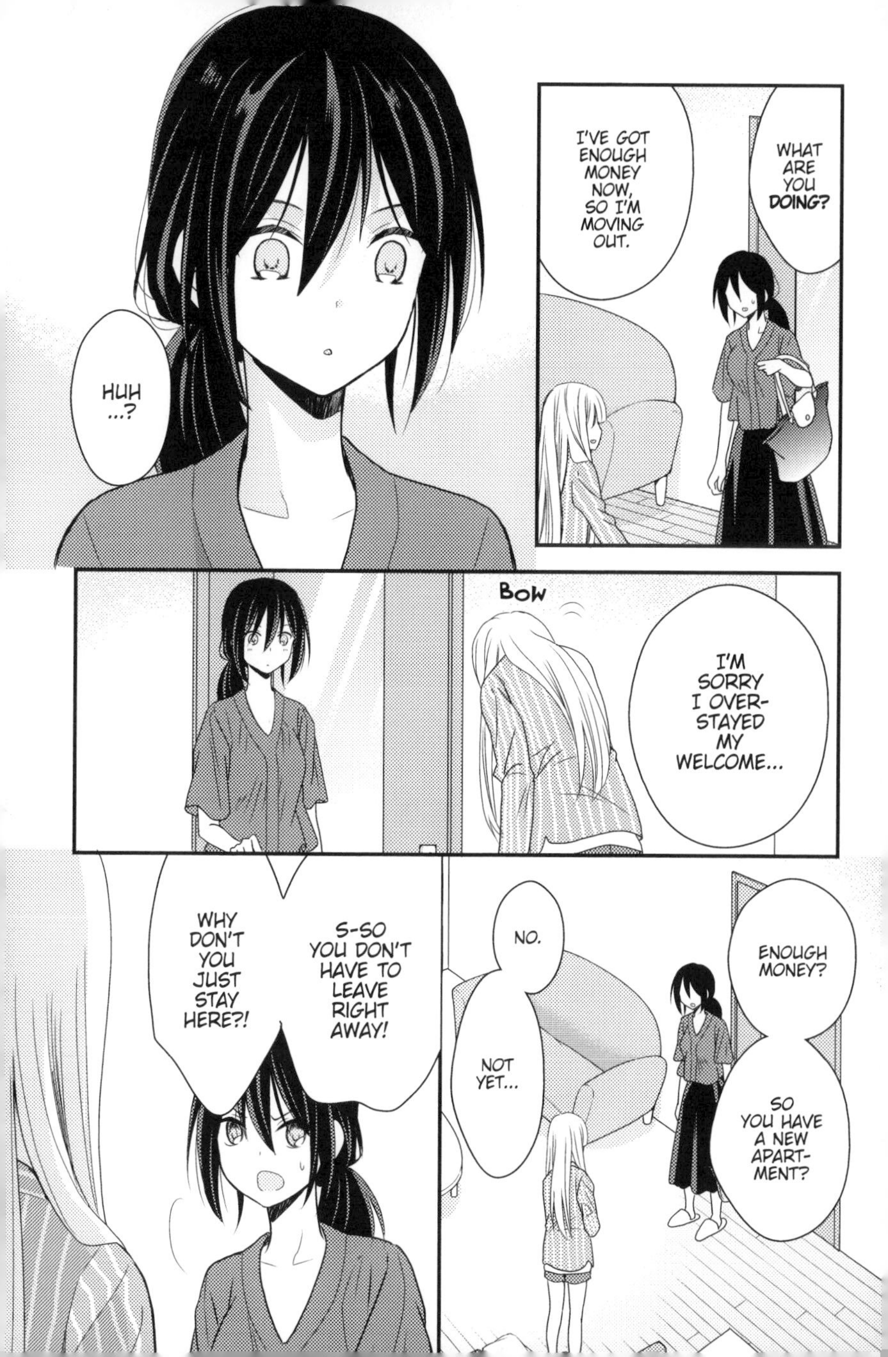
WHAT ARE YOU DOING?
I'VE GOT ENOUGH MONEY NOW, SO I'M MOVING OUT.
HUH ...?
BOW
I'M SORRY I OVERSTAYED MY WELCOME...
ENOUGH MONEY?
SO YOU HAVE A NEW APARTMENT?
NO.
NOT YET...
S-SO YOU DON'T HAVE TO LEAVE RIGHT AWAY!
WHY DON'T YOU JUST STAY HERE?!

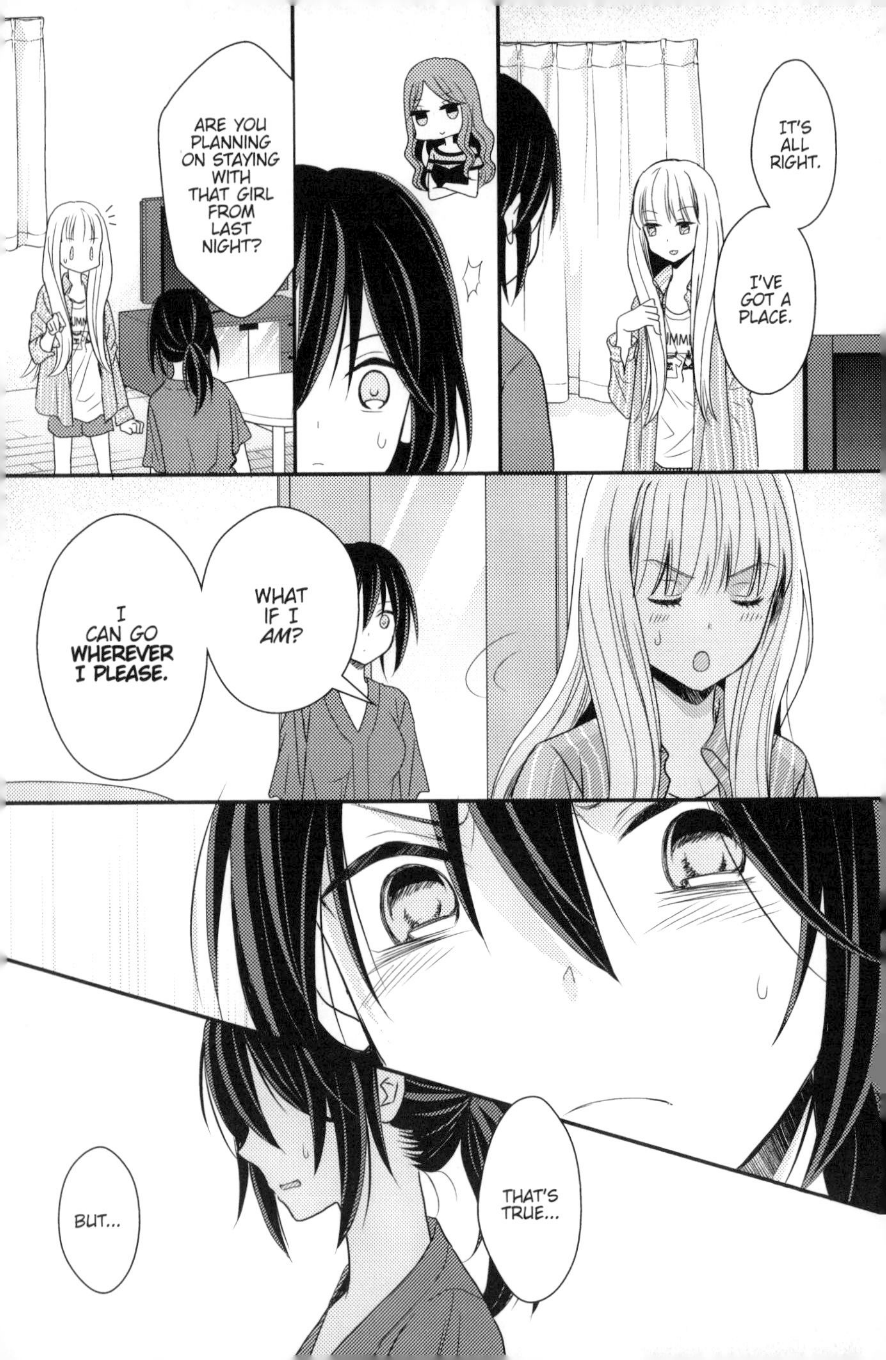
IT'S ALL RIGHT.
I'VE GOT A PLACE.
ARE YOU PLANNING ON STAYING WITH THAT GIRL FROM LAST NIGHT?
WHAT IF I AM?
I CAN GO **WHEREVER I PLEASE.**
THAT'S TRUE...
BUT...

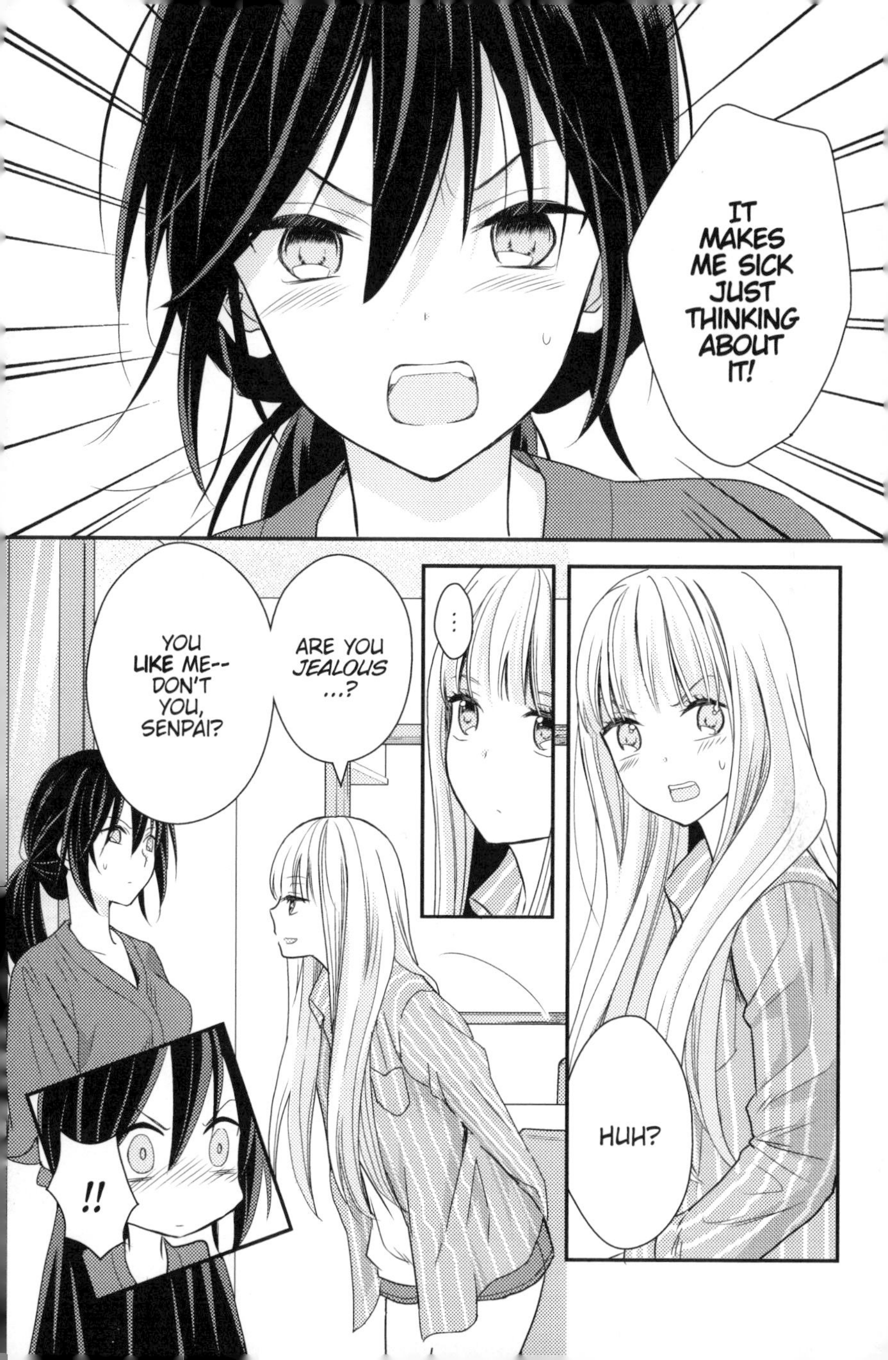
IT MAKES ME SICK JUST THINKING ABOUT IT!
HUH?
...
ARE YOU JEALOUS ...?
YOU LIKE ME-- DON'T YOU, SENPAI?
!!

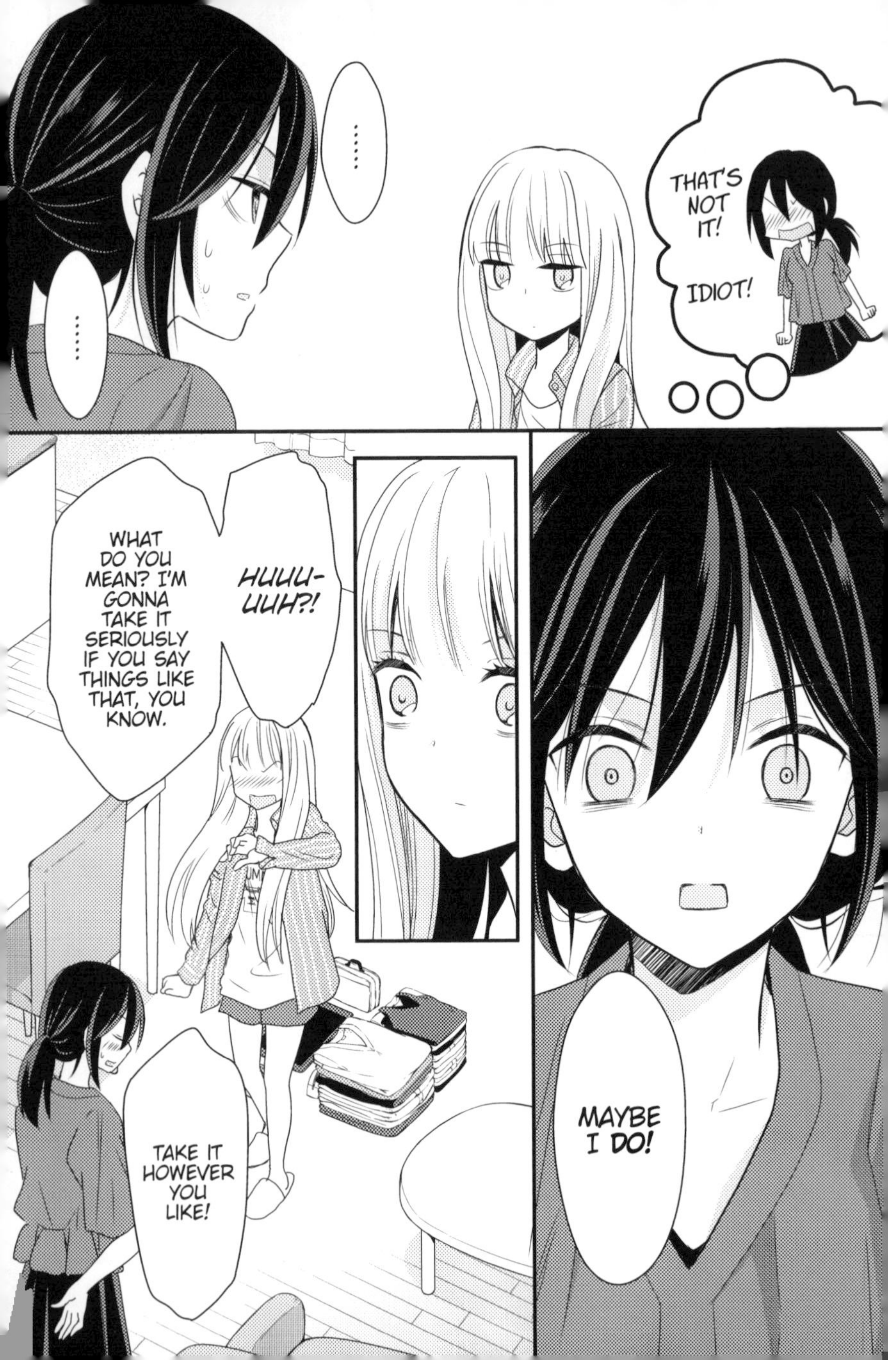
THAT'S NOT IT!
IDIOT!
......
......
MAYBE I DO!
HUUU-UUH?!
WHAT DO YOU MEAN? I'M GONNA TAKE IT SERIOUSLY IF YOU SAY THINGS LIKE THAT, YOU KNOW.
TAKE IT HOWEVER YOU LIKE!

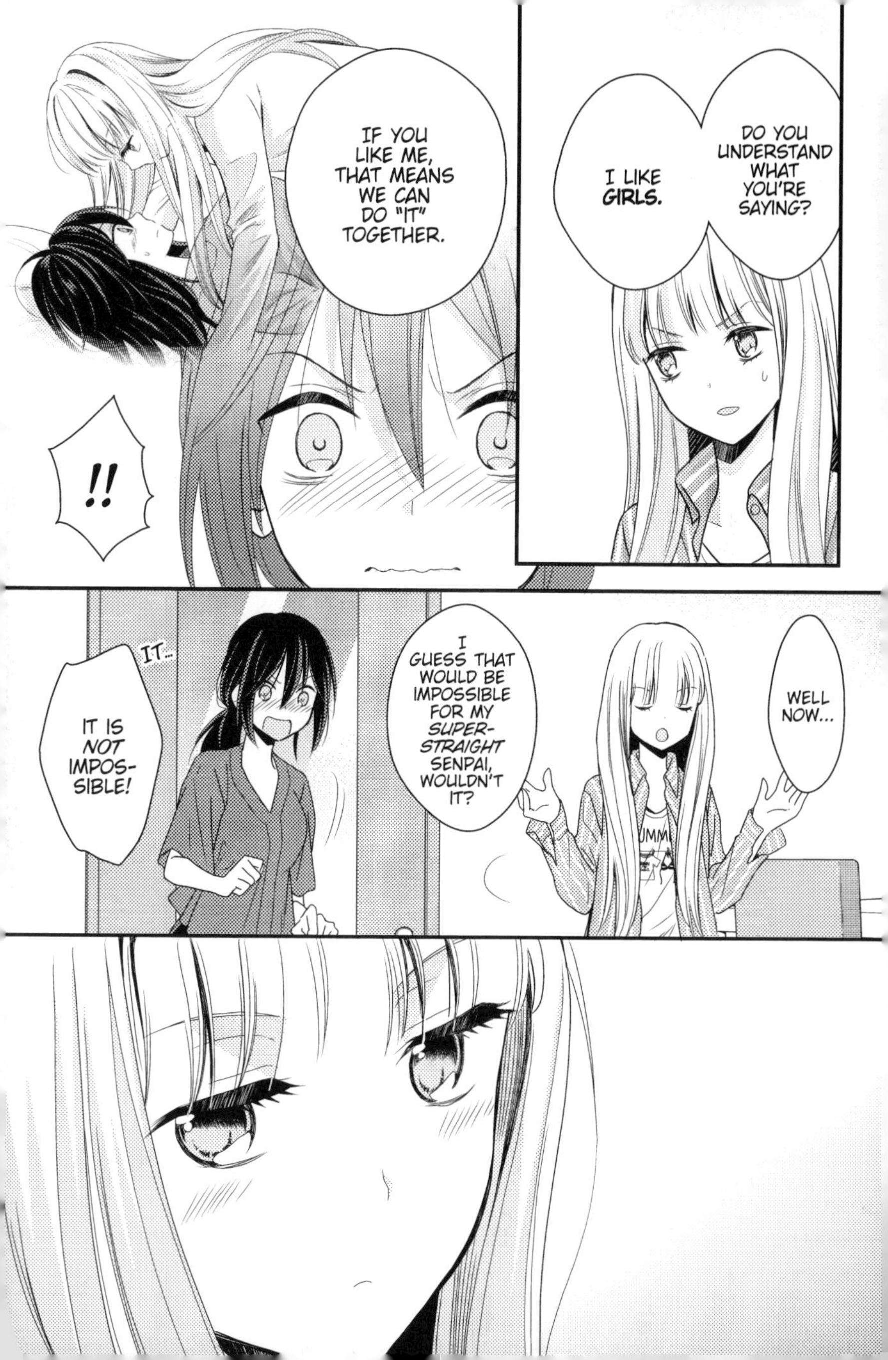
DO YOU UNDERSTAND WHAT YOU'RE SAYING?
I LIKE **GIRLS.**
IF YOU LIKE ME, THAT MEANS WE CAN DO "IT" TOGETHER.
!!
WELL NOW...
I GUESS THAT WOULD BE IMPOSSIBLE FOR MY *SUPER-STRAIGHT* SENPAI, WOULDN'T IT?
IT...
IT IS *NOT* IMPOS-SIBLE!

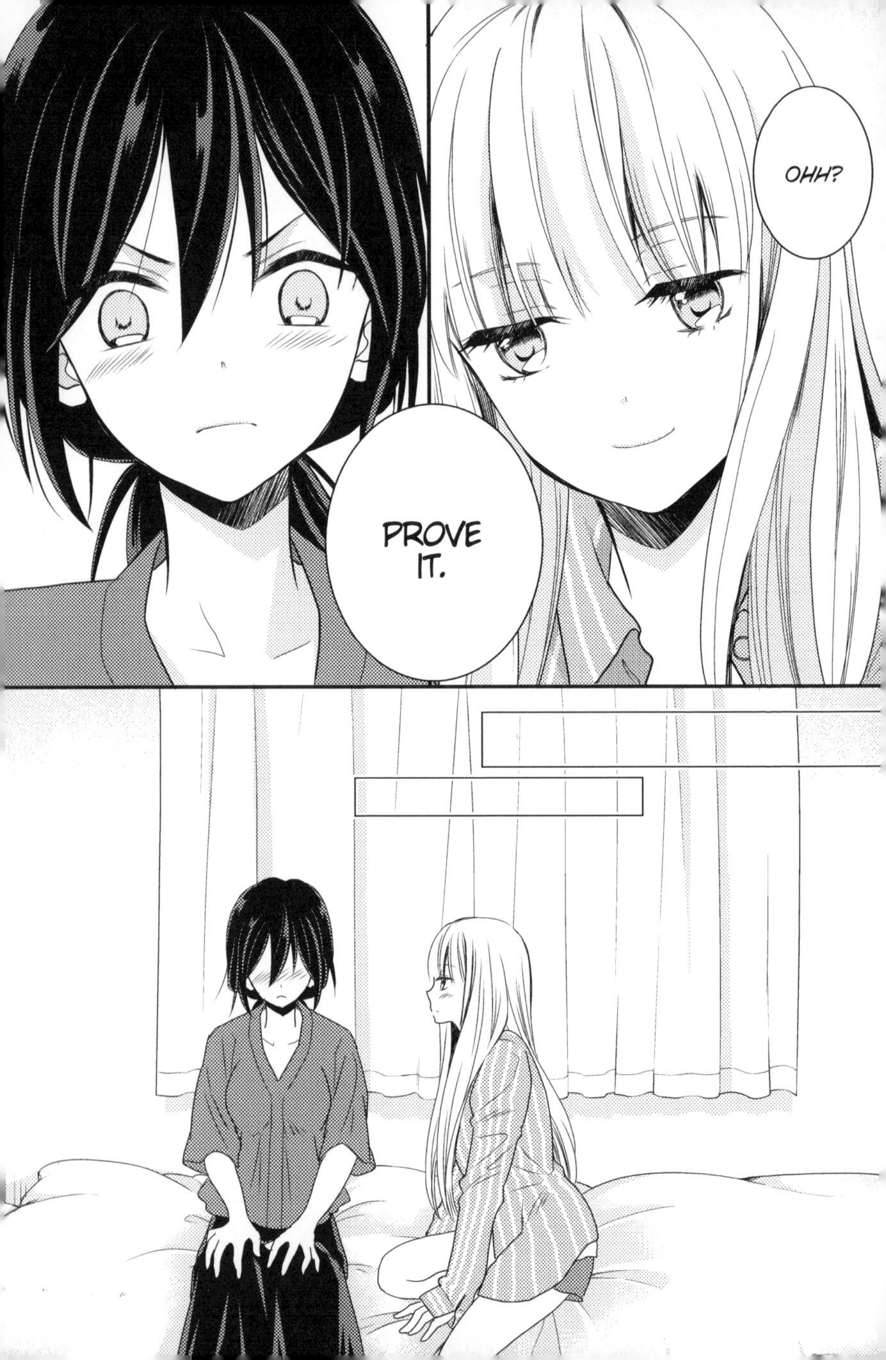
OHH?
PROVE IT.

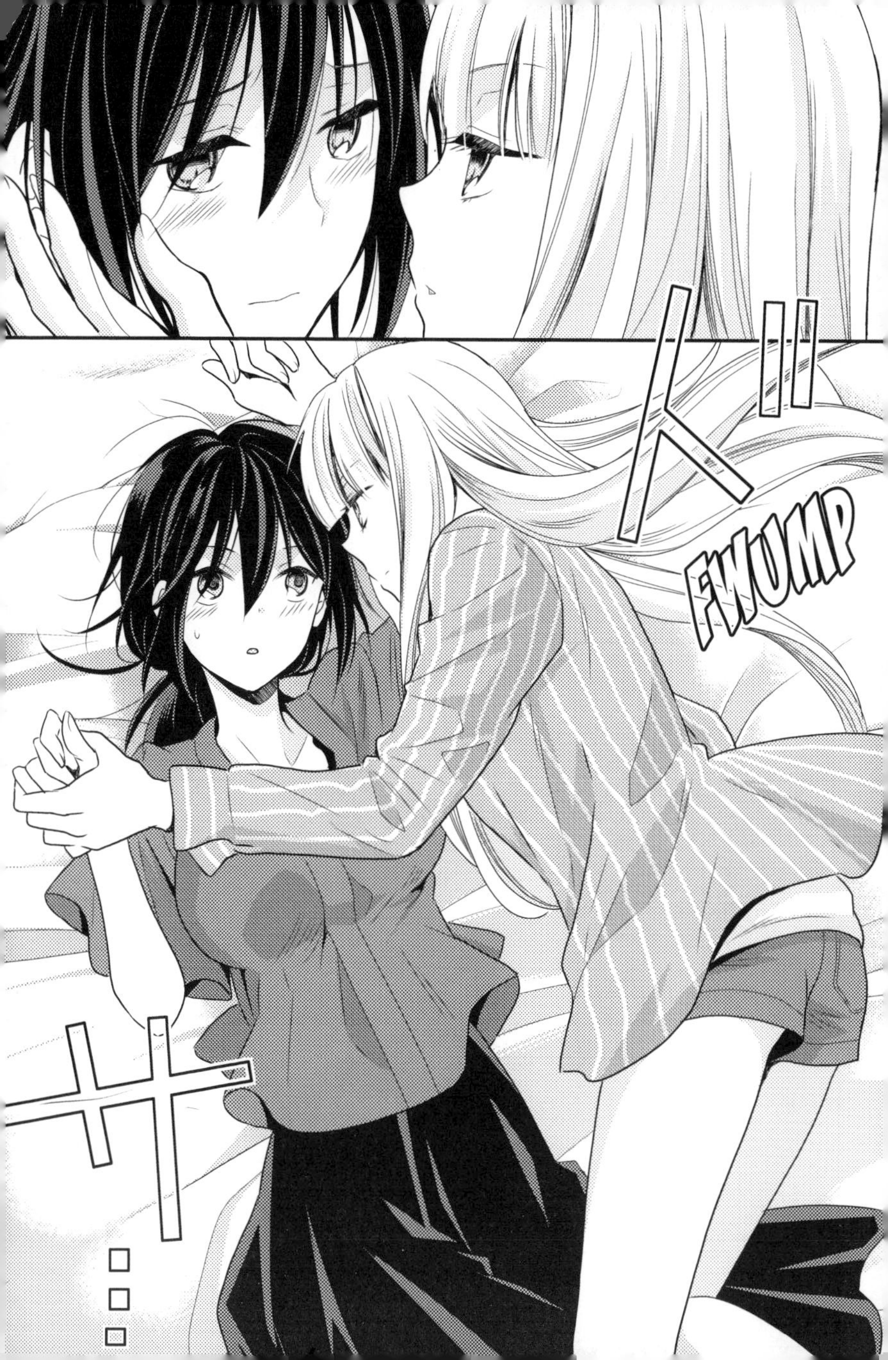
FWUMP

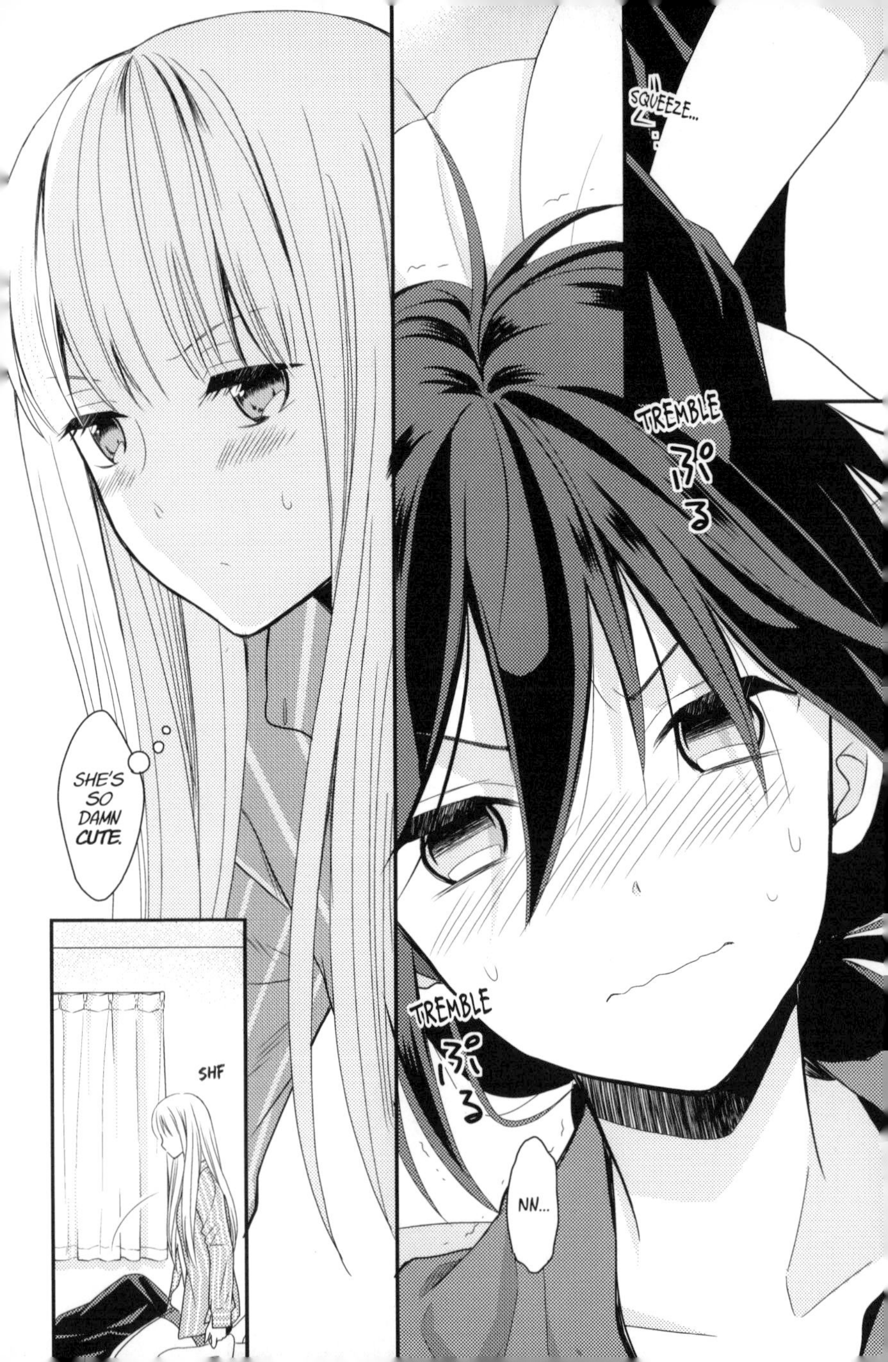
SQUEEZE...
TREMBLE
ぷる
TREMBLE
ぷる
NN...
SHE'S SO DAMN CUTE.
SHF

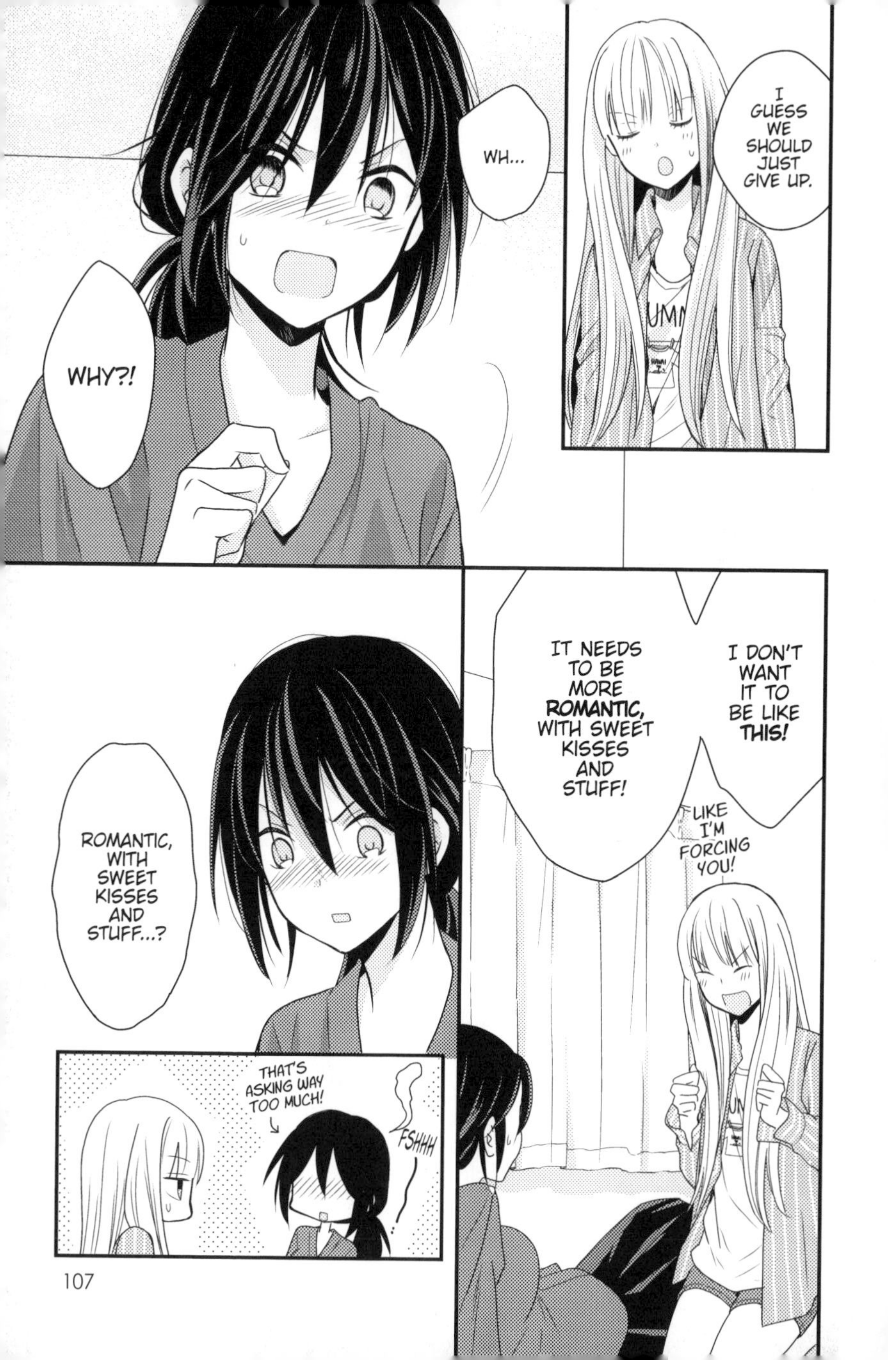
I GUESS WE SHOULD JUST GIVE UP.
WH...
WHY?!
I DON'T WANT IT TO BE LIKE THIS!
IT NEEDS TO BE MORE ROMANTIC, WITH SWEET KISSES AND STUFF!
LIKE I'M FORCING YOU!
ROMANTIC, WITH SWEET KISSES AND STUFF...?
THAT'S ASKING WAY TOO MUCH!
FSHHH

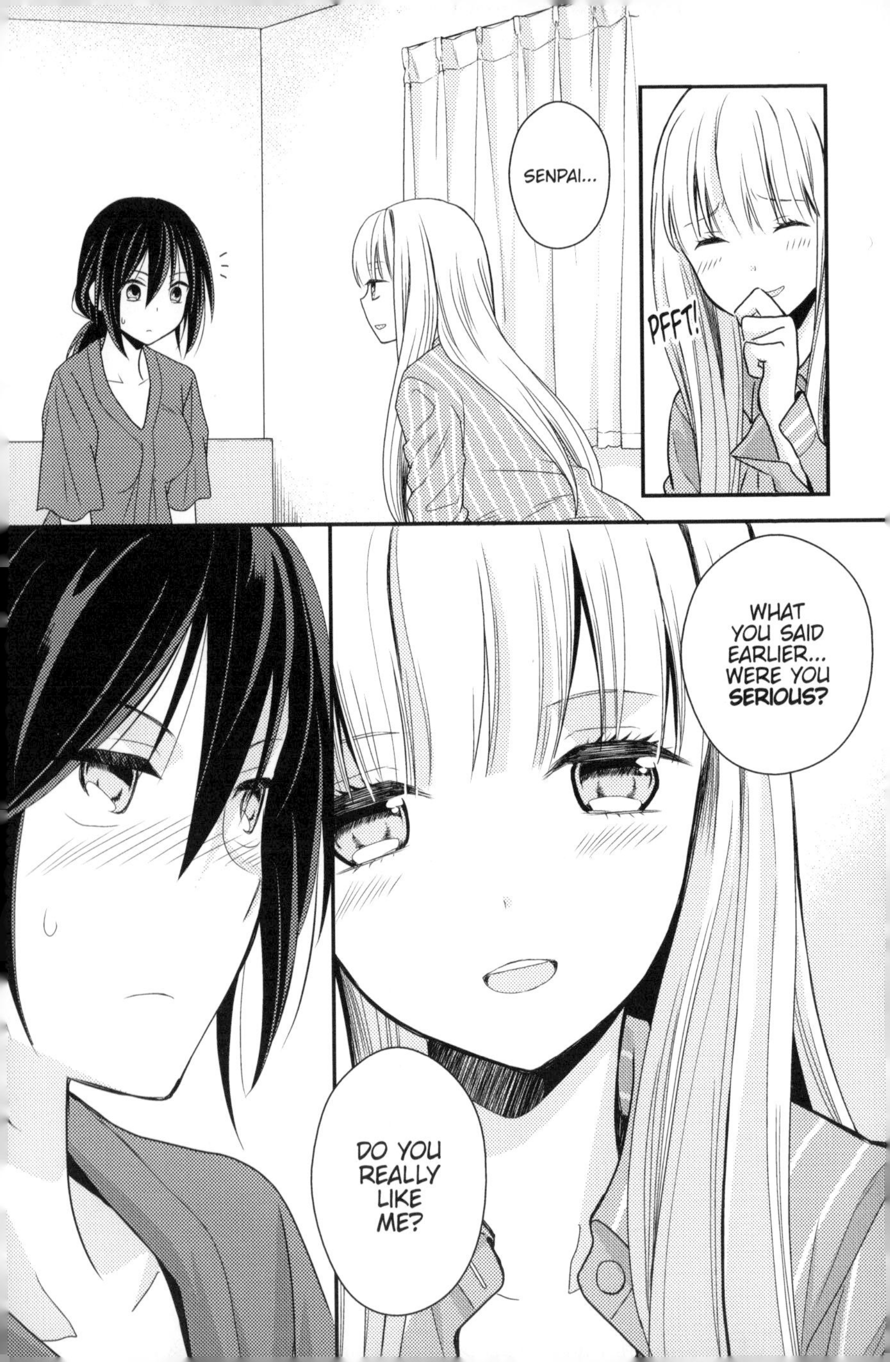
PFFT!
SENPAI...
WHAT YOU SAID EARLIER... WERE YOU SERIOUS?
DO YOU REALLY LIKE ME?

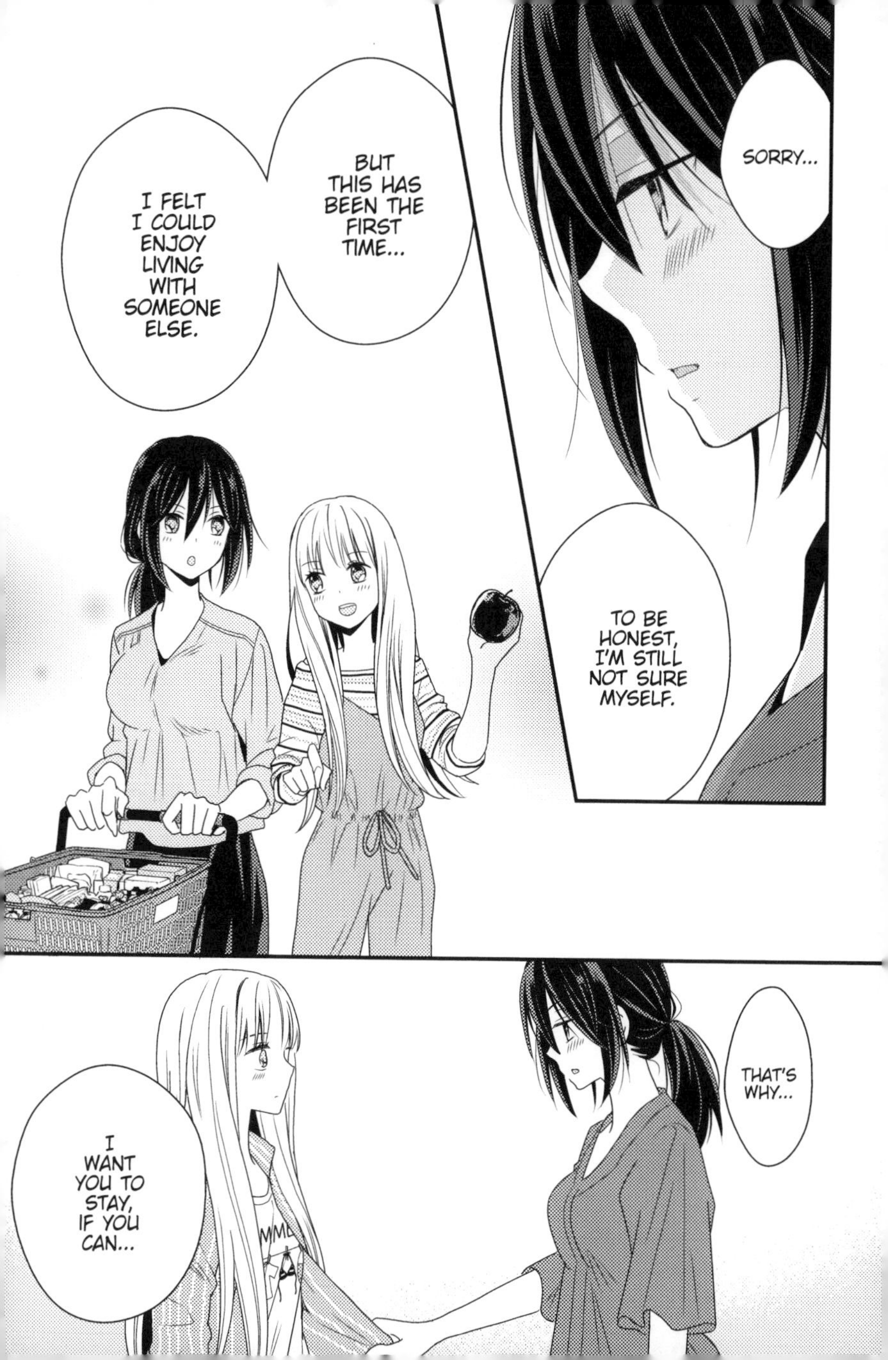
SORRY...
TO BE HONEST, I'M STILL NOT SURE MYSELF.
BUT THIS HAS BEEN THE FIRST TIME...
I FELT I COULD ENJOY LIVING WITH SOMEONE ELSE.
THAT'S WHY...
I WANT YOU TO STAY, IF YOU CAN...

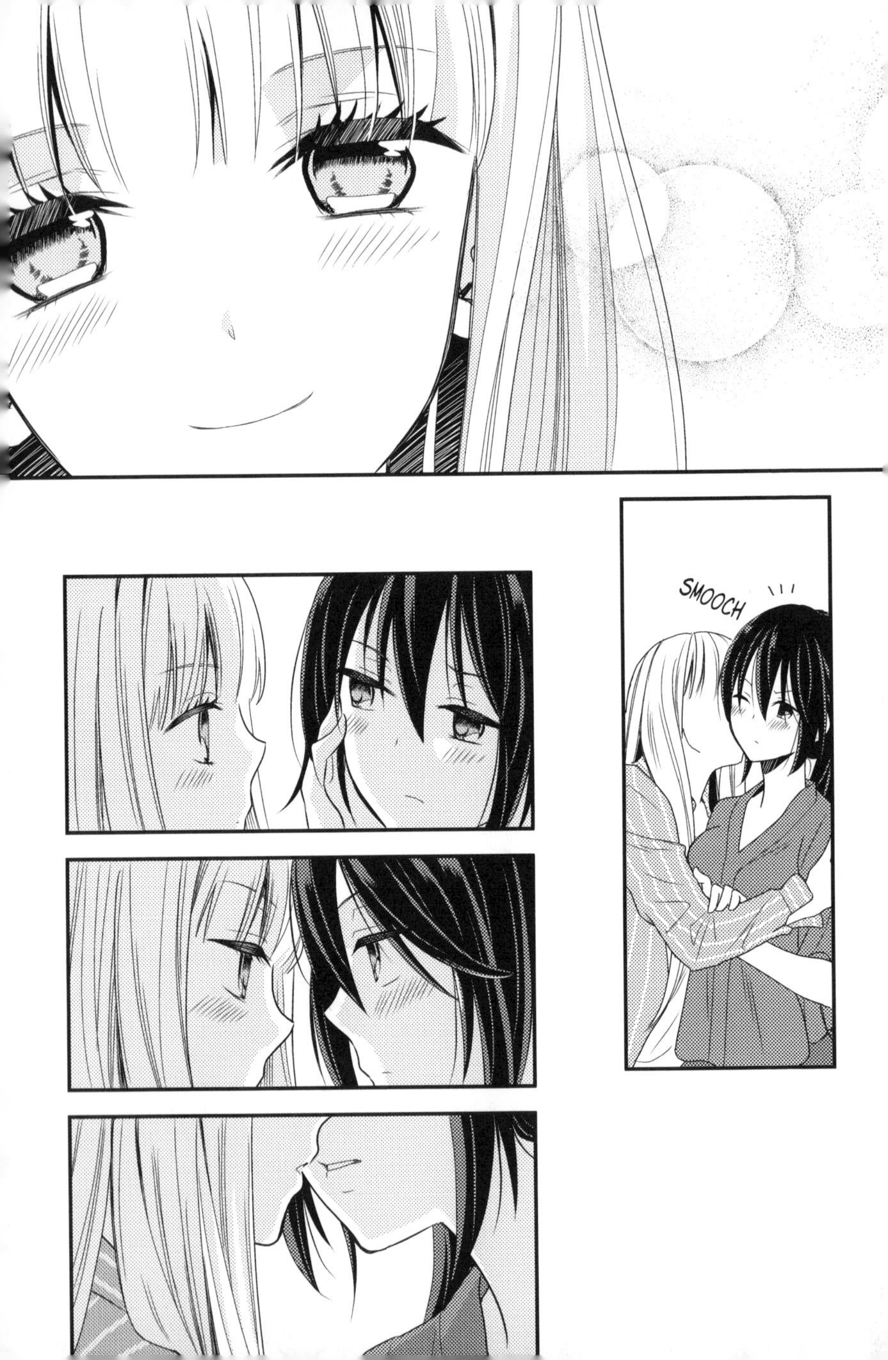
SMOOCH

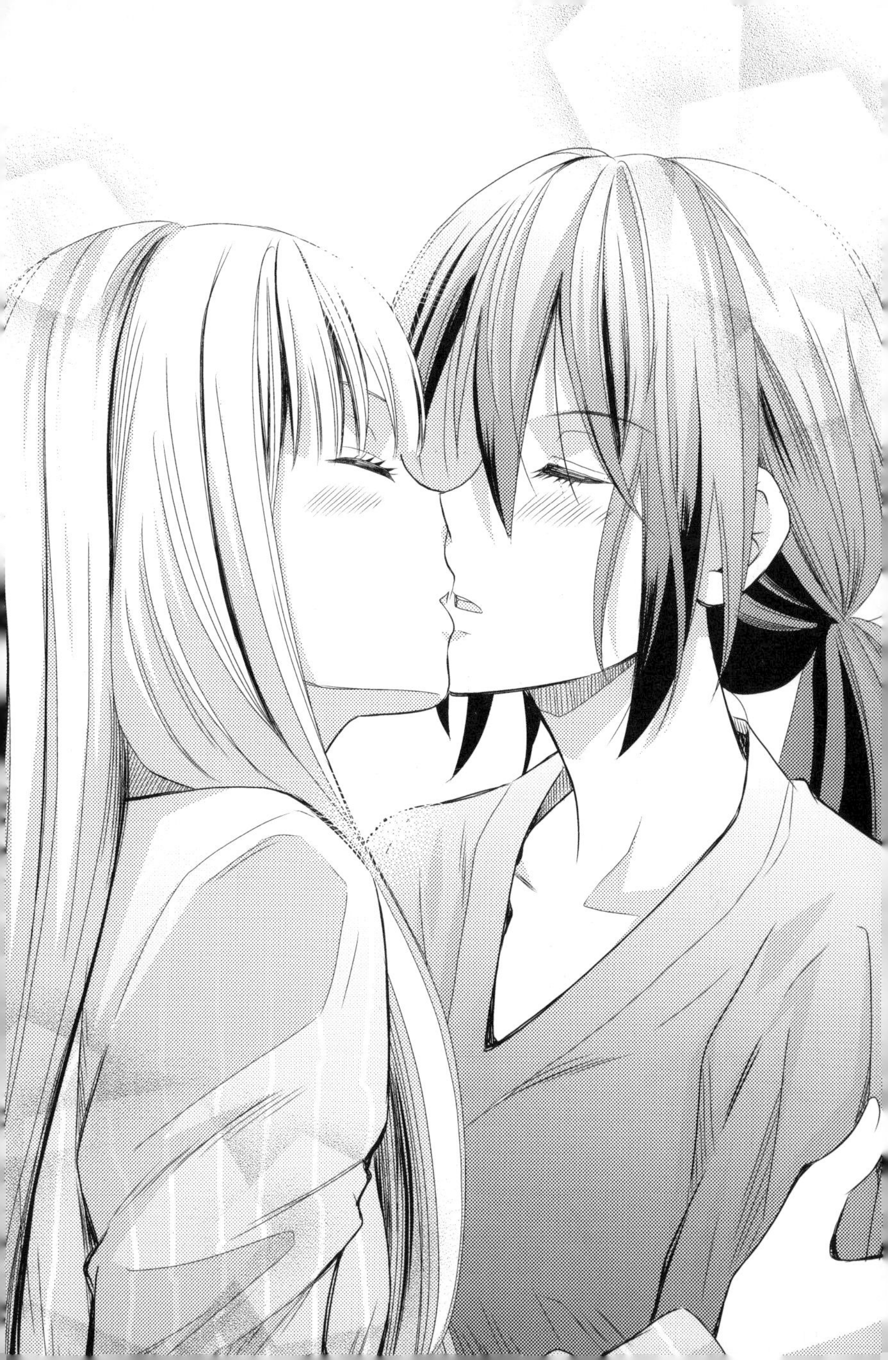

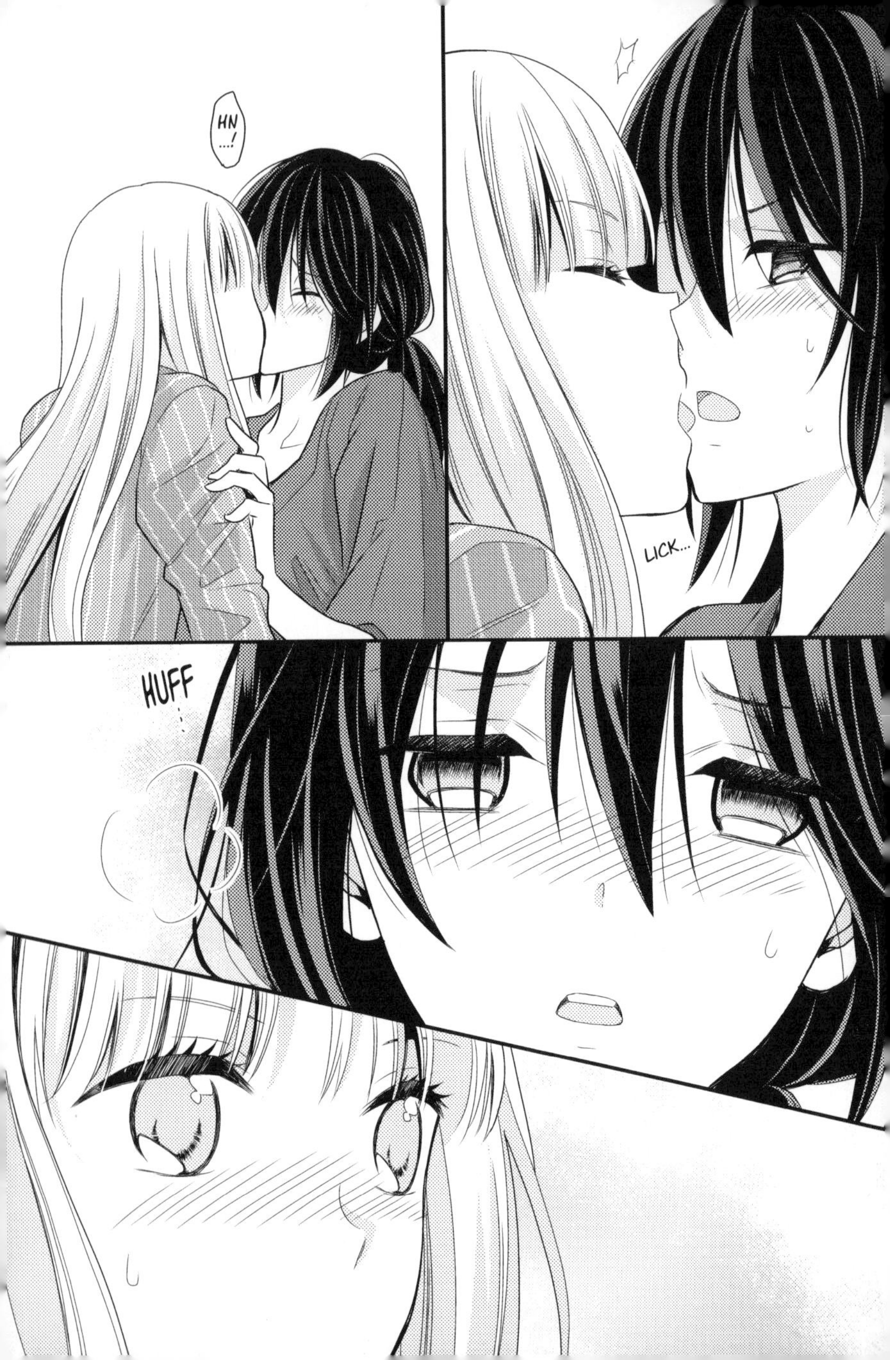
LICK...
HN...!
HUFF

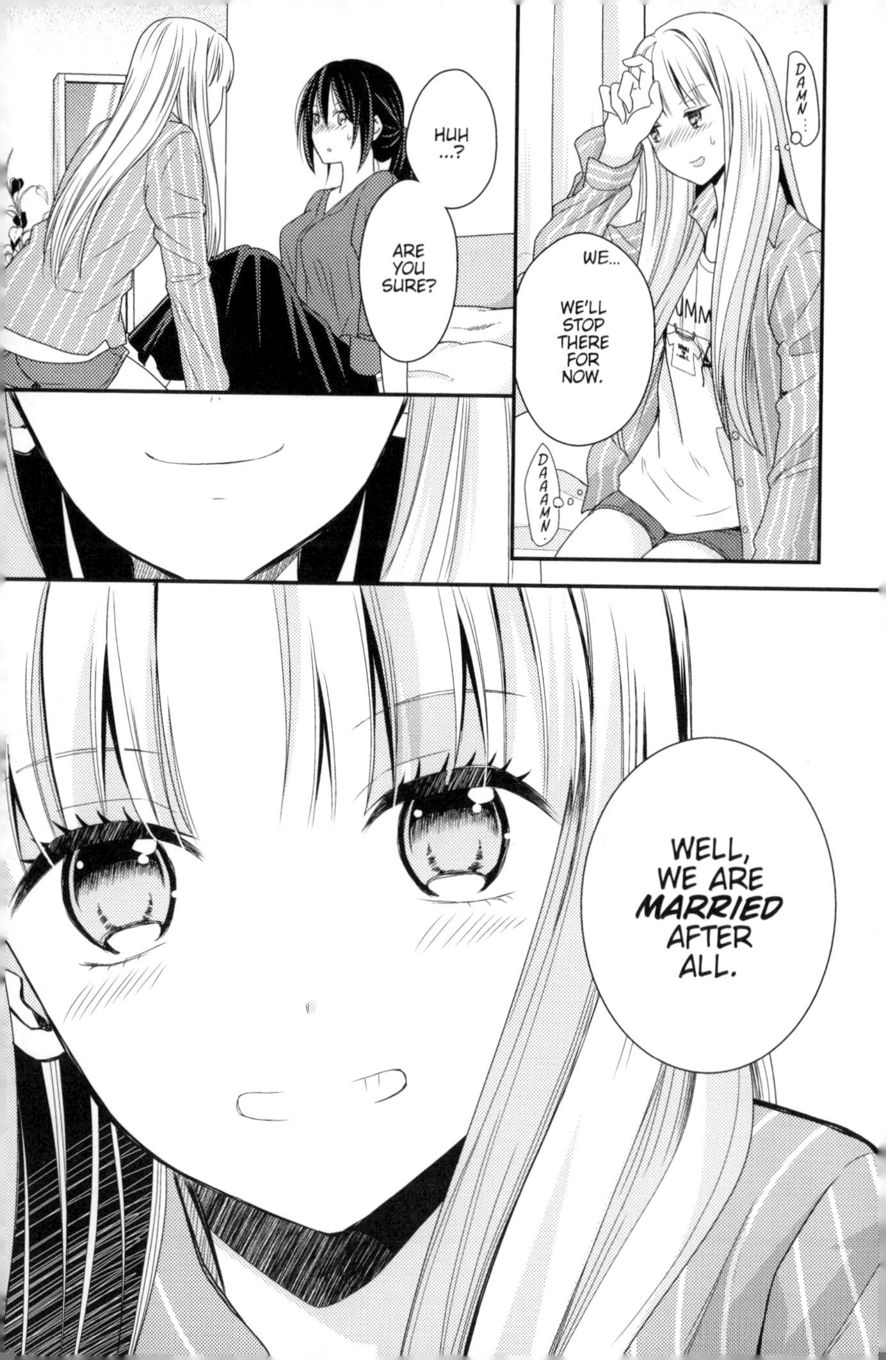
DAMN...
WE...
WE'LL STOP THERE FOR NOW.
DAAAMN.
HUH ...?
ARE YOU SURE?
WELL, WE ARE MARRIED AFTER ALL.

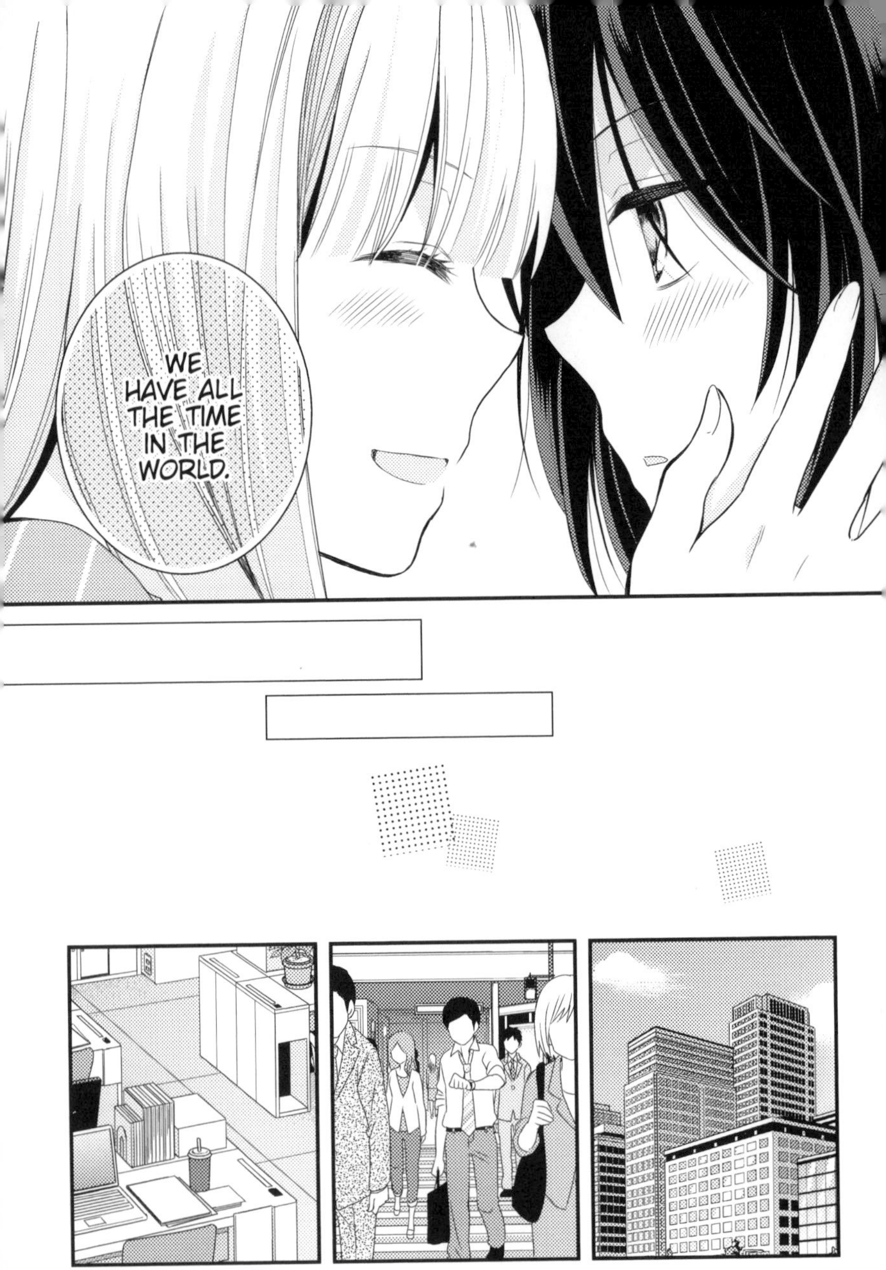
WE HAVE ALL THE TIME IN THE WORLD.

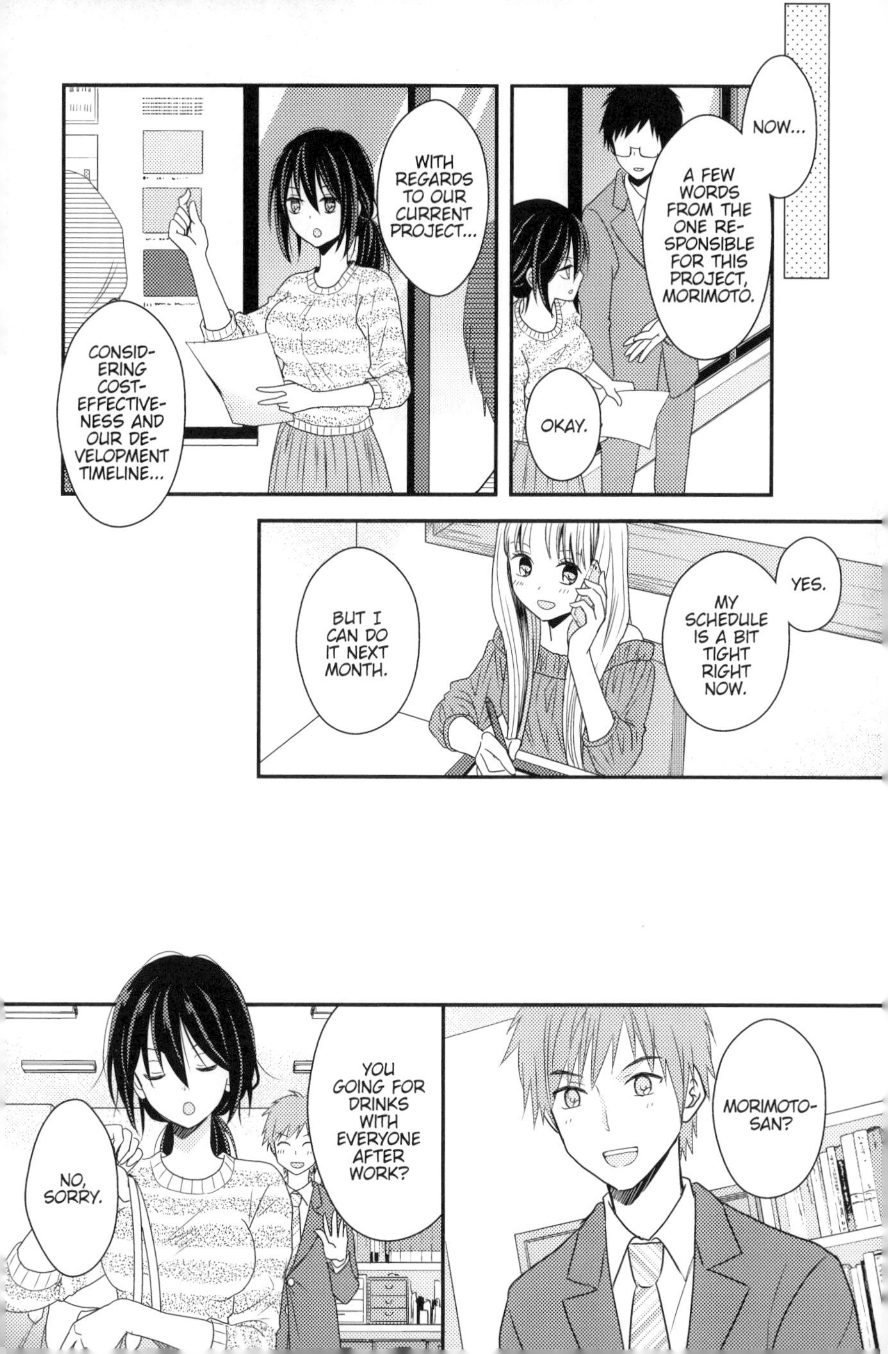
NOW...
A FEW WORDS FROM THE ONE RESPONSIBLE FOR THIS PROJECT, MORIMOTO.
OKAY.
WITH REGARDS TO OUR CURRENT PROJECT...
CONSIDERING COST-EFFECTIVENESS AND OUR DEVELOPMENT TIMELINE...
YES.
MY SCHEDULE IS A BIT TIGHT RIGHT NOW.
BUT I CAN DO IT NEXT MONTH.
MORIMOTO-SAN?
YOU GOING FOR DRINKS WITH EVERYONE AFTER WORK?
NO, SORRY.

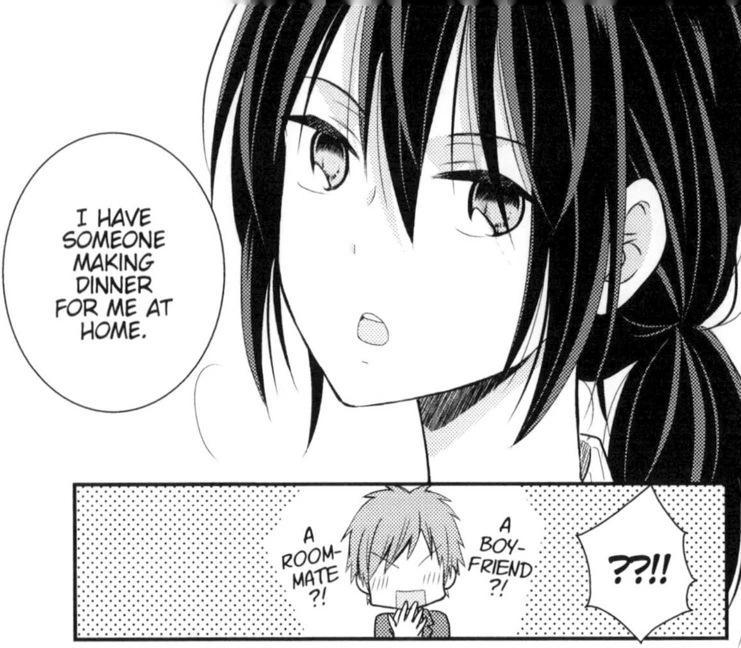
I HAVE SOMEONE MAKING DINNER FOR ME AT HOME.
??!!
A BOY-FRIEND ?!
A ROOM-MATE ?!

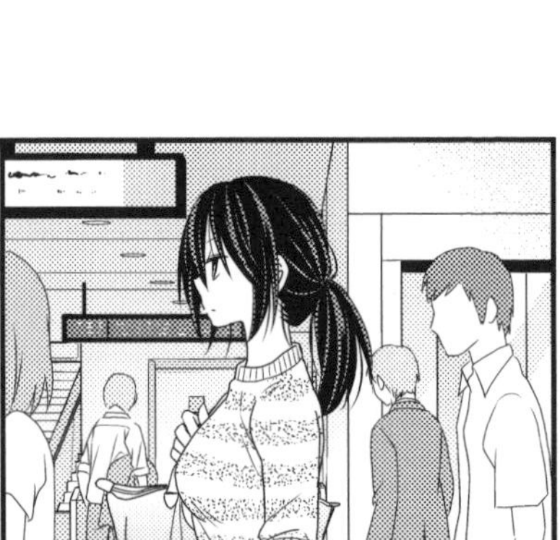

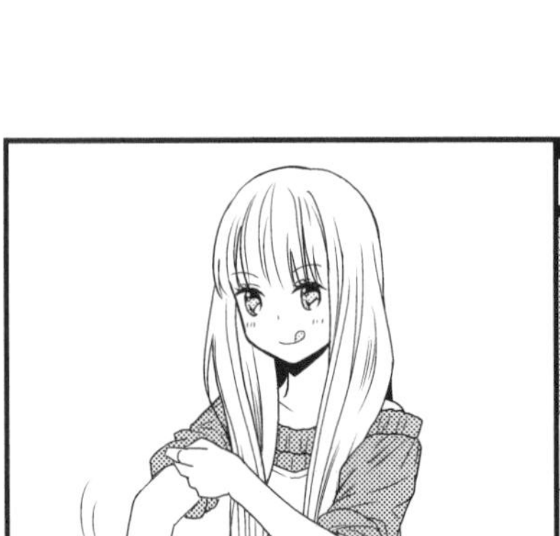

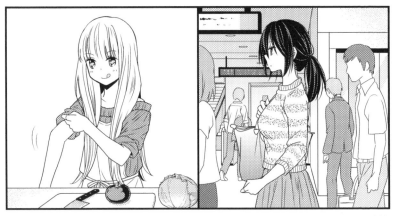

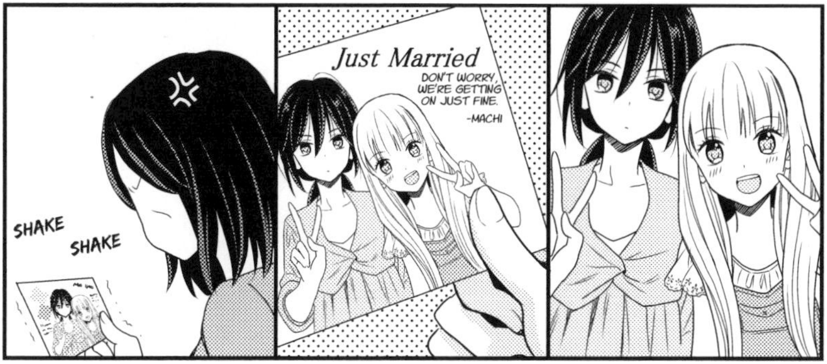
Just Married
DON'T WORRY, WE'RE GETTING ON JUST FINE.
-MACHI
SHAKE
SHAKE

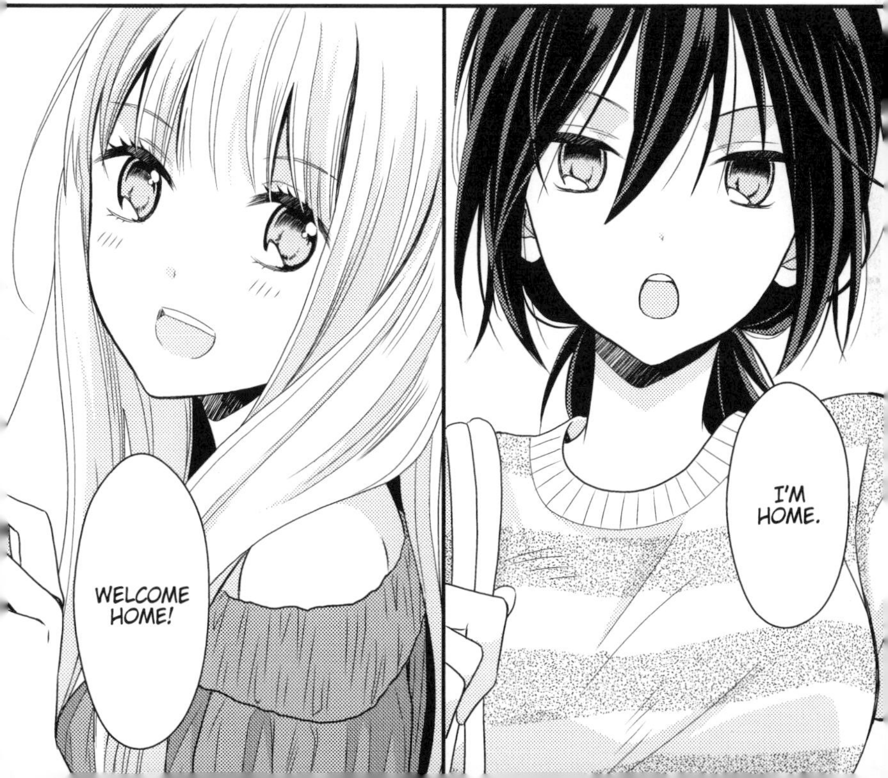
I'M HOME.
WELCOME HOME!

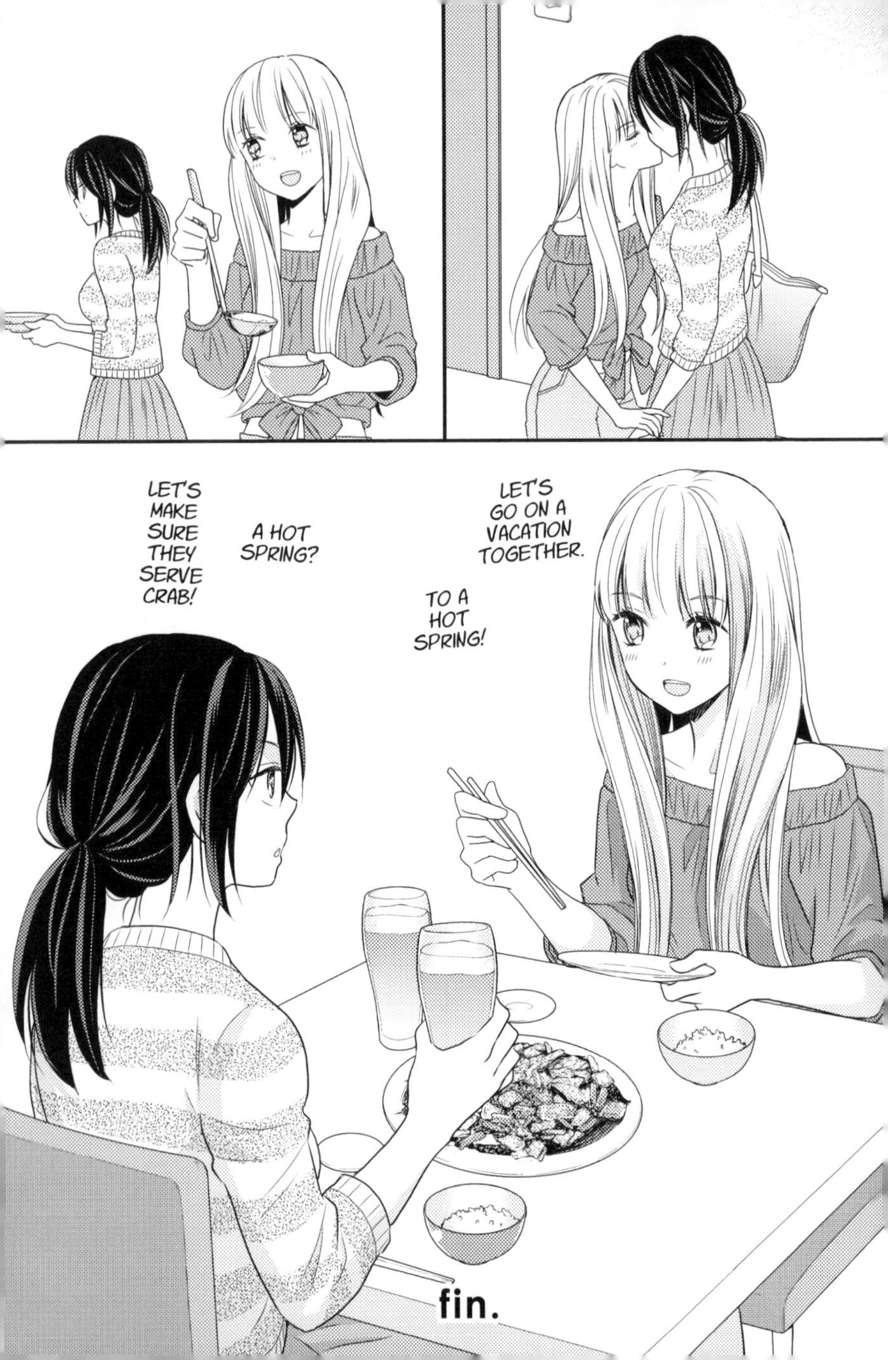
LET'S GO ON A VACATION TOGETHER.
TO A HOT SPRING!
A HOT SPRING?
LET'S MAKE SURE THEY SERVE CRAB!
fin.

I Married My Best Friend(♀)
to Shut My Parents up

I Married My Best Friend (♀)
to Shut My Parents Up

Anaerobic Love

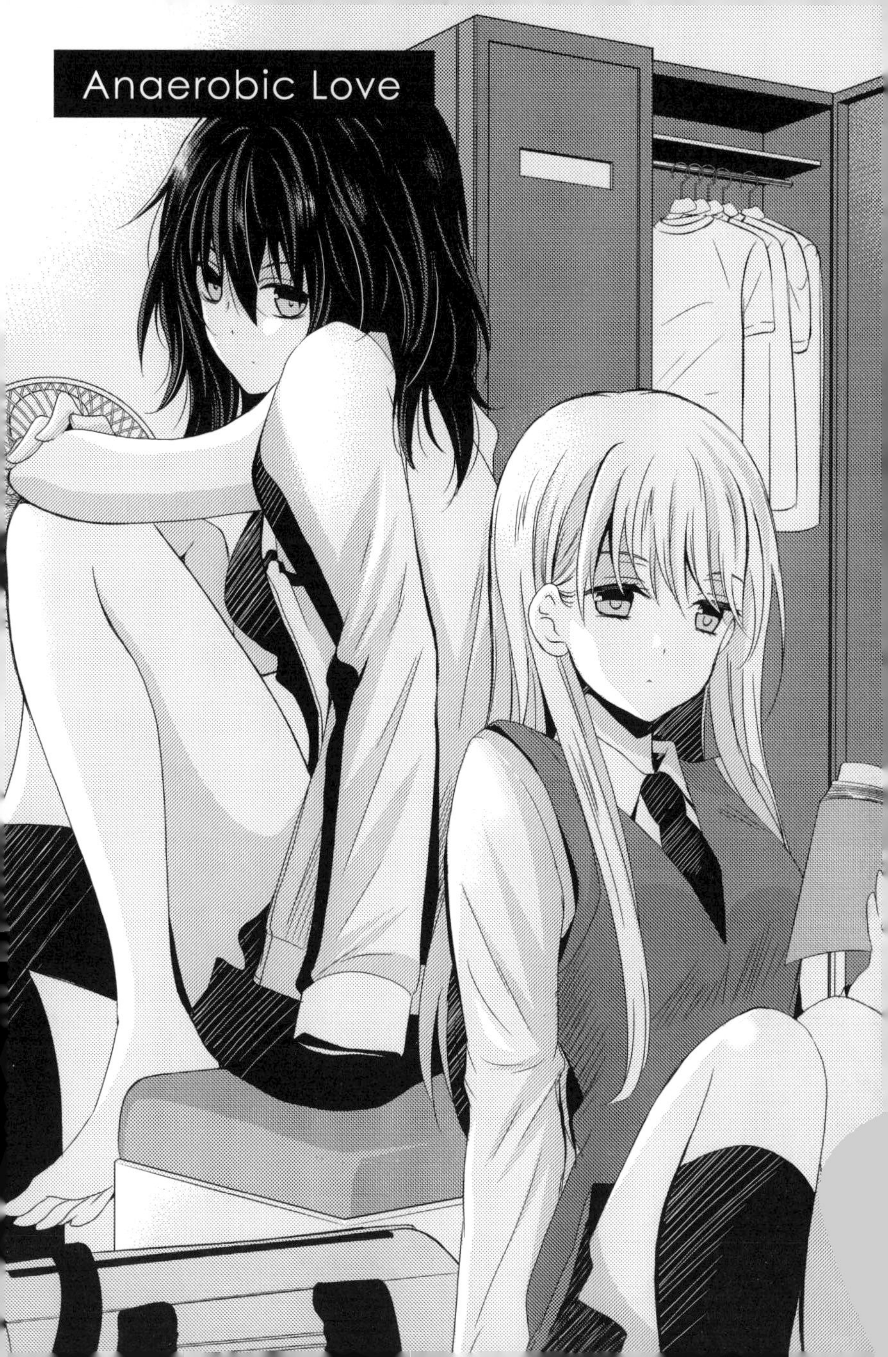

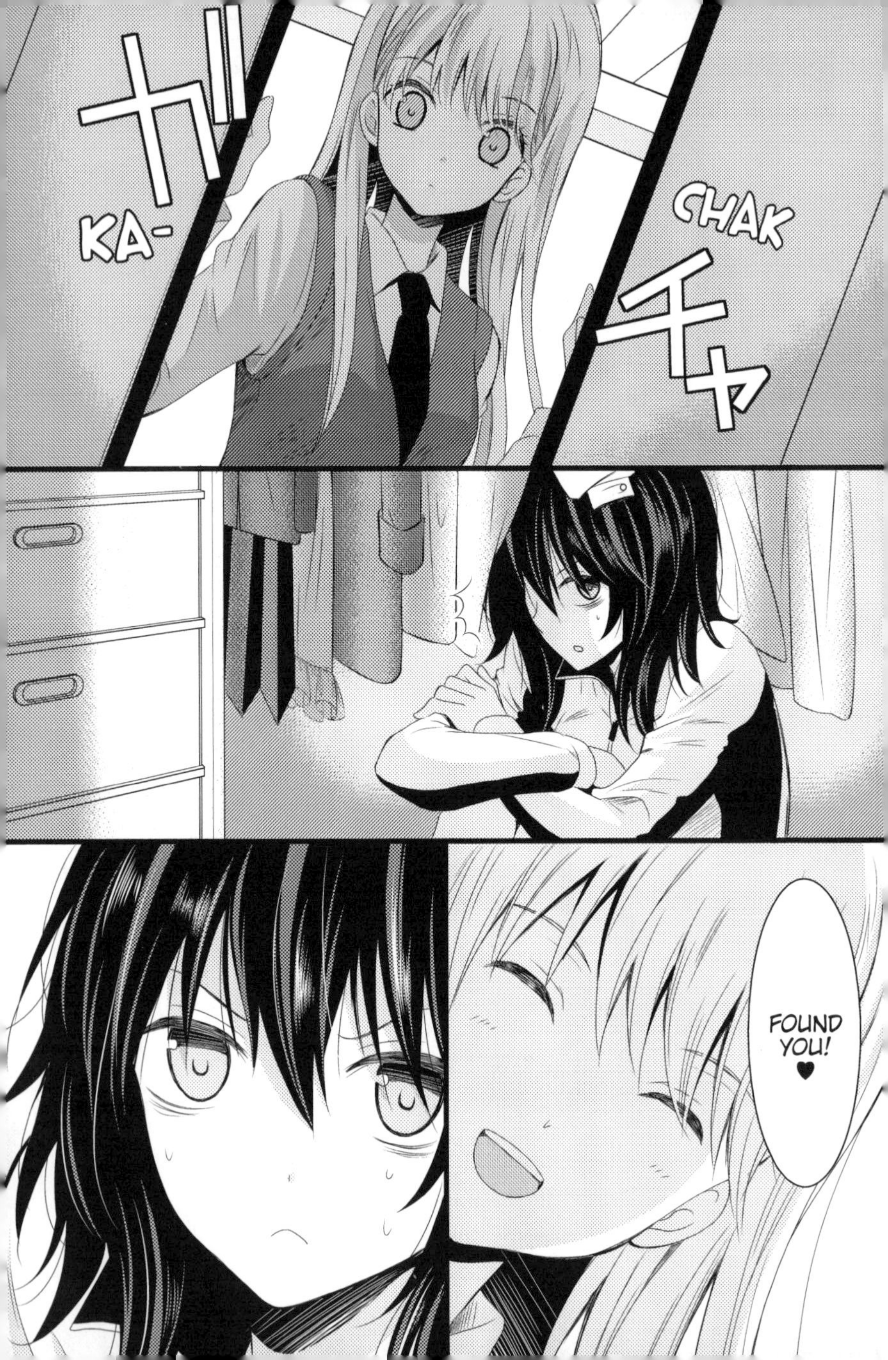
ガ
KA-
CHAK
チャ
FOUND YOU! ♥

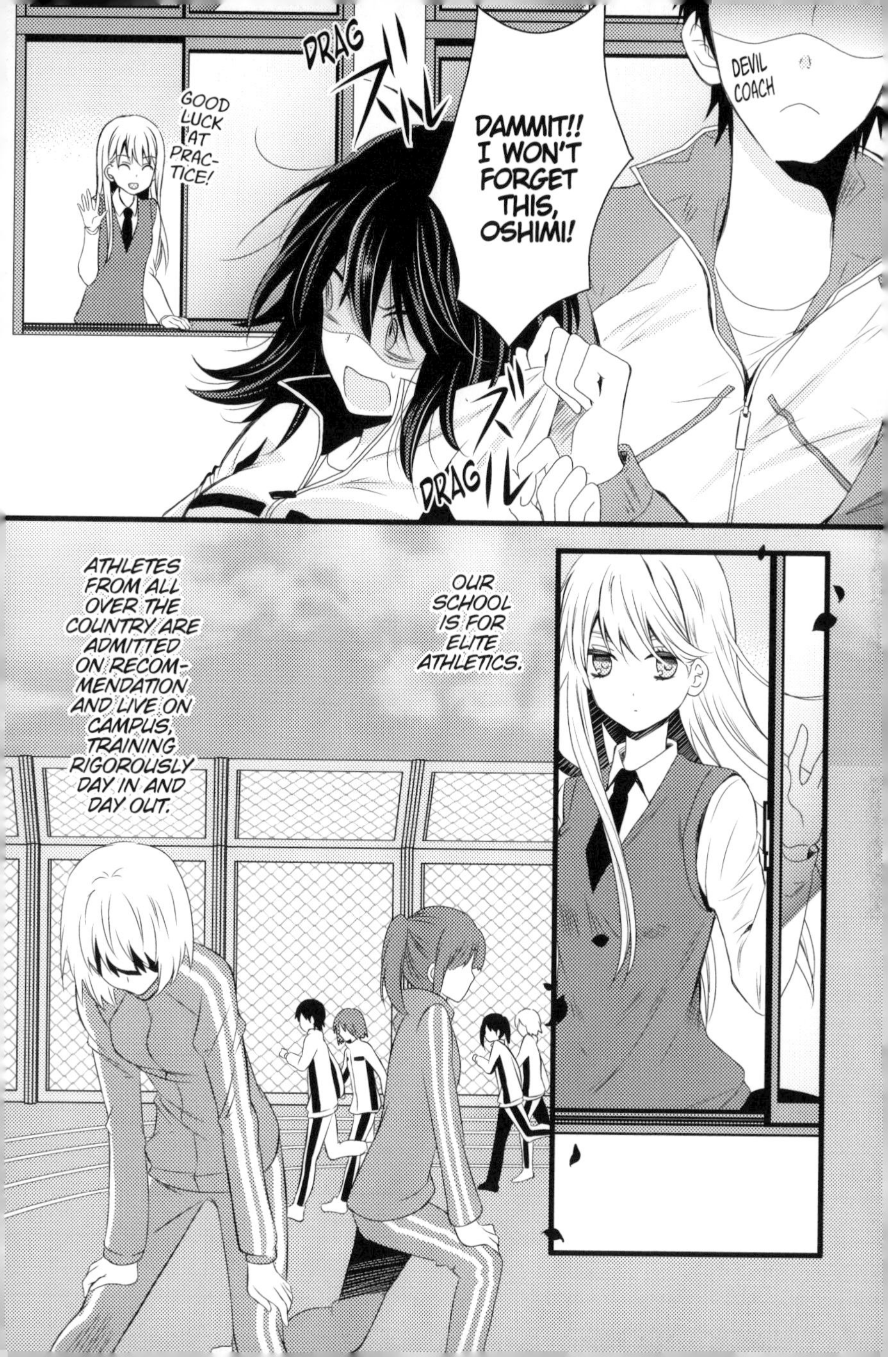
DEVIL COACH
DAMMIT!! I WON'T FORGET THIS, OSHIMI!
DRAG
DRAG
GOOD LUCK AT PRAC-TICE!
OUR SCHOOL IS FOR ELITE ATHLETICS.
ATHLETES FROM ALL OVER THE COUNTRY ARE ADMITTED ON RECOM-MENDATION AND LIVE ON CAMPUS, TRAINING RIGOROUSLY DAY IN AND DAY OUT.

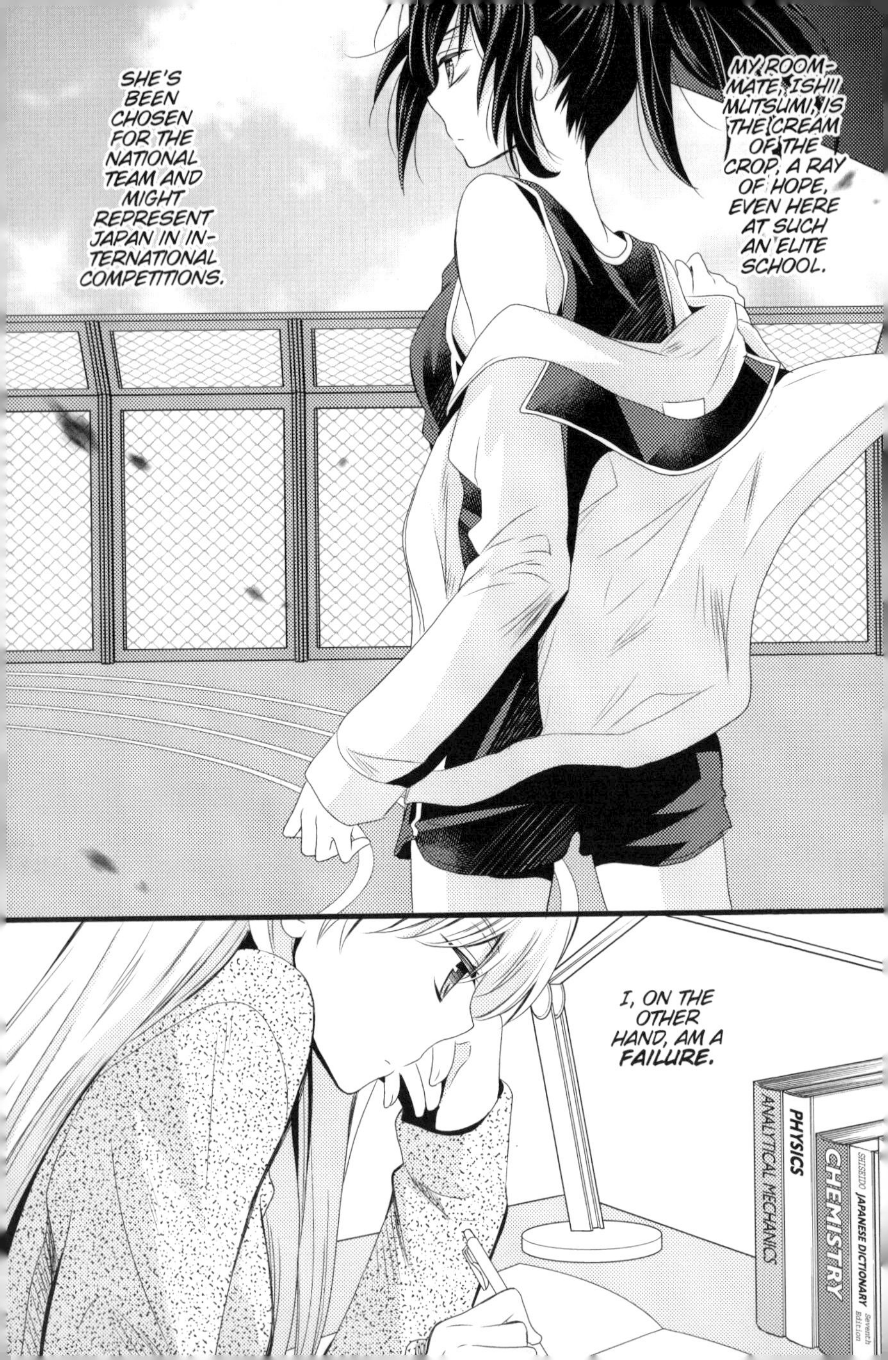
MY ROOM-MATE, ISHII MUTSUMI, IS THE CREAM OF THE CROP, A RAY OF HOPE, EVEN HERE AT SUCH AN ELITE SCHOOL.
SHE'S BEEN CHOSEN FOR THE NATIONAL TEAM AND MIGHT REPRESENT JAPAN IN INTERNATIONAL COMPETITIONS.
I, ON THE OTHER HAND, AM A **FAILURE.**
PHYSICS
ANALYTICAL MECHANICS
CHEMISTRY
JAPANESE DICTIONARY
Seventh Edition

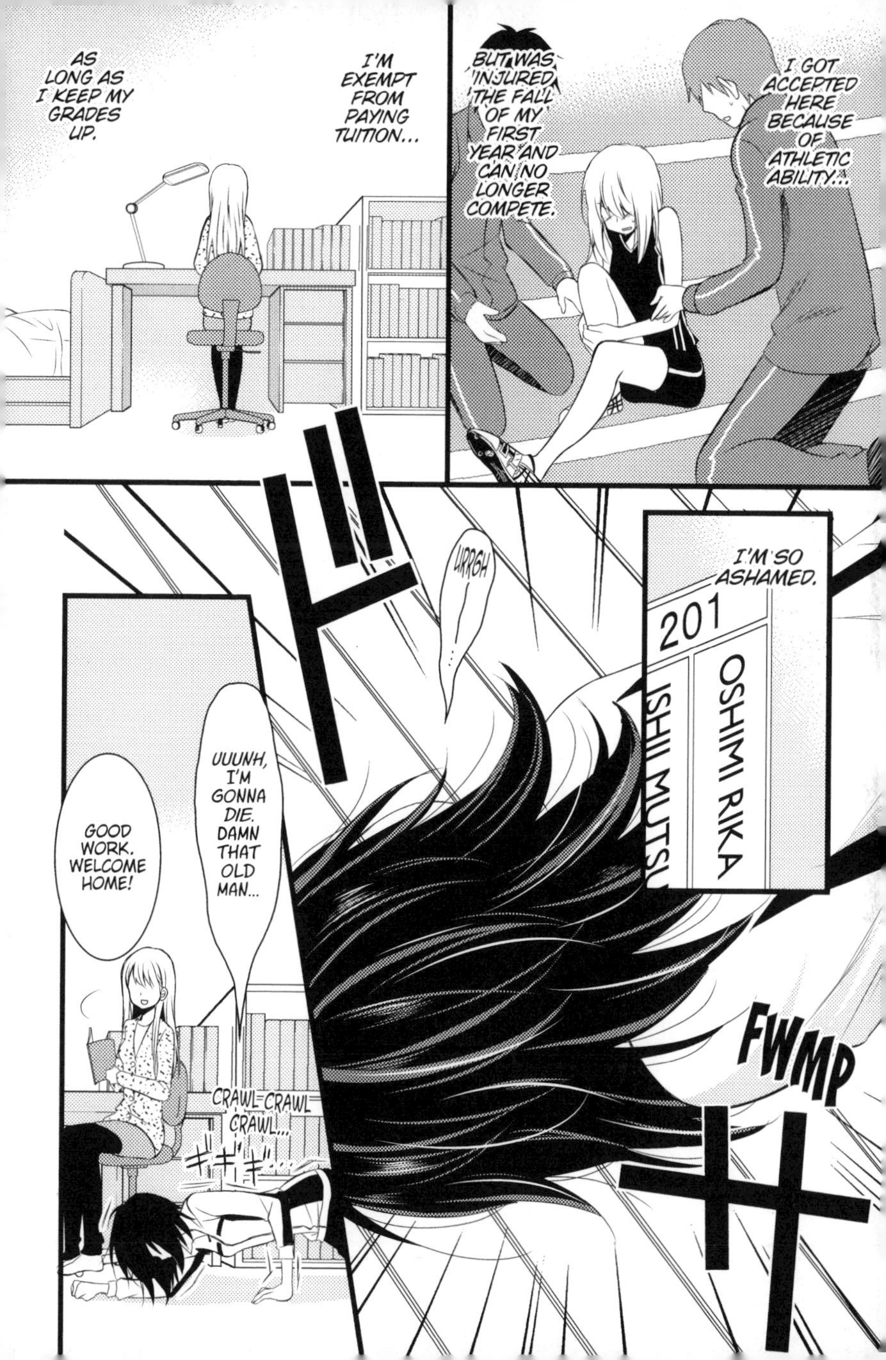
I GOT ACCEPTED HERE BECAUSE OF ATHLETIC ABILITY...
BUT WAS INJURED THE FALL OF MY FIRST YEAR AND CAN NO LONGER COMPETE.
I'M EXEMPT FROM PAYING TUITION...
AS LONG AS I KEEP MY GRADES UP.
I'M SO ASHAMED.
201
OSHIMI RIKA
ISHII MUTSU
FWMP
URRGH
...
UUUNH, I'M GONNA DIE. DAMN THAT OLD MAN...
GOOD WORK. WELCOME HOME!
CRAWL CRAWL CRAWL...
ギギギ...

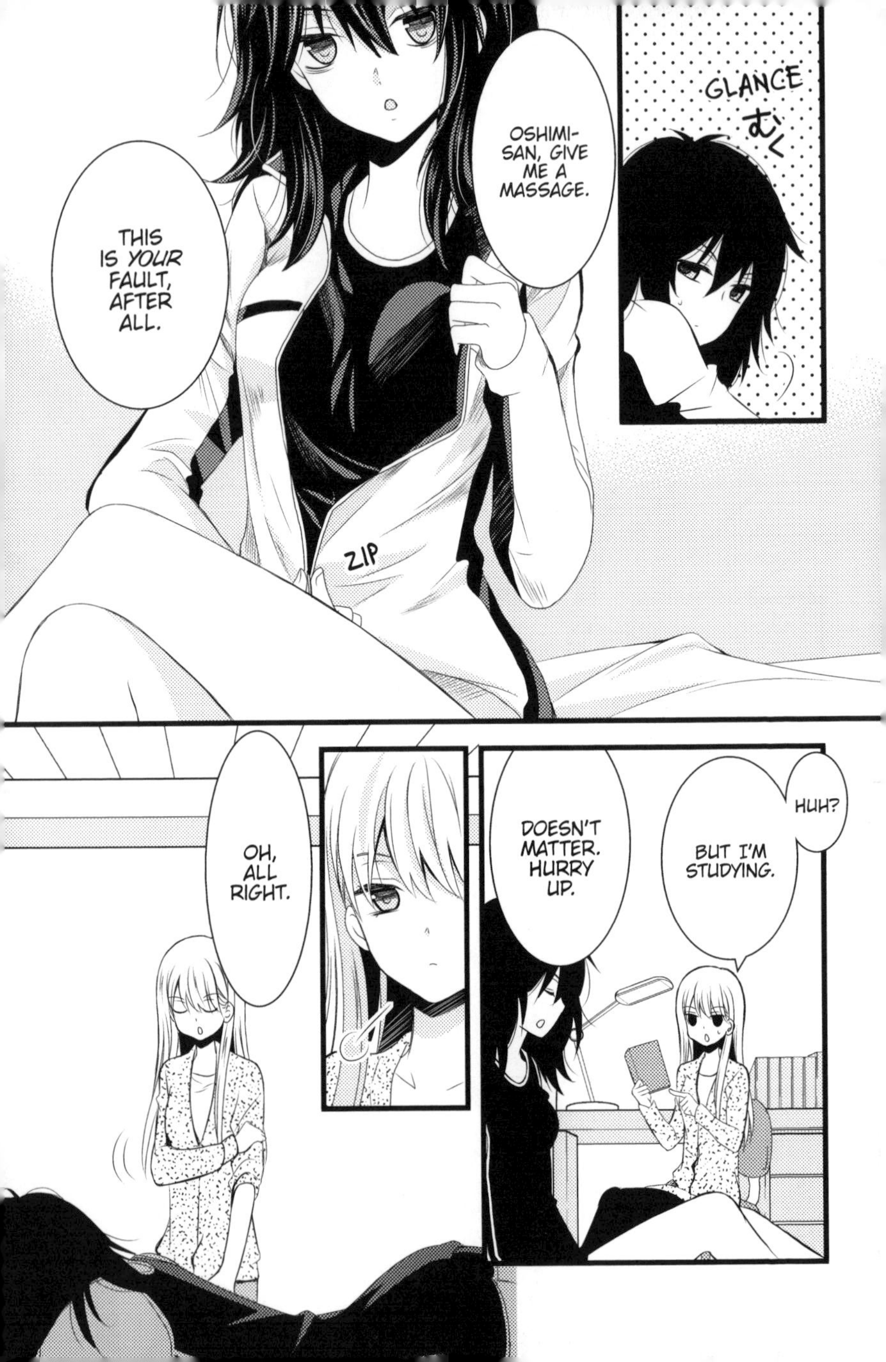
GLANCE
むく
OSHIMI-SAN, GIVE ME A MASSAGE.
THIS IS *YOUR* FAULT, AFTER ALL.
ZIP
HUH?
BUT I'M STUDYING.
DOESN'T MATTER. HURRY UP.
OH, ALL RIGHT.

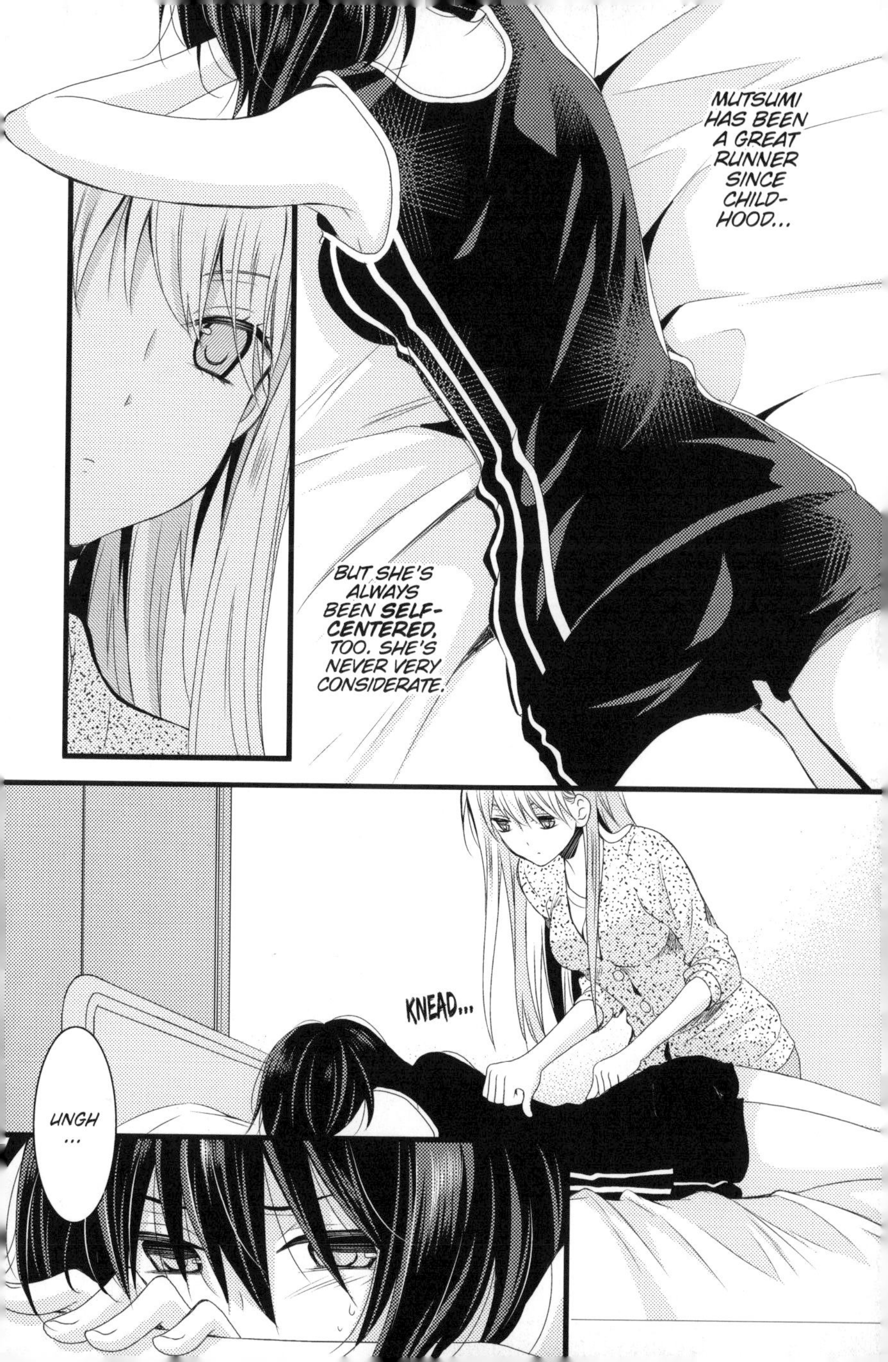
MUTSUMI HAS BEEN A GREAT RUNNER SINCE CHILD-HOOD...
BUT SHE'S ALWAYS BEEN **SELF-CENTERED,** TOO. SHE'S NEVER VERY CONSIDERATE.
KNEAD...
UNGH...

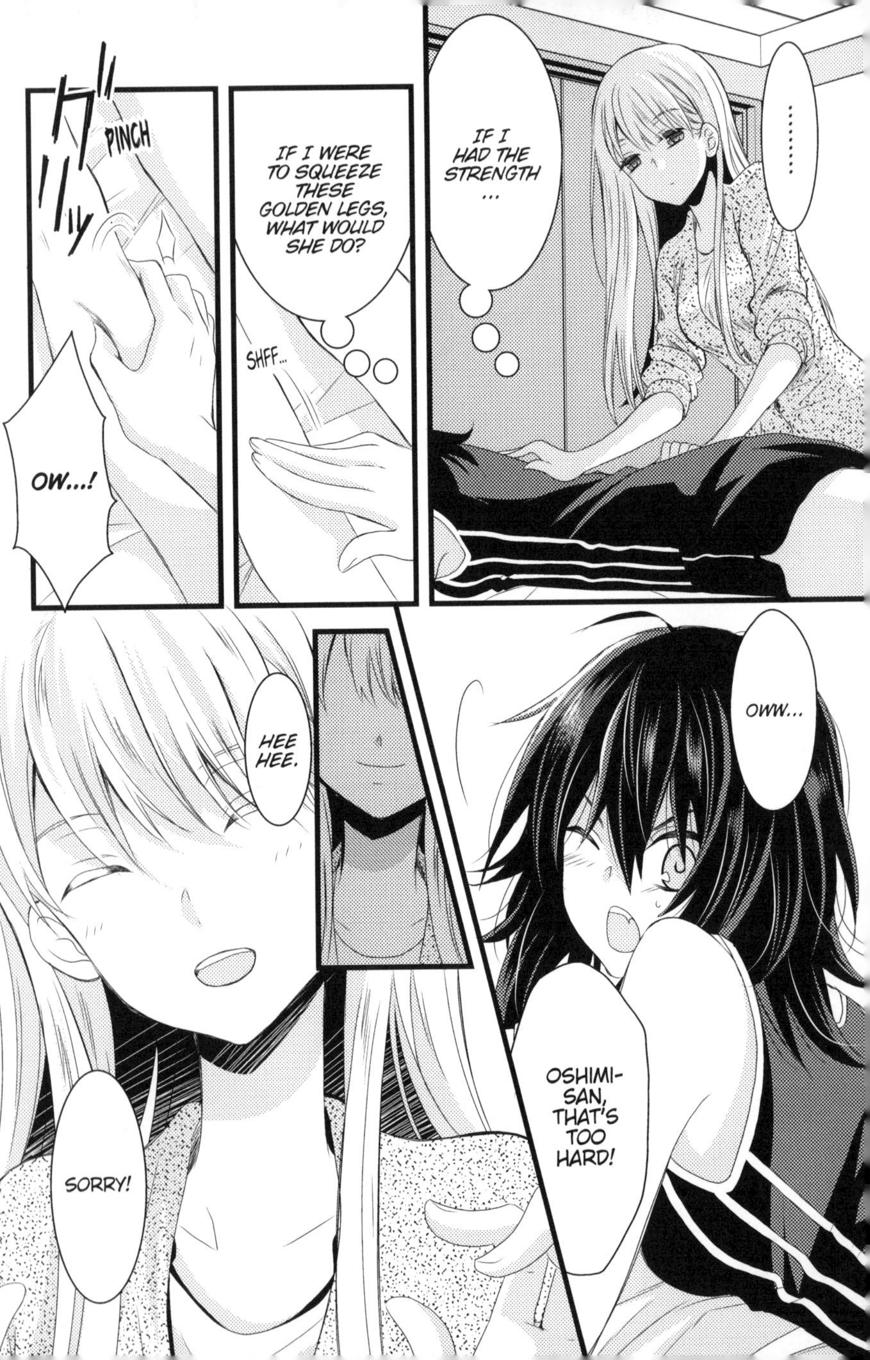
......
IF I HAD THE STRENGTH ...
IF I WERE TO SQUEEZE THESE GOLDEN LEGS, WHAT WOULD SHE DO?
SHFF...
PINCH
OW...!
OWW...
OSHIMI-SAN, THAT'S TOO HARD!
HEE HEE.
SORRY!

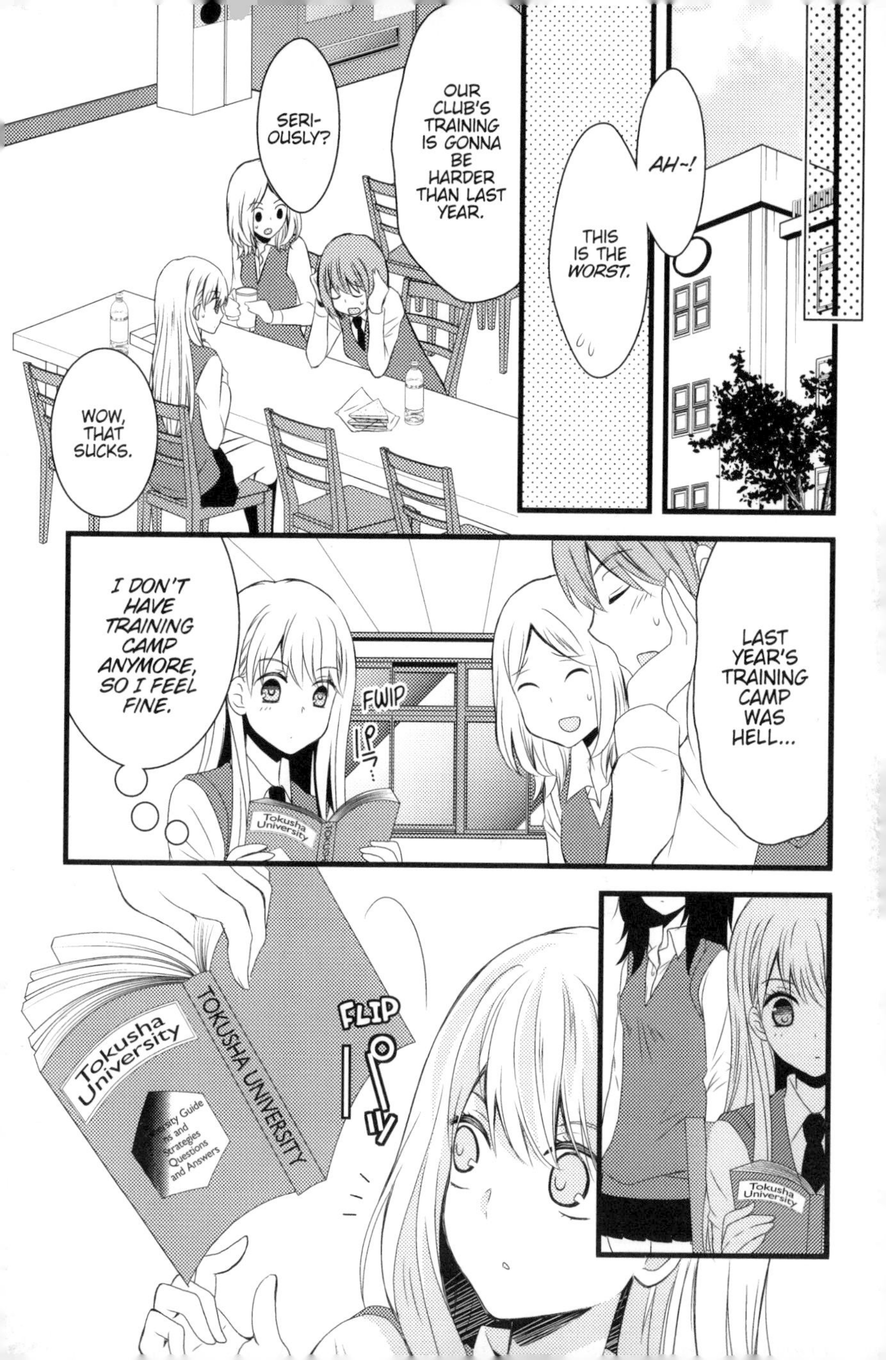
AH~!
THIS IS THE WORST.
OUR CLUB'S TRAINING IS GONNA BE HARDER THAN LAST YEAR.
SERI-OUSLY?
WOW, THAT SUCKS.
LAST YEAR'S TRAINING CAMP WAS HELL...
I DON'T HAVE TRAINING CAMP ANYMORE, SO I FEEL FINE.
FWIP
Tokusha University
Tokusha University
FLIP
Tokusha University
TOKUSHA UNIVERSITY
Strategies
Questions
and Answers

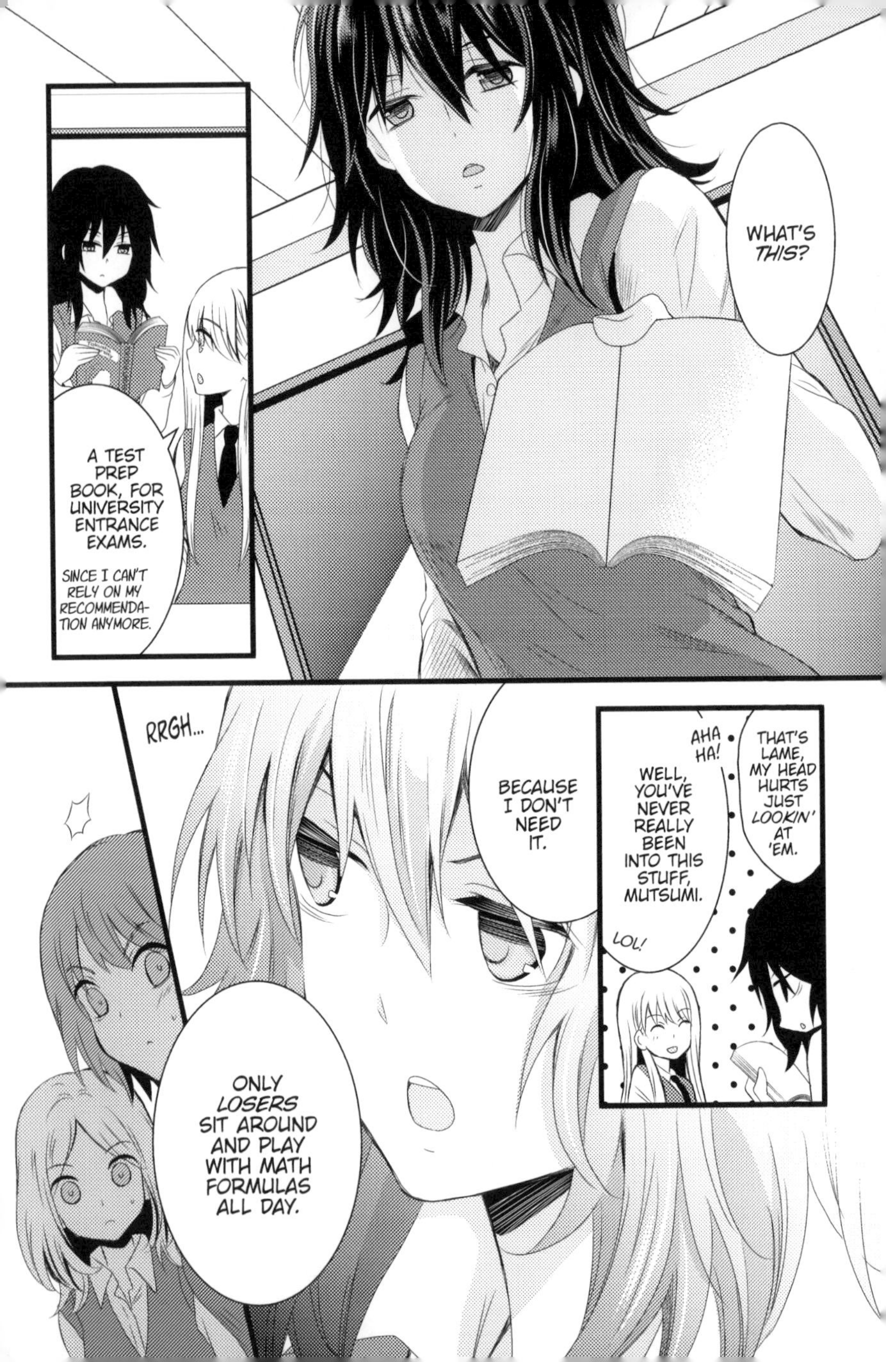
WHAT'S *THIS?*
A TEST PREP BOOK, FOR UNIVERSITY ENTRANCE EXAMS.
SINCE I CAN'T RELY ON MY RECOMMENDATION ANYMORE.
THAT'S LAME, MY HEAD HURTS JUST *LOOKIN'* AT 'EM.
AHA HA!
WELL, YOU'VE NEVER REALLY BEEN INTO THIS STUFF, MUTSUMI.
LOL!
BECAUSE I DON'T NEED IT.
RRGH...
ONLY *LOSERS* SIT AROUND AND PLAY WITH MATH FORMULAS ALL DAY.

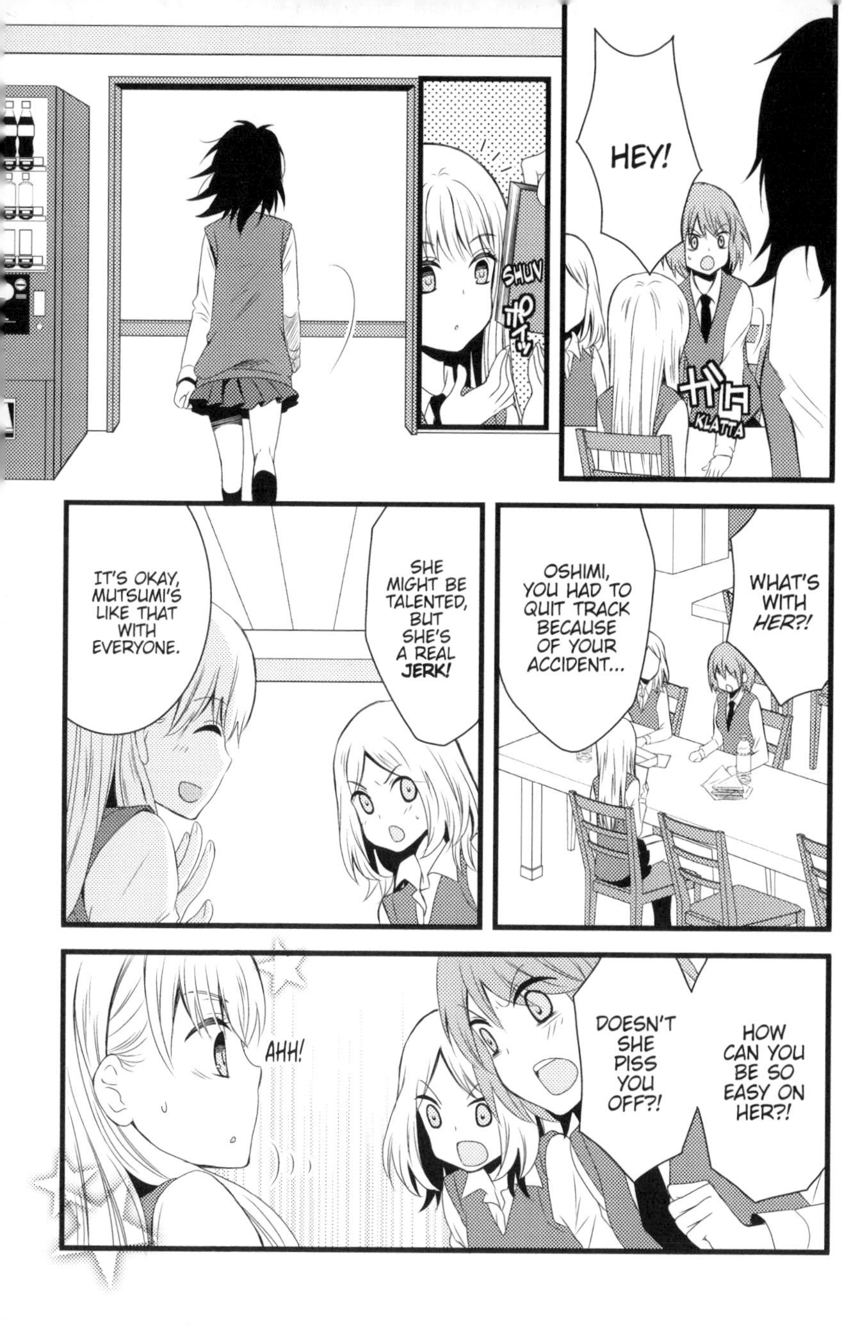
HEY!
ガタ
KLATTA
SHUV
ポイッ
WHAT'S WITH HER?!
OSHIMI, YOU HAD TO QUIT TRACK BECAUSE OF YOUR ACCIDENT...
SHE MIGHT BE TALENTED, BUT SHE'S A REAL JERK!
IT'S OKAY, MUTSUMI'S LIKE THAT WITH EVERYONE.
HOW CAN YOU BE SO EASY ON HER?!
DOESN'T SHE PISS YOU OFF?!
AHH!

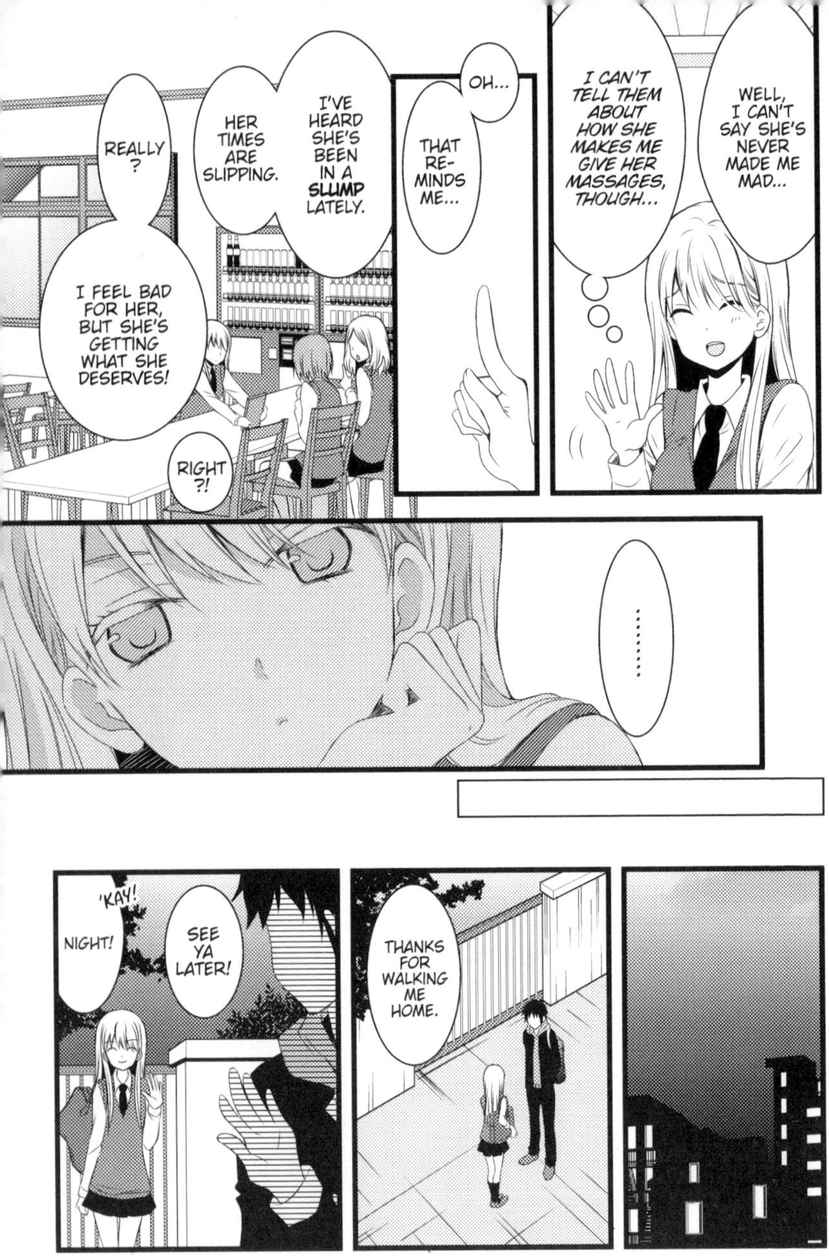
WELL, I CAN'T SAY SHE'S NEVER MADE ME MAD...
I CAN'T TELL THEM ABOUT HOW SHE MAKES ME GIVE HER MASSAGES, THOUGH...
OH...
THAT RE-MINDS ME...
I'VE HEARD SHE'S BEEN IN A SLUMP LATELY.
HER TIMES ARE SLIPPING.
REALLY?
I FEEL BAD FOR HER, BUT SHE'S GETTING WHAT SHE DESERVES!
RIGHT?!
....
THANKS FOR WALKING ME HOME.
SEE YA LATER!
'KAY!
NIGHT!

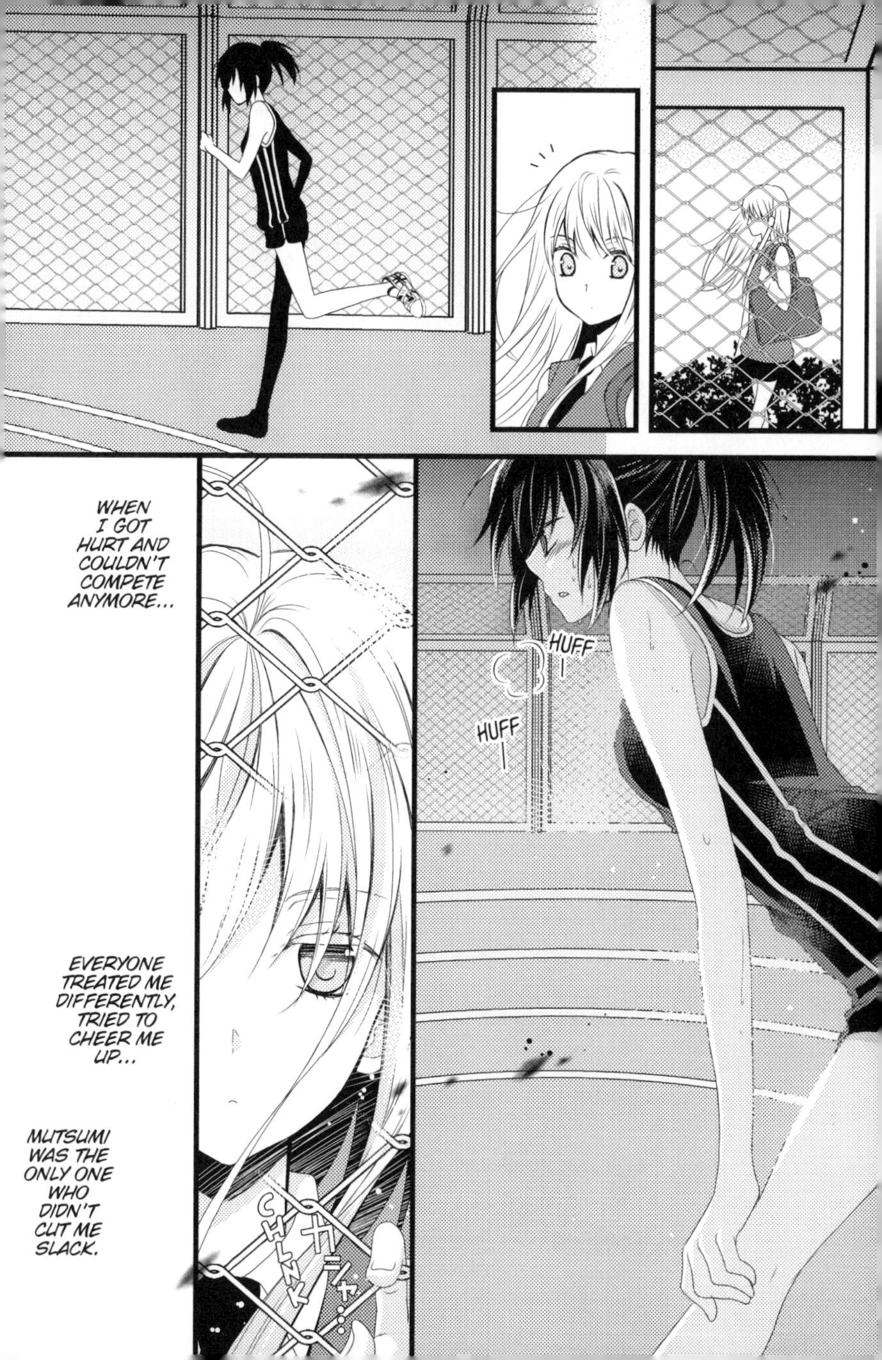
HUFF
HUFF
CHLNK
WHEN I GOT HURT AND COULDN'T COMPETE ANYMORE...
EVERYONE TREATED ME DIFFERENTLY, TRIED TO CHEER ME UP...
MUTSUMI WAS THE ONLY ONE WHO DIDN'T CUT ME SLACK.

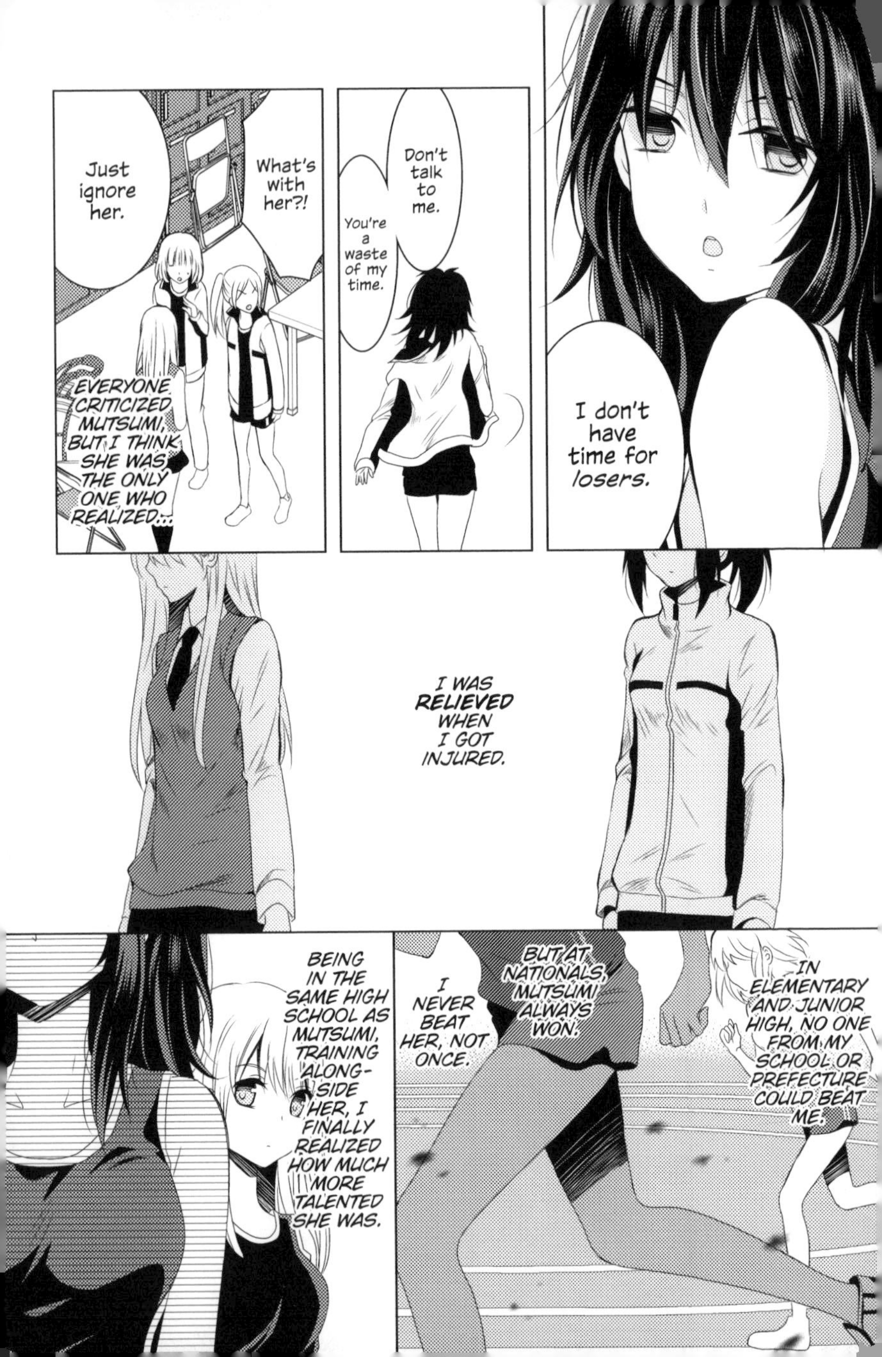
I don't have time for losers.
Don't talk to me.
You're a waste of my time.
What's with her?!
Just ignore her.
EVERYONE CRITICIZED MUTSUMI, BUT I THINK SHE WAS THE ONLY ONE WHO REALIZED...
I WAS **RELIEVED** WHEN I GOT INJURED.
IN ELEMENTARY AND JUNIOR HIGH, NO ONE FROM MY SCHOOL OR PREFECTURE COULD BEAT ME.
BUT AT NATIONALS, MUTSUMI ALWAYS WON.
I NEVER BEAT HER, NOT ONCE.
BEING IN THE SAME HIGH SCHOOL AS MUTSUMI, TRAINING ALONG-SIDE HER, I FINALLY REALIZED HOW MUCH MORE TALENTED SHE WAS.

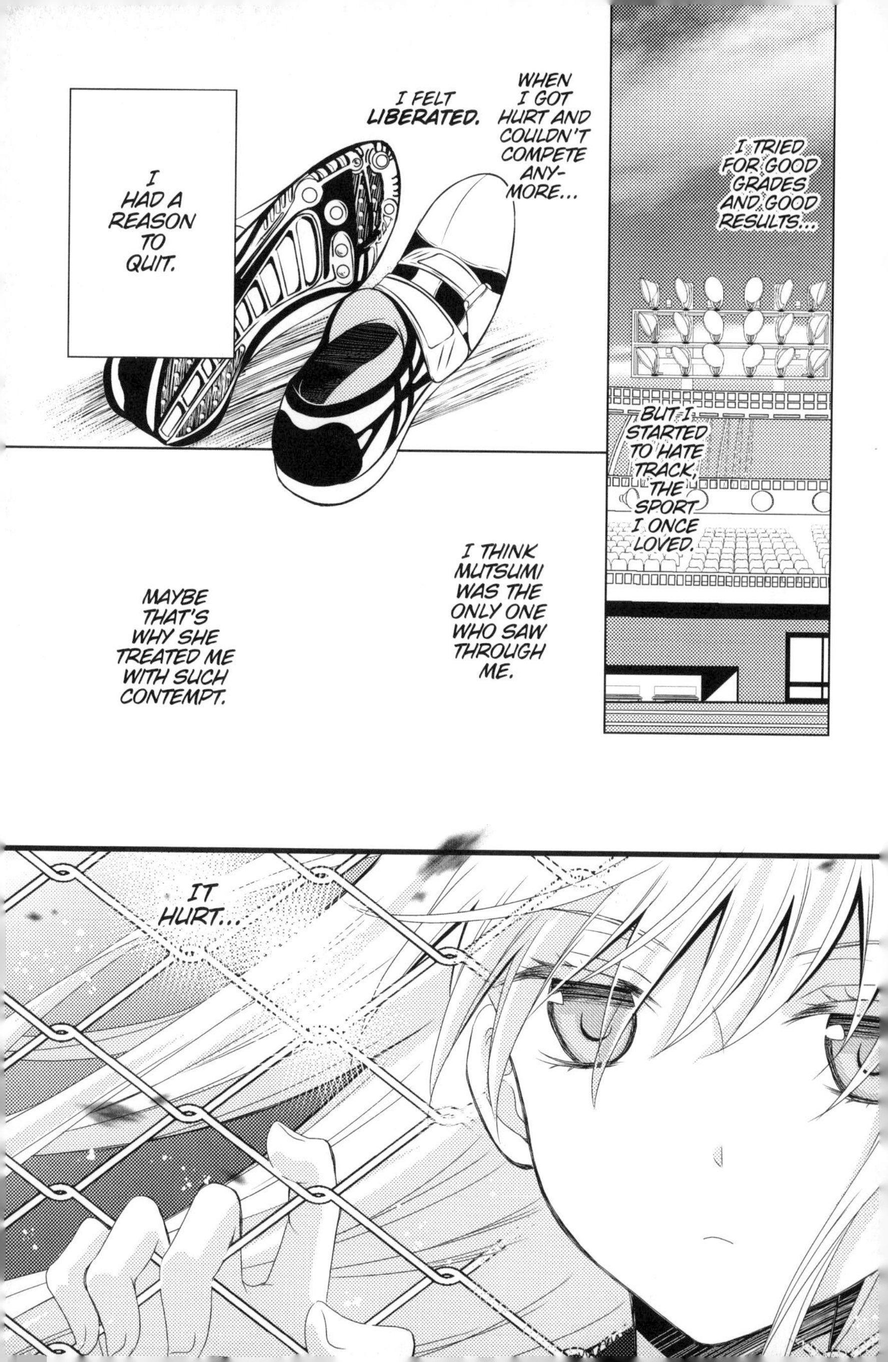
I TRIED FOR GOOD GRADES AND GOOD RESULTS...
BUT I STARTED TO HATE TRACK, THE SPORT I ONCE LOVED.
WHEN I GOT HURT AND COULDN'T COMPETE ANYMORE...
I FELT **LIBERATED.**
I HAD A REASON TO QUIT.
I THINK MUTSUMI WAS THE ONLY ONE WHO SAW THROUGH ME.
MAYBE THAT'S WHY SHE TREATED ME WITH SUCH CONTEMPT.
IT HURT...

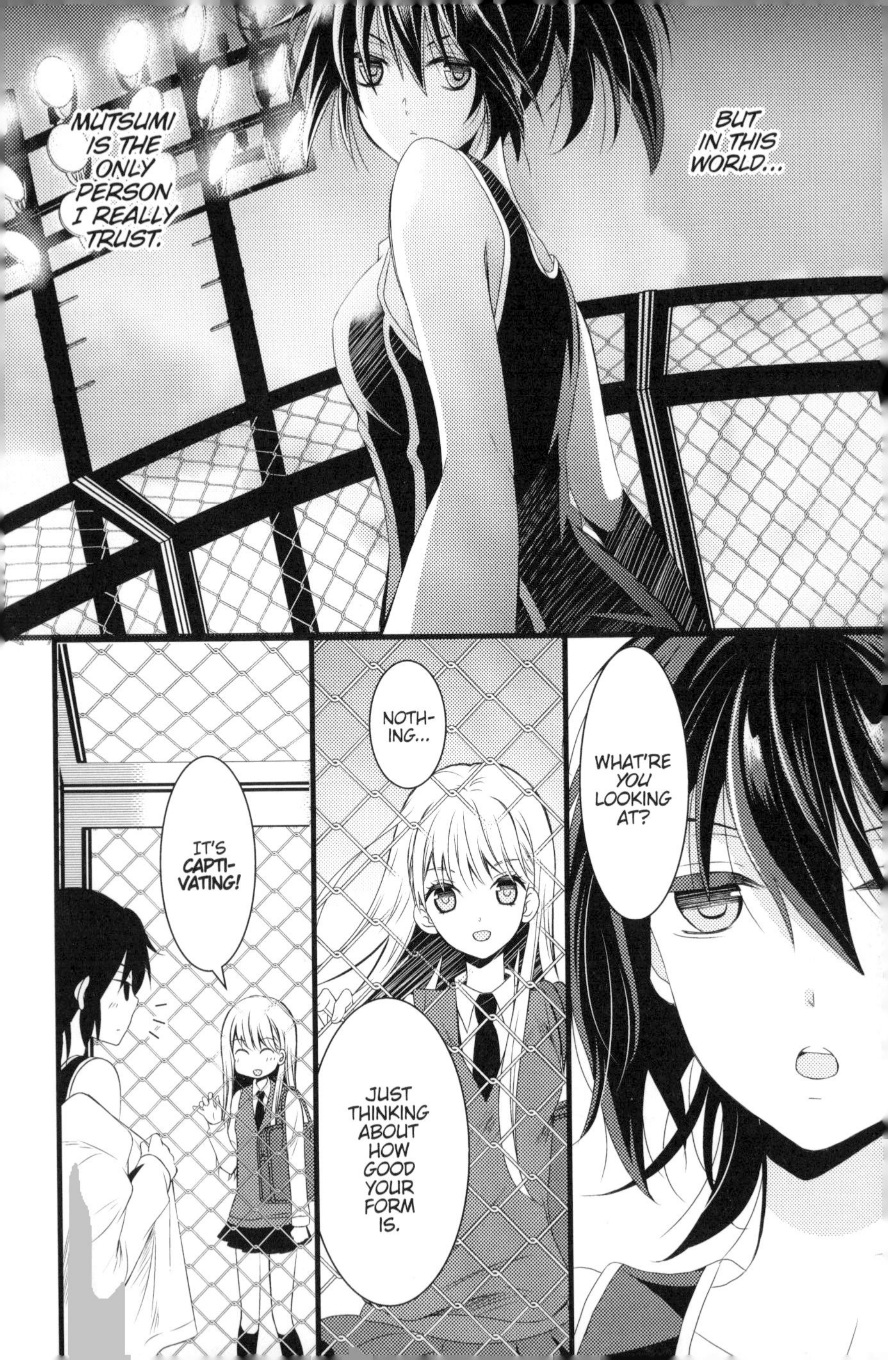
BUT IN THIS WORLD...
MUTSUMI IS THE ONLY PERSON I REALLY TRUST.
WHAT'RE YOU LOOKING AT?
NOTH-ING...
JUST THINKING ABOUT HOW GOOD YOUR FORM IS.
IT'S CAPTI-VATING!

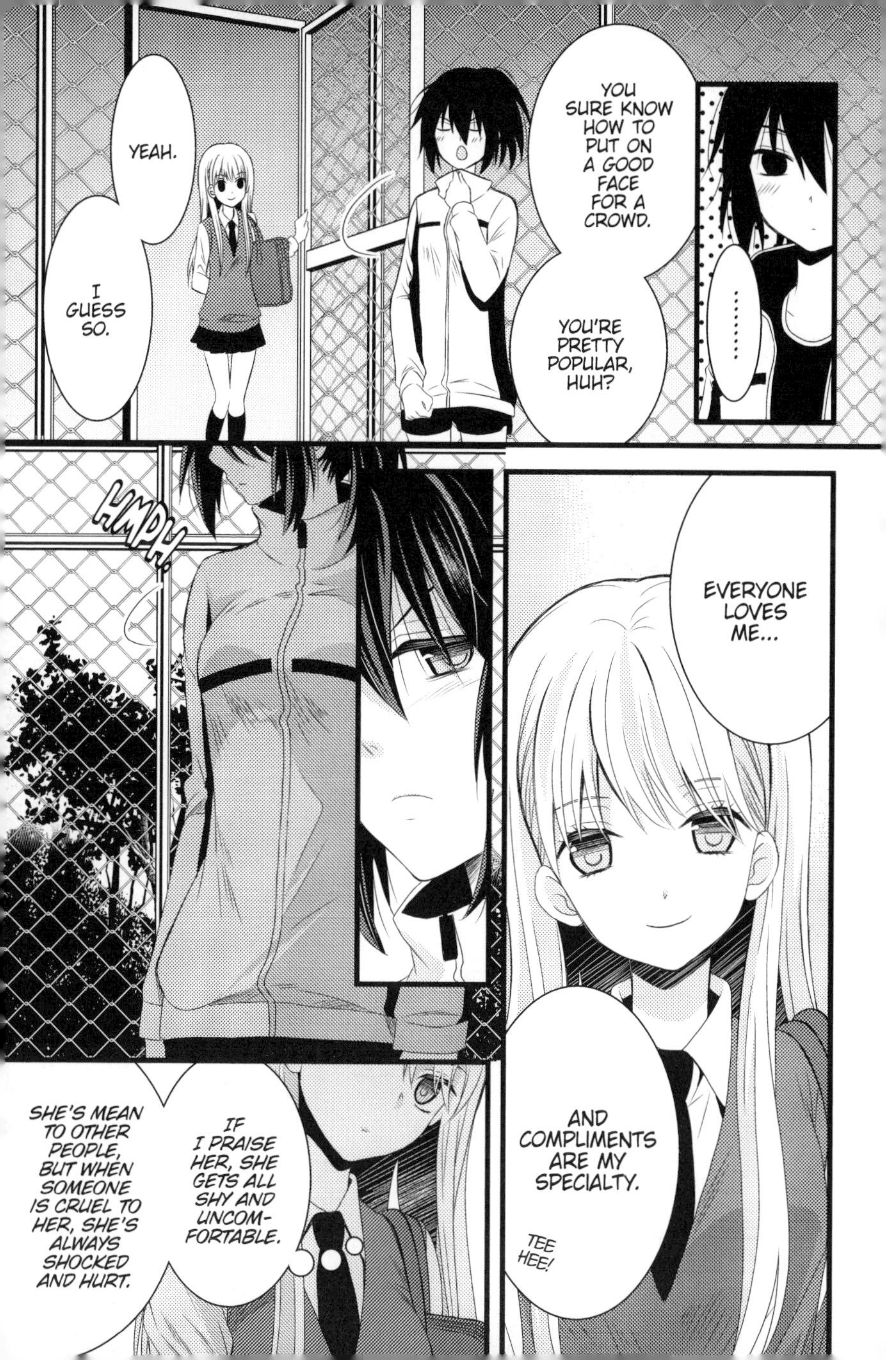

......
YOU SURE KNOW HOW TO PUT ON A GOOD FACE FOR A CROWD.
YOU'RE PRETTY POPULAR, HUH?
YEAH.
I GUESS SO.
EVERYONE LOVES ME...
AND COMPLIMENTS ARE MY SPECIALTY.
TEE HEE!
HMPH
IF I PRAISE HER, SHE GETS ALL SHY AND UNCOM-FORTABLE.
SHE'S MEAN TO OTHER PEOPLE, BUT WHEN SOMEONE IS CRUEL TO HER, SHE'S ALWAYS SHOCKED AND HURT.

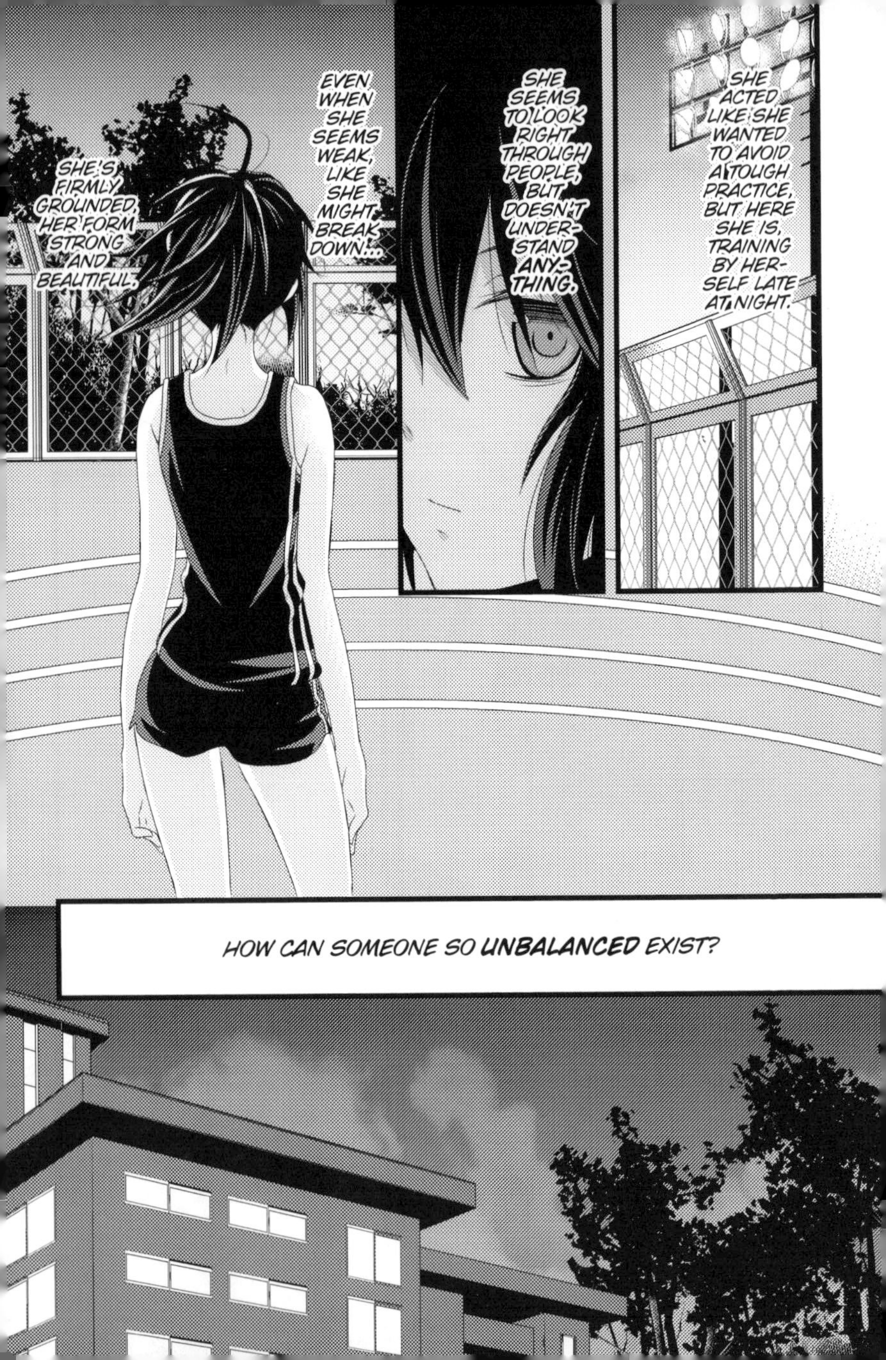
SHE ACTED LIKE SHE WANTED TO AVOID A TOUGH PRACTICE, BUT HERE SHE IS, TRAINING BY HER-SELF LATE AT NIGHT.
SHE SEEMS TO LOOK RIGHT THROUGH PEOPLE, BUT DOESN'T UNDER-STAND ANY-THING.
EVEN WHEN SHE SEEMS WEAK, LIKE SHE MIGHT BREAK DOWN...
SHE'S FIRMLY GROUNDED, HER FORM STRONG AND BEAUTIFUL.
HOW CAN SOMEONE SO **UNBALANCED** EXIST?

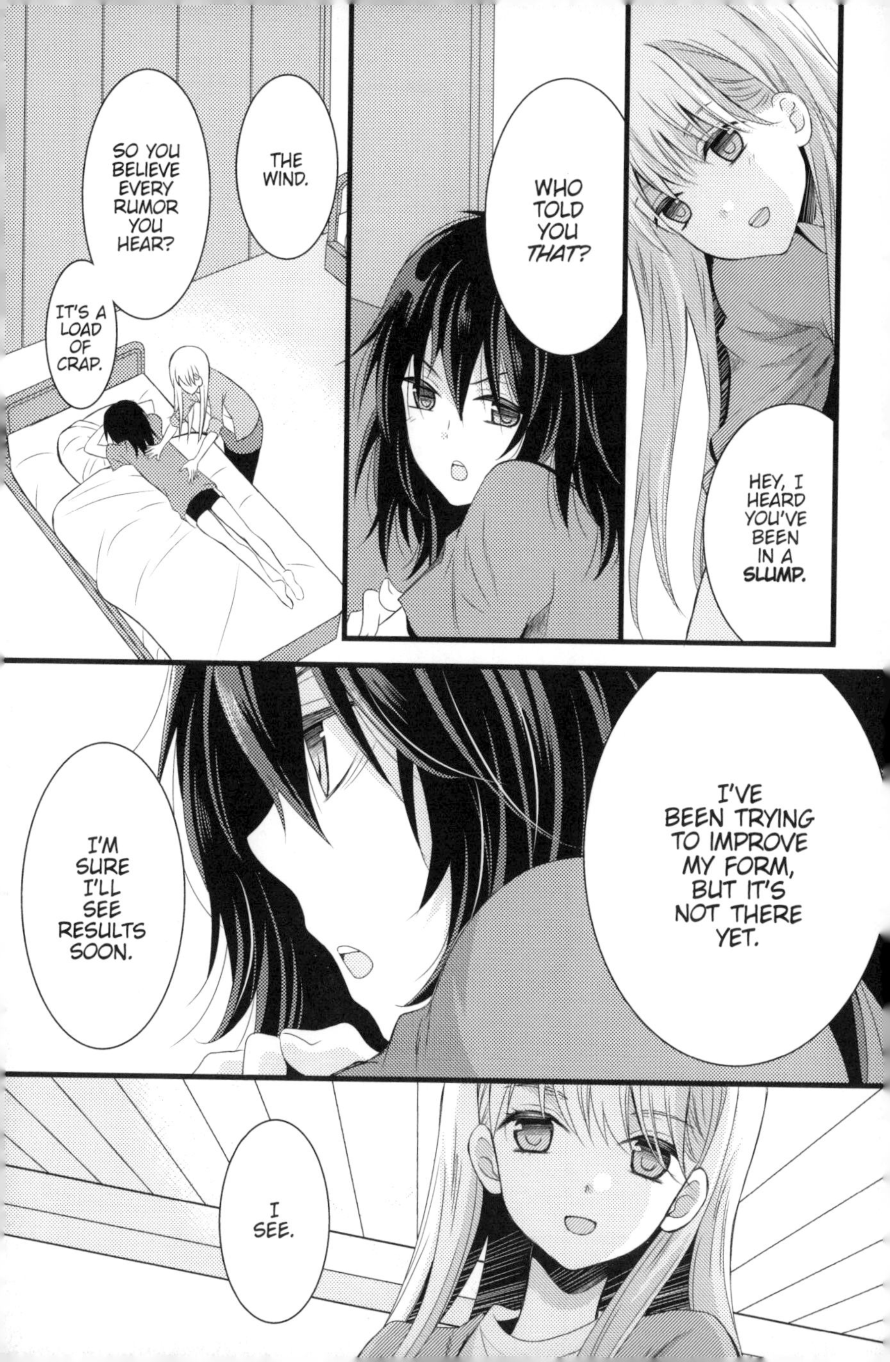
HEY, I HEARD YOU'VE BEEN IN A SLUMP.
WHO TOLD YOU THAT?
THE WIND.
SO YOU BELIEVE EVERY RUMOR YOU HEAR?
IT'S A LOAD OF CRAP.
I'VE BEEN TRYING TO IMPROVE MY FORM, BUT IT'S NOT THERE YET.
I'M SURE I'LL SEE RESULTS SOON.
I SEE.

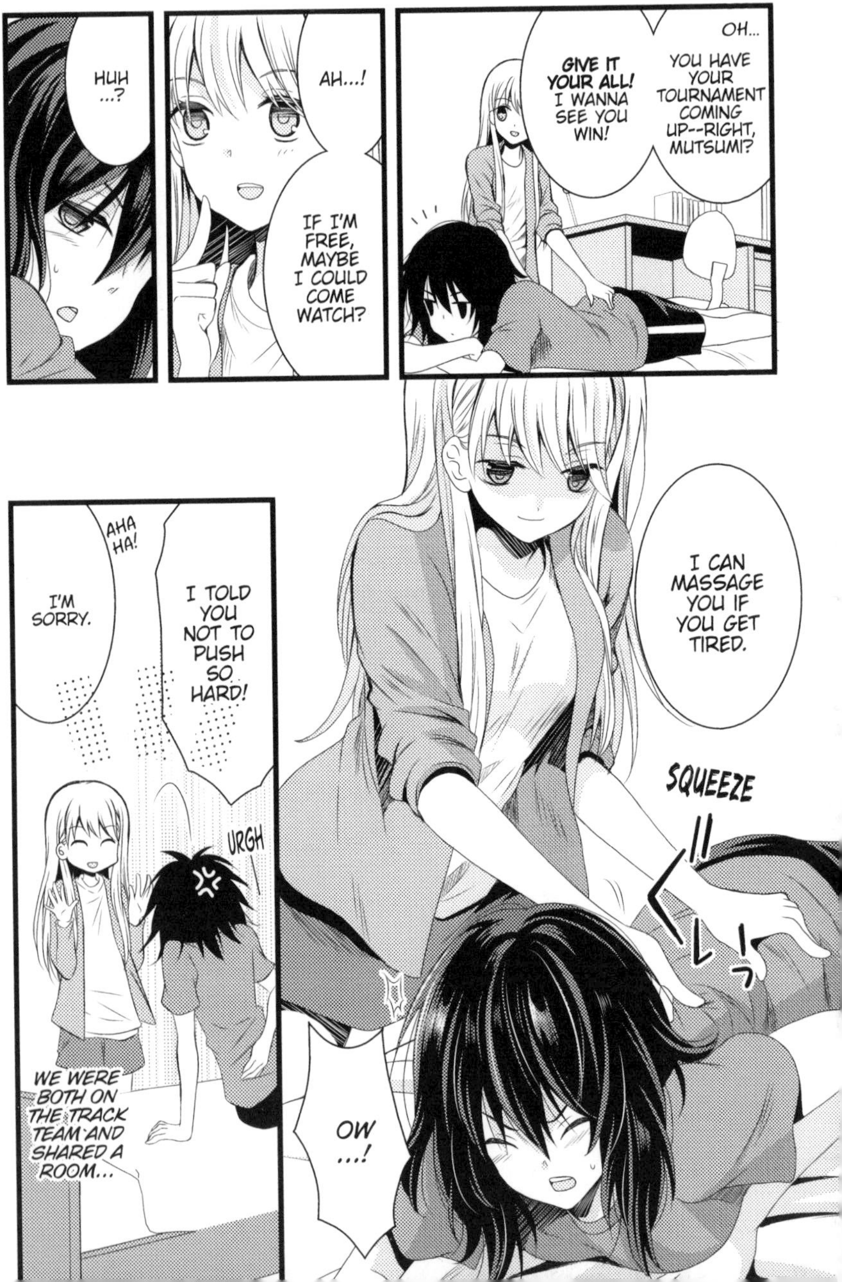
OH...
YOU HAVE YOUR TOURNAMENT COMING UP--RIGHT, MUTSUMI?
GIVE IT YOUR ALL! I WANNA SEE YOU WIN!
AH...!
IF I'M FREE, MAYBE I COULD COME WATCH?
HUH...?
I CAN MASSAGE YOU IF YOU GET TIRED.
SQUEEZE
OW...!
I TOLD YOU NOT TO PUSH SO HARD!
AHA HA!
I'M SORRY.
URGH
WE WERE BOTH ON THE TRACK TEAM AND SHARED A ROOM...

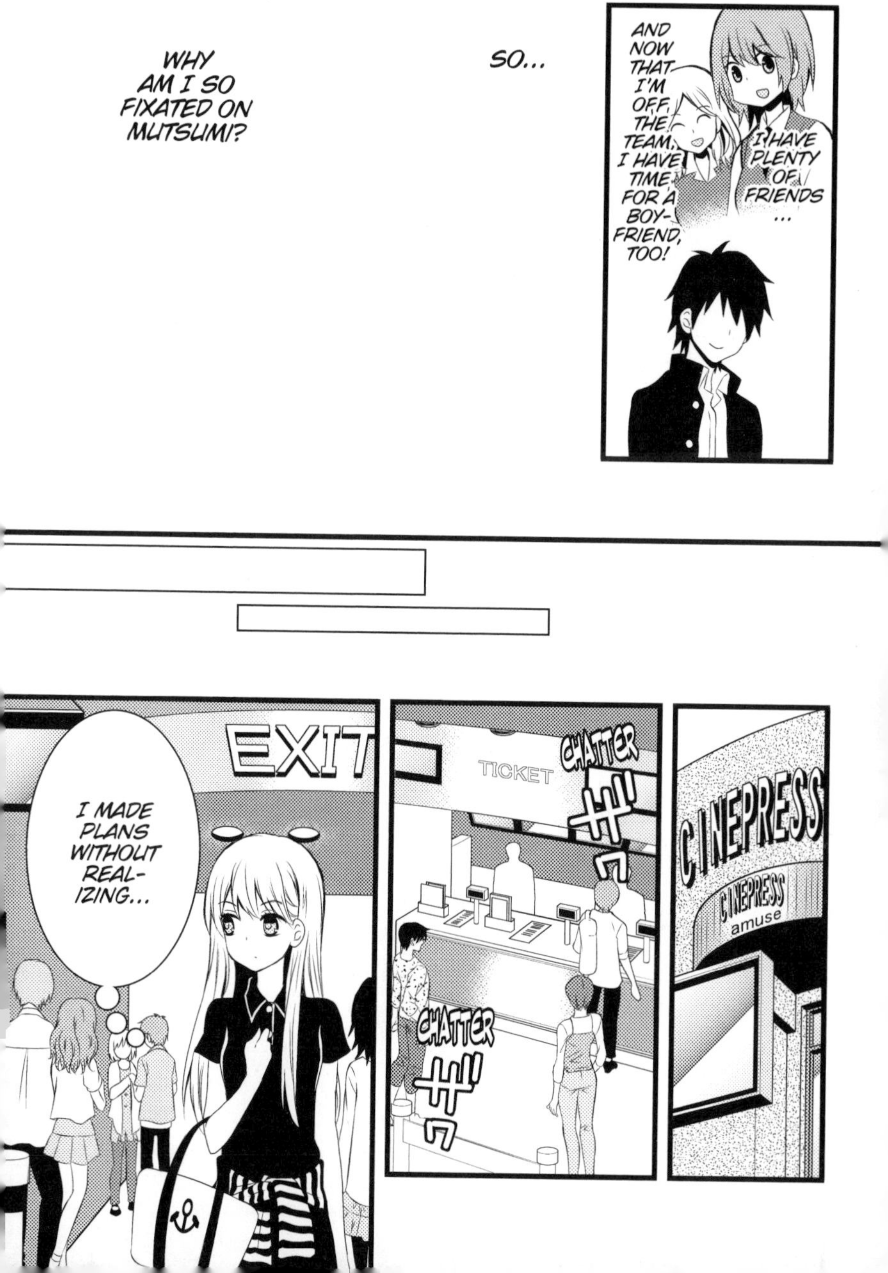
I HAVE PLENTY OF FRIENDS...
AND NOW THAT I'M OFF THE TEAM, I HAVE TIME FOR A BOY-FRIEND, TOO!
SO...
WHY AM I SO FIXATED ON MUTSUMI!?
CINEPRESS
CINEPRESS
amuse
CHATTER
TICKET
CHATTER
EXIT
I MADE PLANS WITHOUT REAL-IZING...

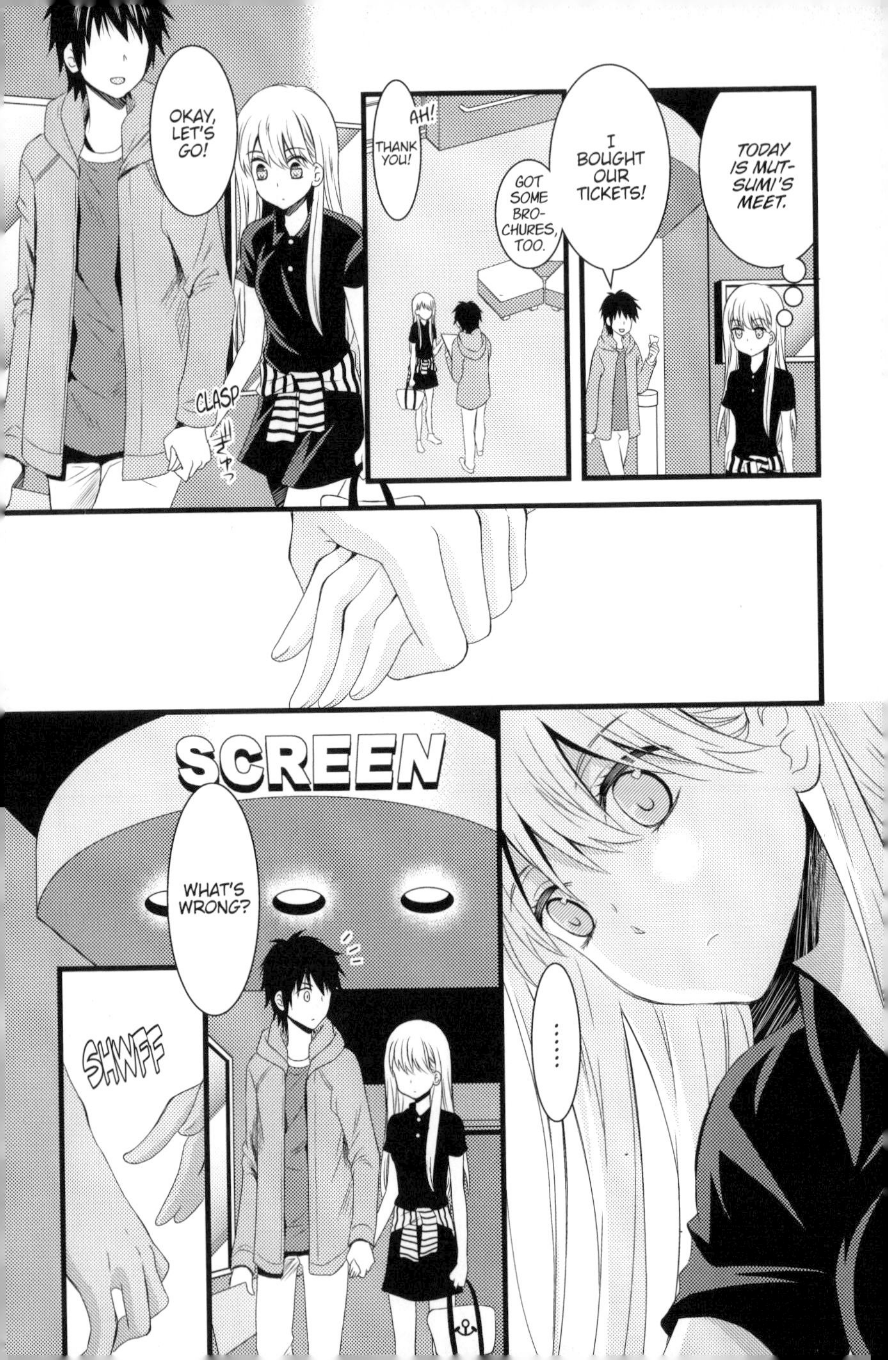
TODAY IS MUT-SUMI'S MEET.
I BOUGHT OUR TICKETS!
GOT SOME BRO-CHURES, TOO.
AH!
THANK YOU!
OKAY, LET'S GO!
CLASP
ぎゅっ
......
SCREEN
WHAT'S WRONG?
SHNFF

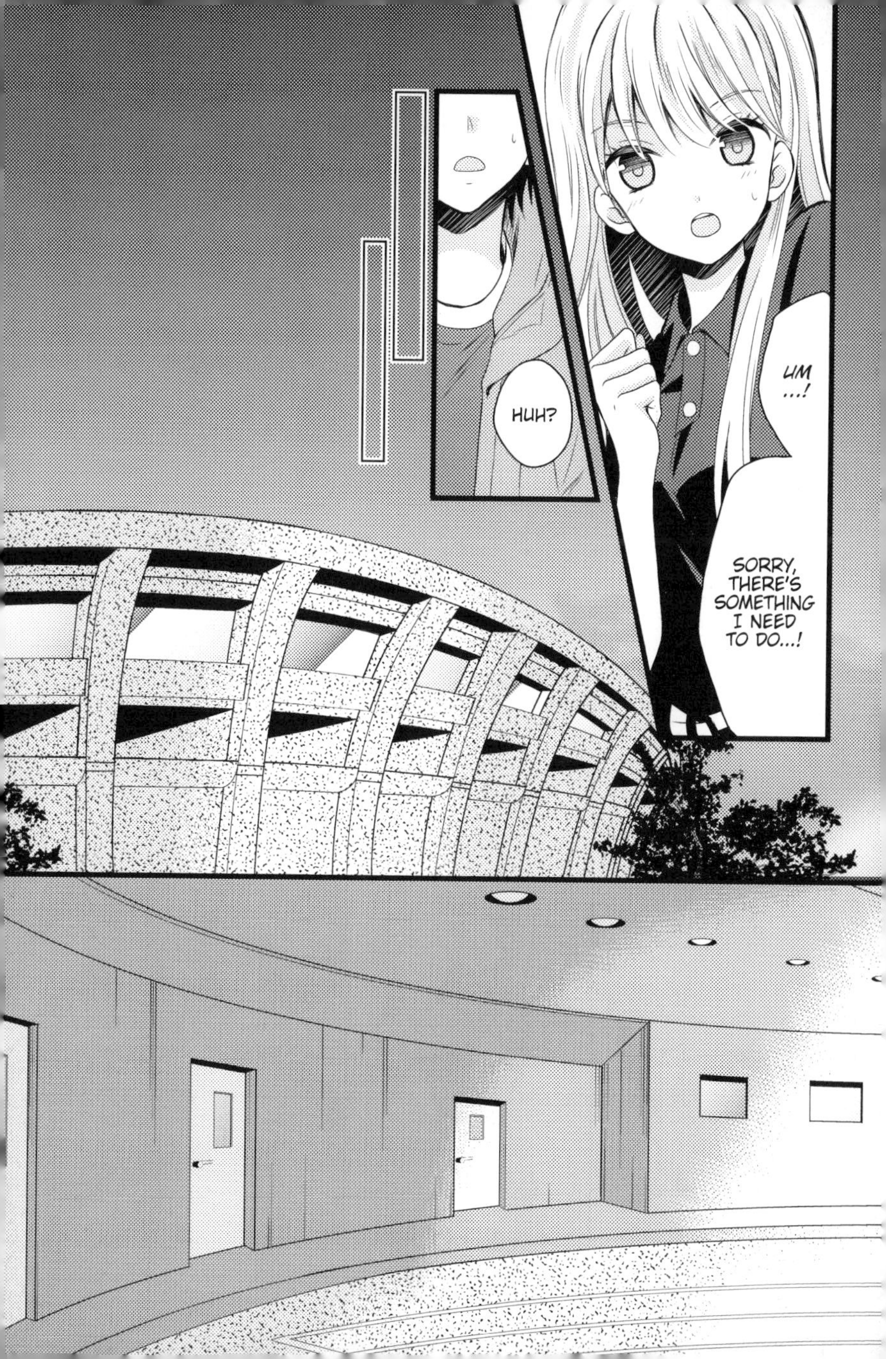
UM ...!
SORRY, THERE'S SOMETHING I NEED TO DO...!
HUH?

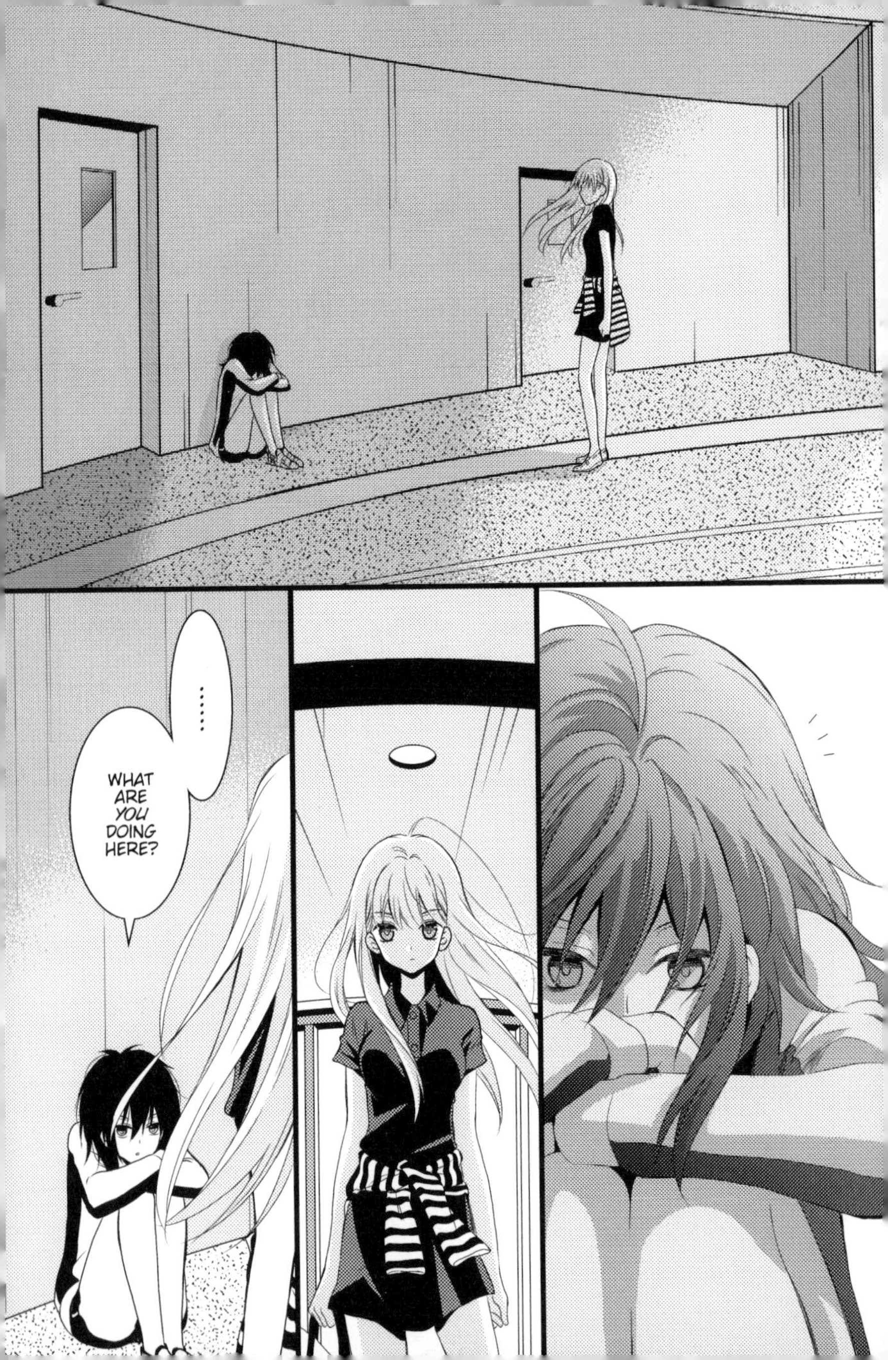
......
WHAT ARE *YOU* DOING HERE?

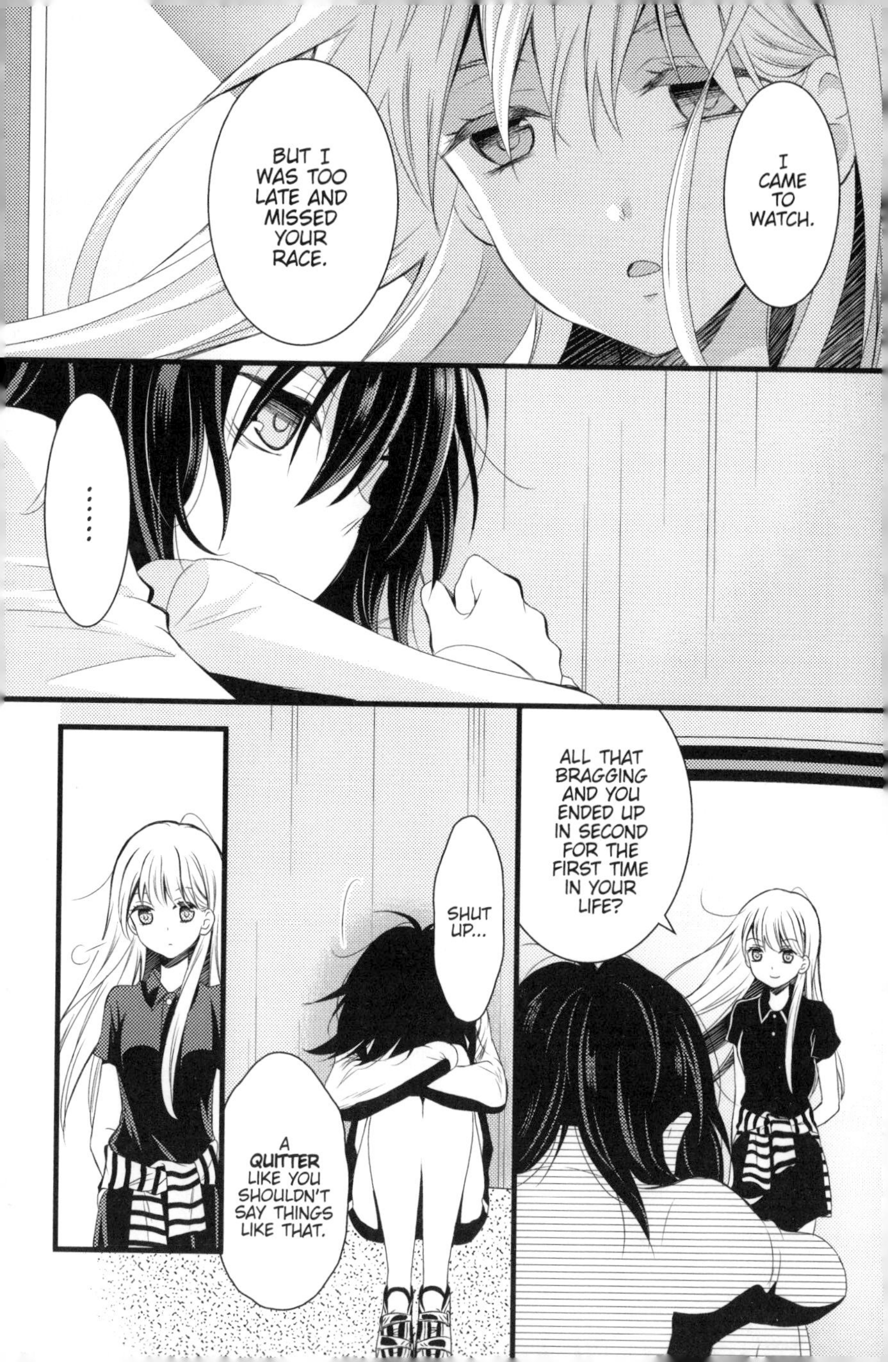
I CAME TO WATCH.
BUT I WAS TOO LATE AND MISSED YOUR RACE.
......
ALL THAT BRAGGING AND YOU ENDED UP IN SECOND FOR THE FIRST TIME IN YOUR LIFE?
SHUT UP...
A **QUITTER** LIKE YOU SHOULDN'T SAY THINGS LIKE THAT.

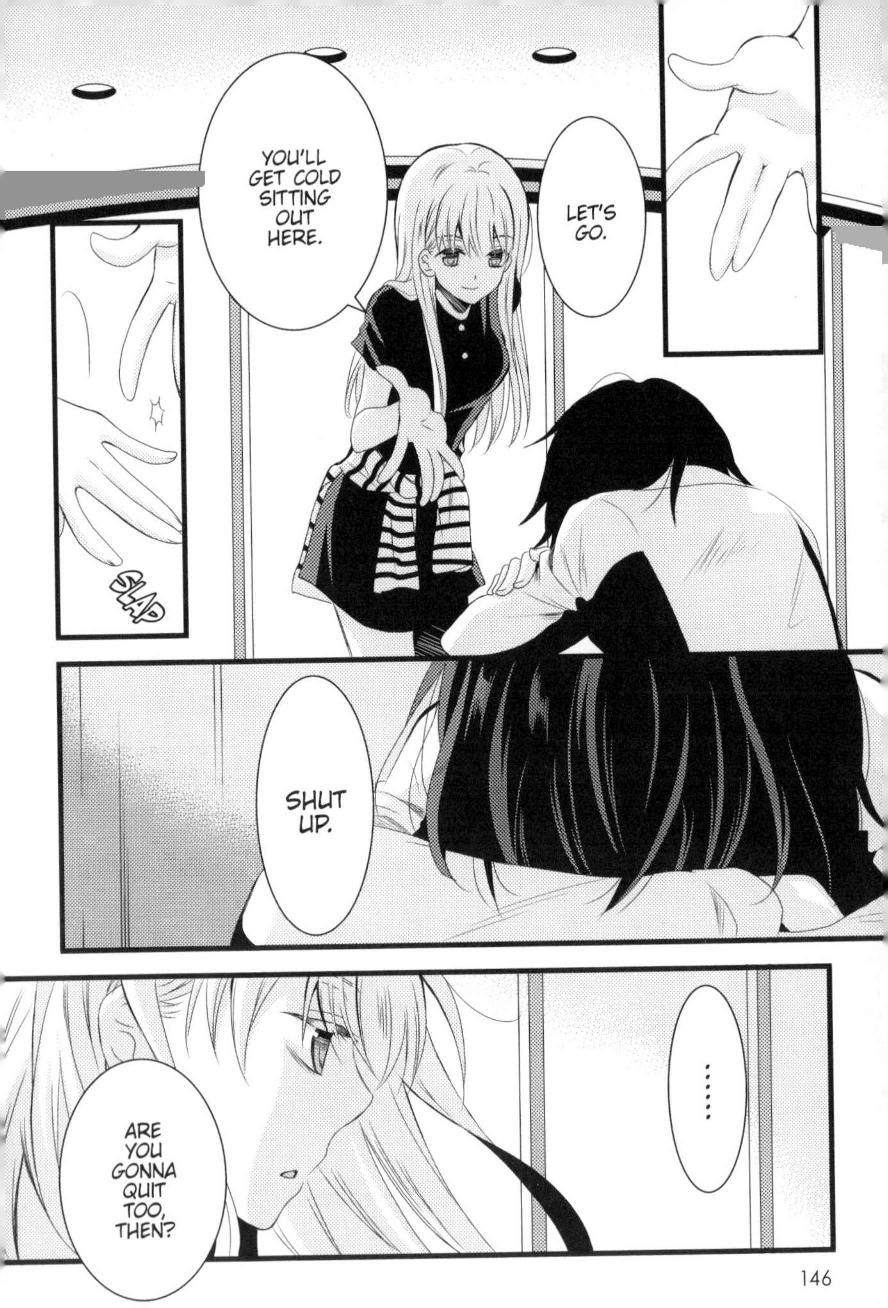
LET'S GO.
YOU'LL GET COLD SITTING OUT HERE.
SLAP
SHUT UP.
……
ARE YOU GONNA QUIT TOO, THEN?

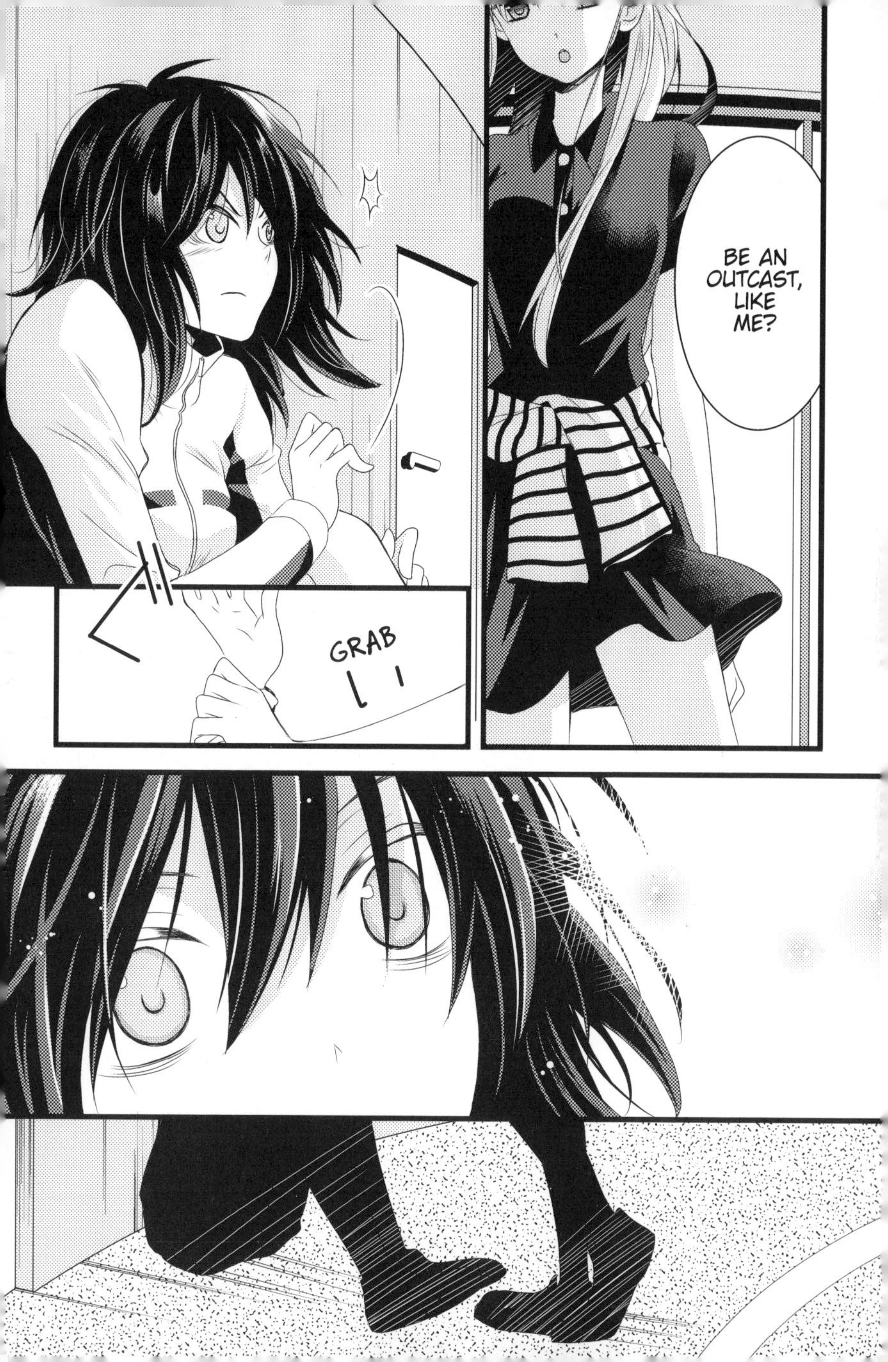
BE AN OUTCAST, LIKE ME?
GRAB

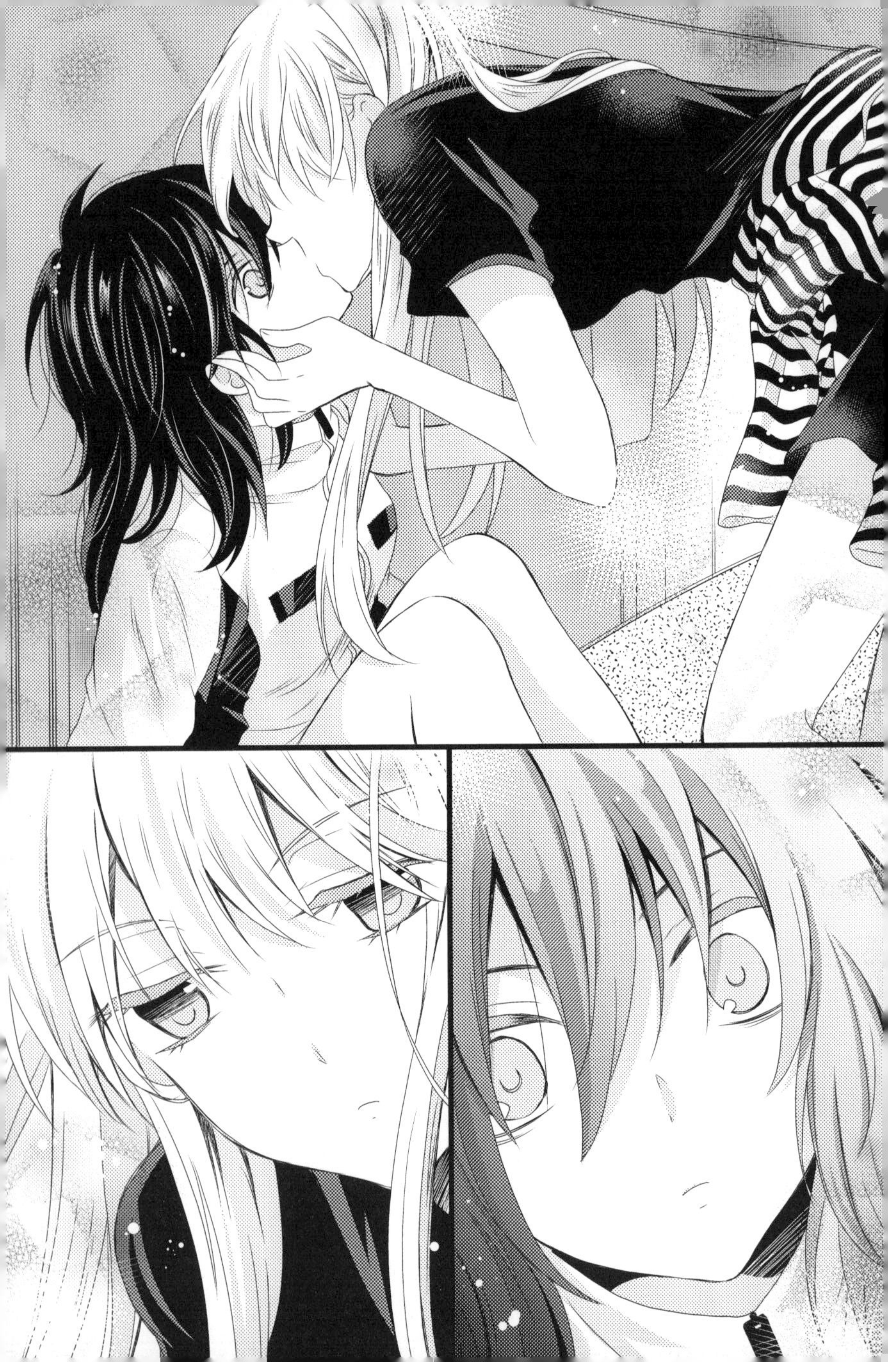

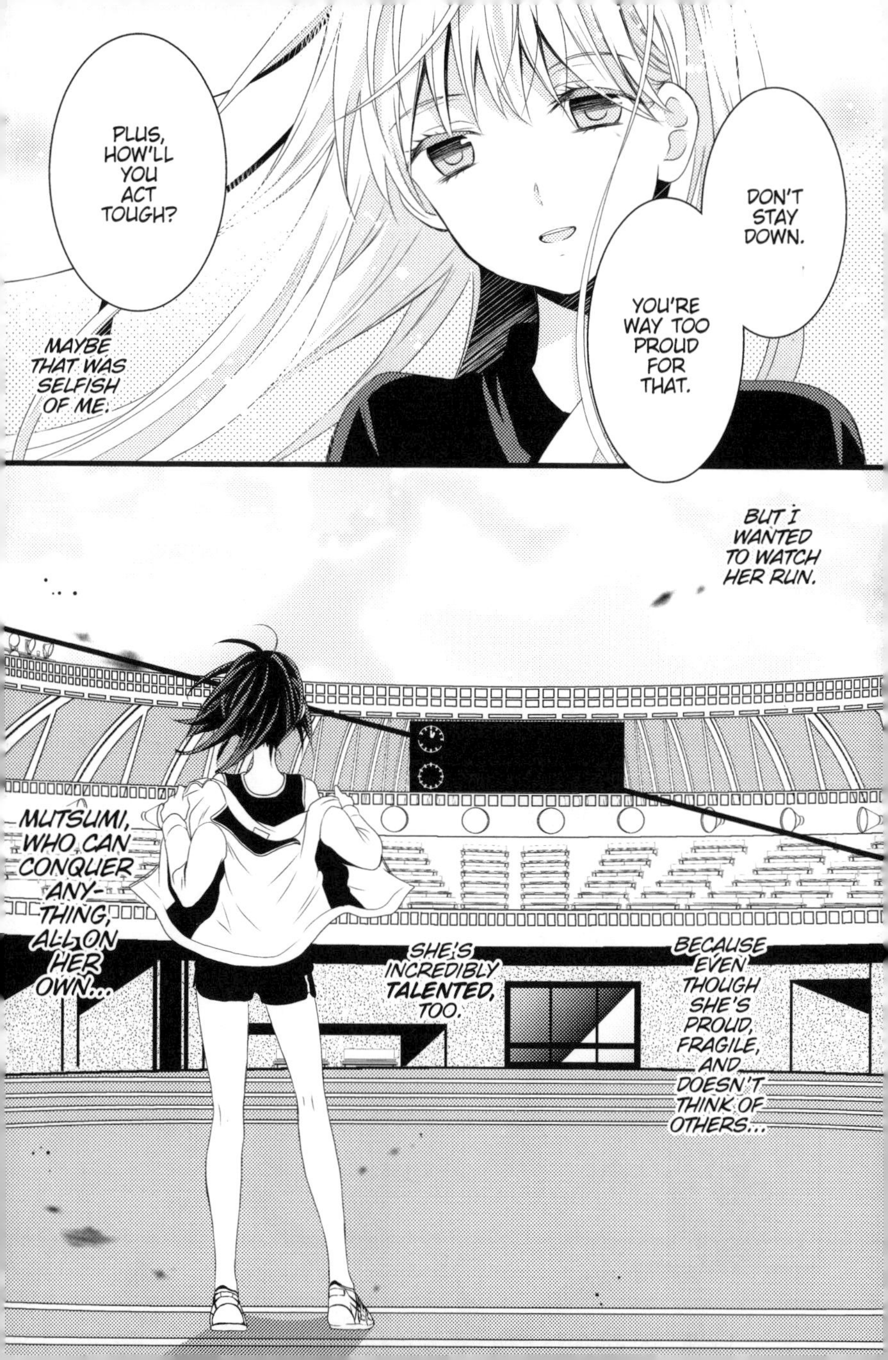
DON'T STAY DOWN.
YOU'RE WAY TOO PROUD FOR THAT.
PLUS, HOW'LL YOU ACT TOUGH?
MAYBE THAT WAS SELFISH OF ME.
BUT I WANTED TO WATCH HER RUN.
...
BECAUSE EVEN THOUGH SHE'S PROUD, FRAGILE, AND DOESN'T THINK OF OTHERS...
SHE'S INCREDIBLY TALENTED, TOO.
MUTSUMI, WHO CAN CONQUER ANY-THING, ALL ON HER OWN...

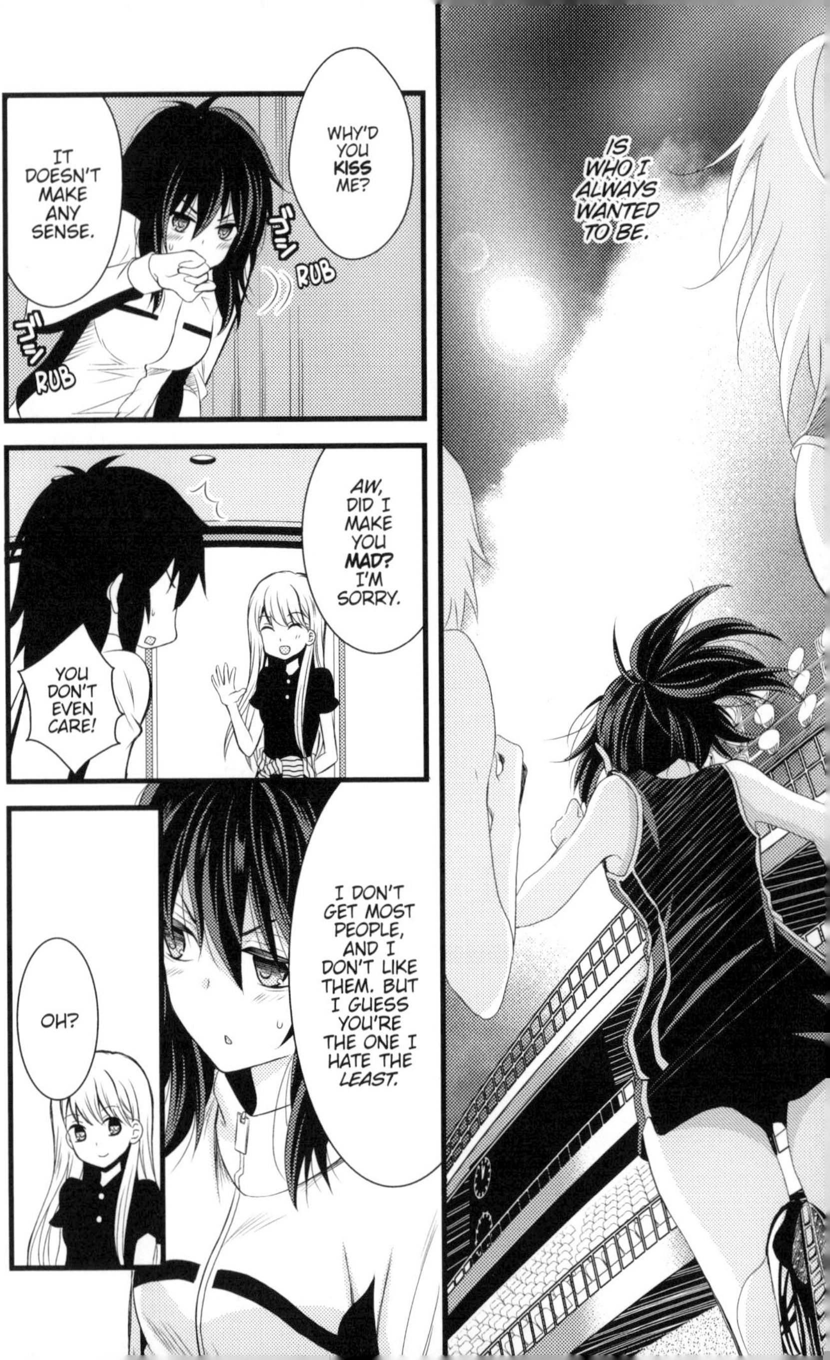
IS WHO I ALWAYS WANTED TO BE.
WHY'D YOU KISS ME?
IT DOESN'T MAKE ANY SENSE.
RUB
RUB
AW, DID I MAKE YOU MAD? I'M SORRY.
YOU DON'T EVEN CARE!
I DON'T GET MOST PEOPLE, AND I DON'T LIKE THEM. BUT I GUESS YOU'RE THE ONE I HATE THE LEAST.
OH?

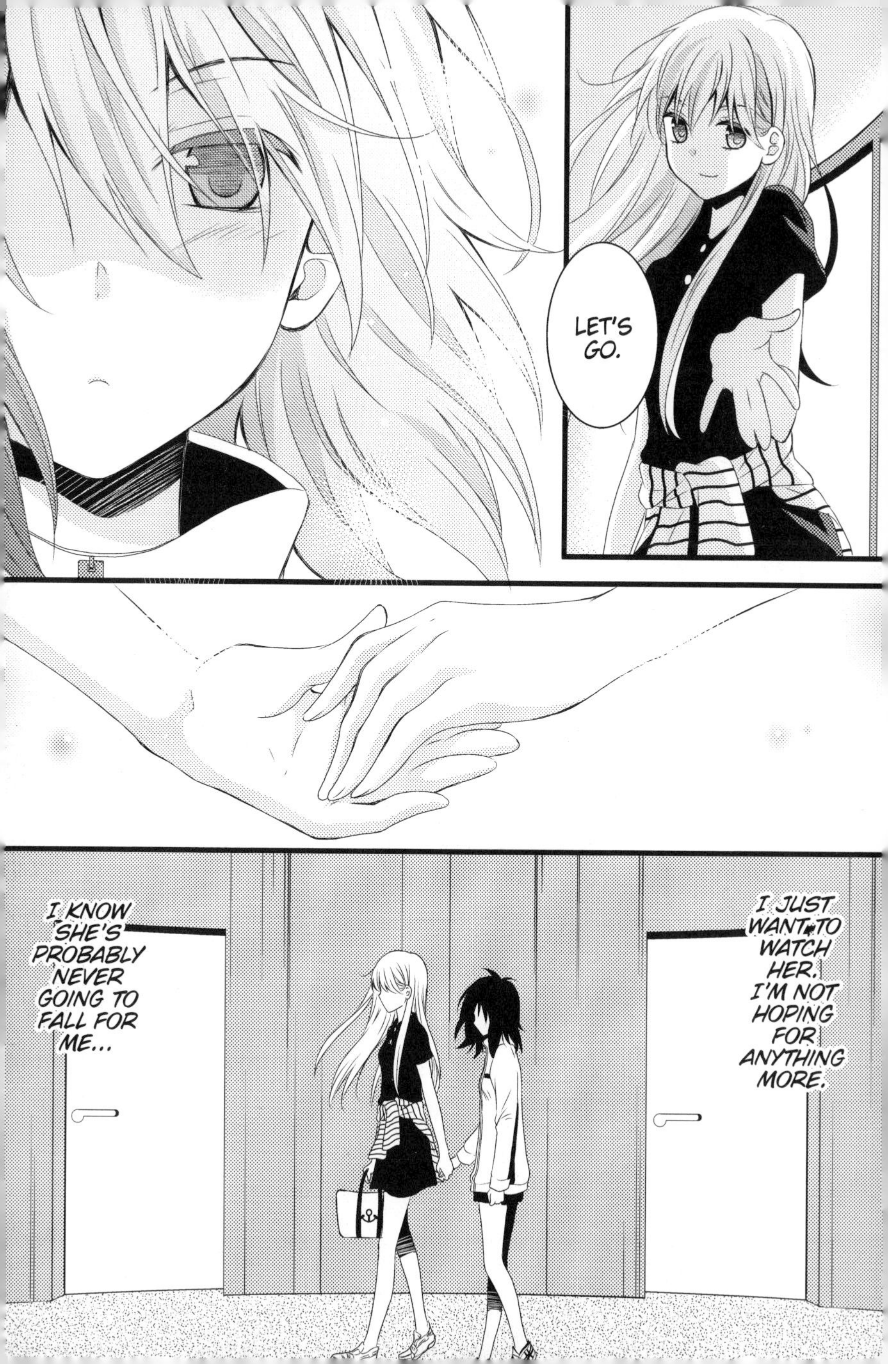
LET'S GO.
I JUST WANT TO WATCH HER. I'M NOT HOPING FOR ANYTHING MORE.
I KNOW SHE'S PROBABLY NEVER GOING TO FALL FOR ME...

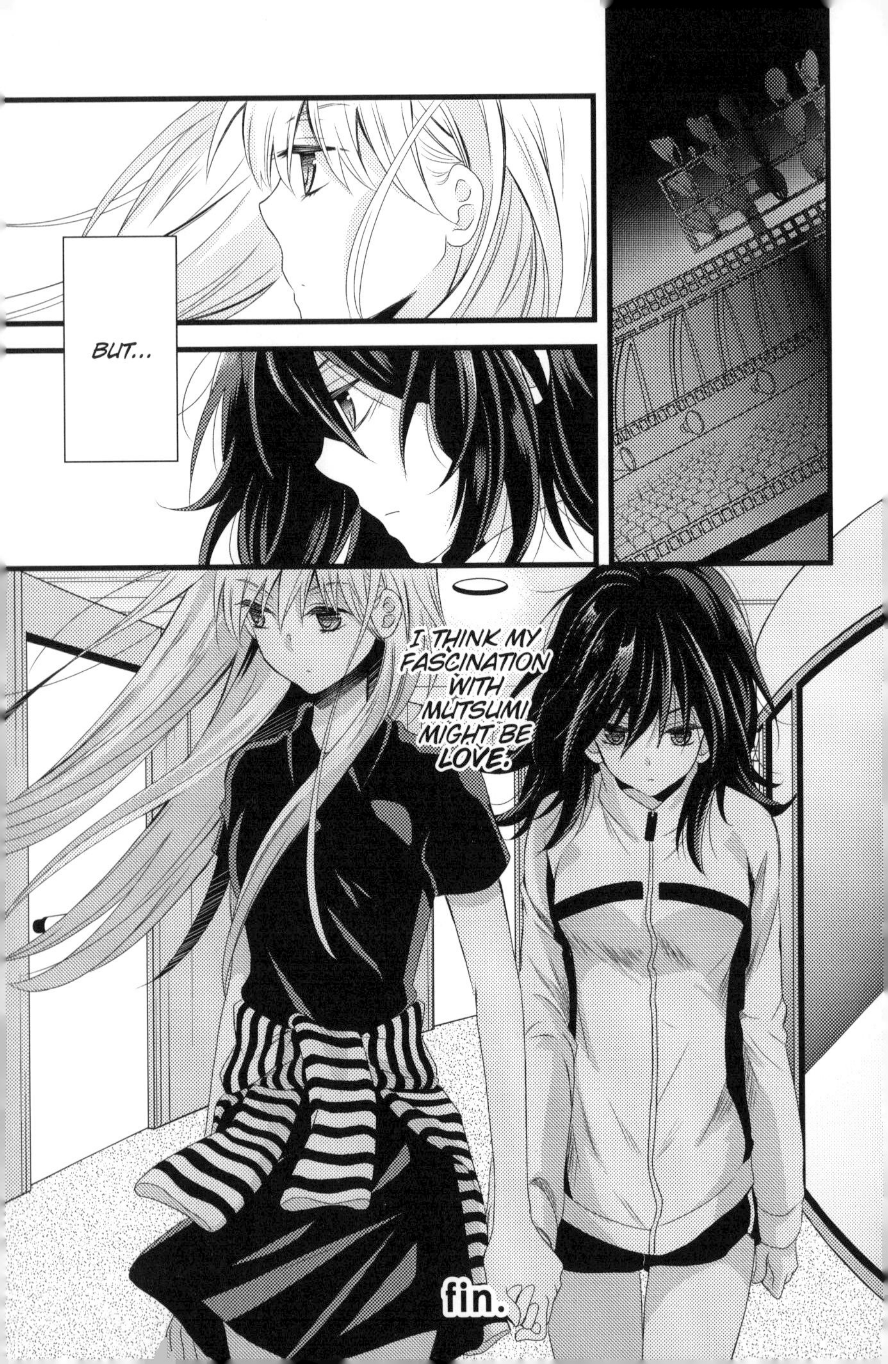
BUT...
I THINK MY FASCINATION WITH MUTSUMI MIGHT BE LOVE.
fin.

I Married My Best Friend(♀)
to Shut My Parents up

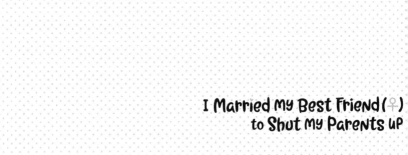

I Married My Best Friend (♀)
to Shut My Parents up

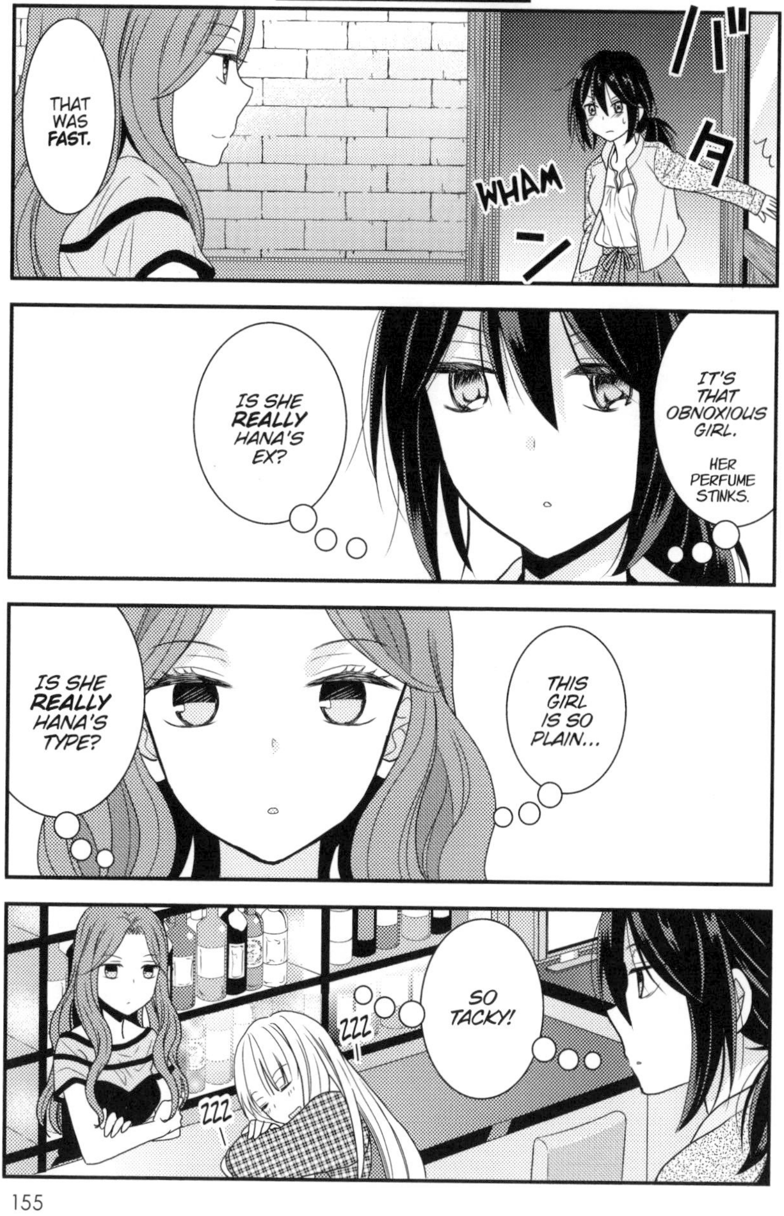
バ
タ
WHAM
THAT WAS FAST.
IT'S THAT OBNOXIOUS GIRL.
HER PERFUME STINKS.
IS SHE REALLY HANA'S EX?
THIS GIRL IS SO PLAIN...
IS SHE REALLY HANA'S TYPE?
SO TACKY!
ZZZ
ZZZ

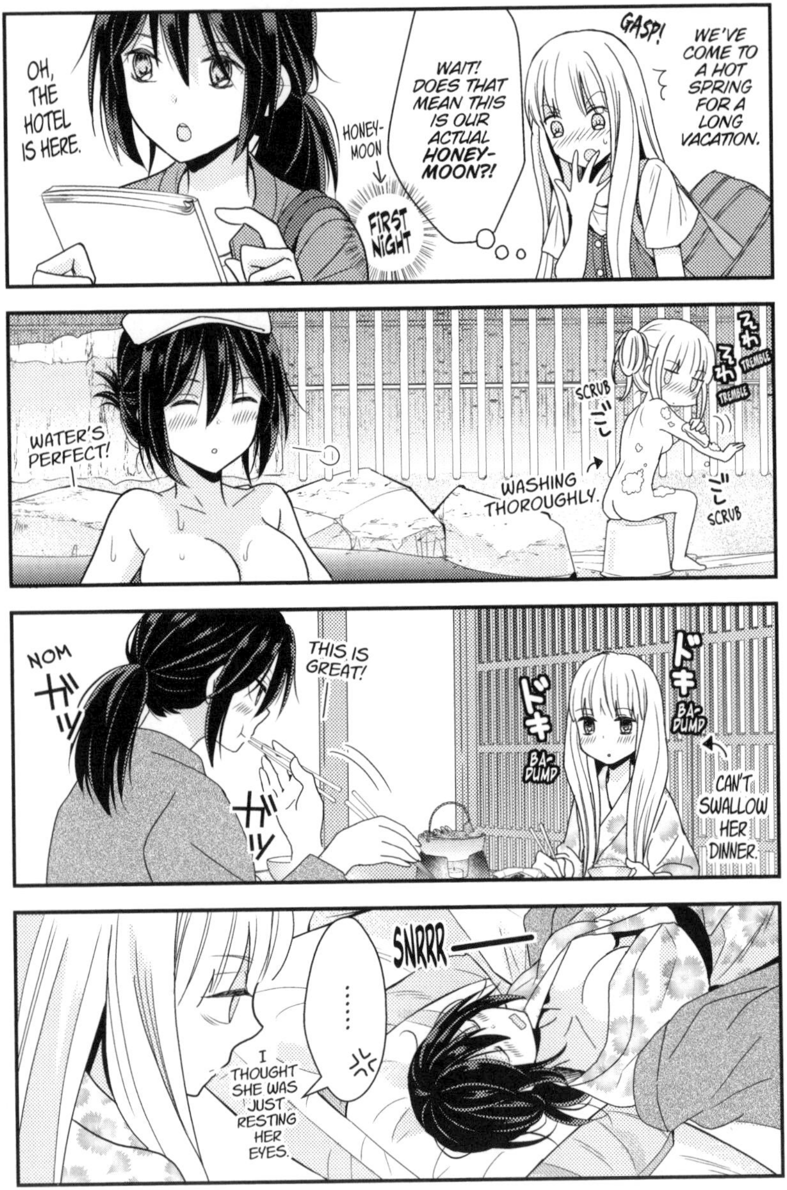
WE'VE COME TO A HOT SPRING FOR A LONG VACATION.
GASP!
WAIT! DOES THAT MEAN THIS IS OUR ACTUAL HONEY-MOON?!
HONEY-MOON
FIRST NIGHT
OH, THE HOTEL IS HERE.
TREMBLE
TREMBLE
SCRUB
ごし
WASHING THOROUGHLY.
ごし
SCRUB
WATER'S PERFECT!
ドキ
BA-DUMP
CAN'T SWALLOW HER DINNER.
ドキ
BA-DUMP
THIS IS GREAT!
NOM
SNRRR
......
I THOUGHT SHE WAS JUST RESTING HER EYES.

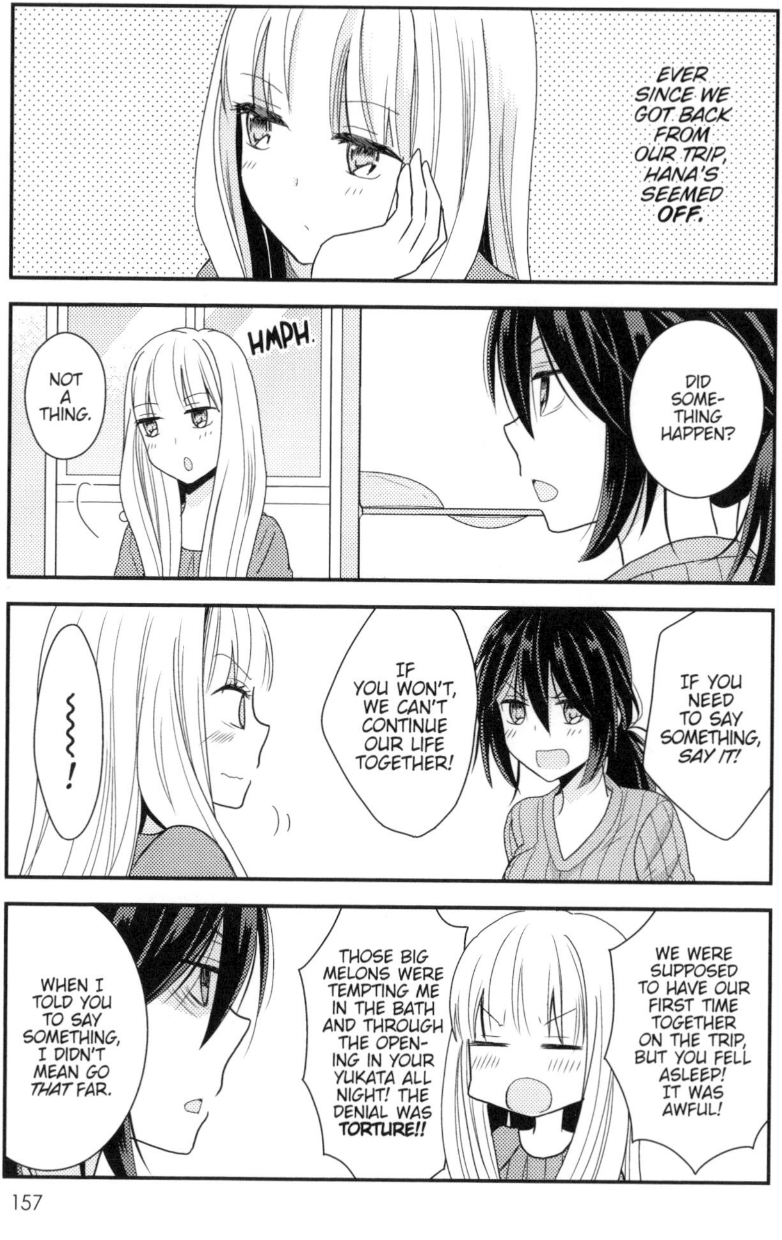
EVER SINCE WE GOT BACK FROM OUR TRIP, HANA'S SEEMED **OFF.**
DID SOMETHING HAPPEN?
HMPH.
NOT A THING.
IF YOU NEED TO SAY SOMETHING, *SAY IT!*
IF YOU WON'T, WE CAN'T CONTINUE OUR LIFE TOGETHER!
~~~!
WE WERE SUPPOSED TO HAVE OUR FIRST TIME TOGETHER ON THE TRIP, BUT YOU FELL ASLEEP! IT WAS AWFUL!
THOSE BIG MELONS WERE TEMPTING ME IN THE BATH AND THROUGH THE OPENING IN YOUR YUKATA ALL NIGHT! THE DENIAL WAS **TORTURE!!**
WHEN I TOLD YOU TO SAY SOMETHING, I DIDN'T MEAN GO *THAT* FAR.
~~~

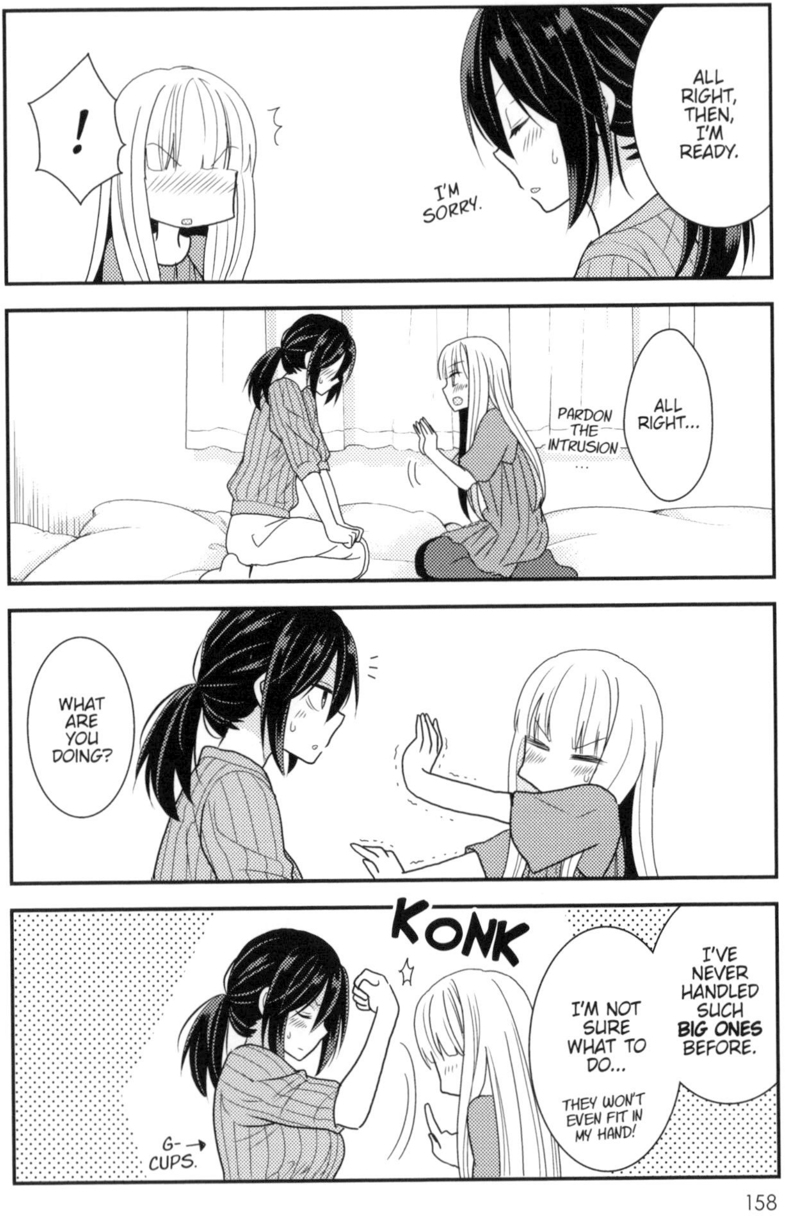
ALL RIGHT, THEN, I'M READY.
I'M SORRY.
!
ALL RIGHT...
PARDON THE INTRUSION...
WHAT ARE YOU DOING?
I'VE NEVER HANDLED SUCH **BIG ONES** BEFORE.
I'M NOT SURE WHAT TO DO...
THEY WON'T EVEN FIT IN MY HAND!
KONK
G- CUPS.

I Married My Best Friend (♀)
to Shut My Parents up

Afterword

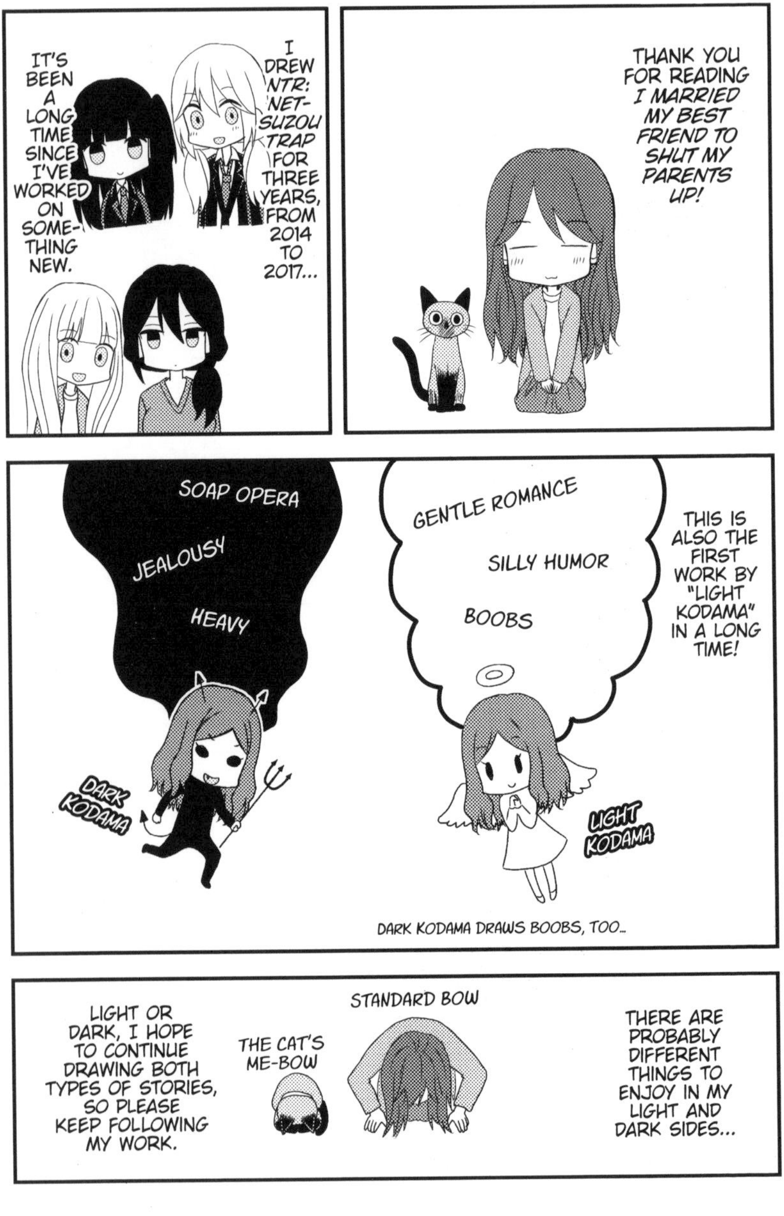
THANK YOU FOR READING *I MARRIED MY BEST FRIEND TO SHUT MY PARENTS UP!*
I DREW *NTR: NET-SUZOU TRAP* FOR THREE YEARS, FROM 2014 TO 2017...
IT'S BEEN A LONG TIME SINCE I'VE WORKED ON SOMETHING NEW.
THIS IS ALSO THE FIRST WORK BY "LIGHT KODAMA" IN A LONG TIME!
GENTLE ROMANCE
SILLY HUMOR
BOOBS
LIGHT KODAMA
SOAP OPERA
JEALOUSY
HEAVY
DARK KODAMA
DARK KODAMA DRAWS BOOBS, TOO..
THERE ARE PROBABLY DIFFERENT THINGS TO ENJOY IN MY LIGHT AND DARK SIDES...
STANDARD BOW
THE CAT'S ME-BOW
LIGHT OR DARK, I HOPE TO CONTINUE DRAWING BOTH TYPES OF STORIES, SO PLEASE KEEP FOLLOWING MY WORK.

SEVEN SEAS ENTERTAINMENT PRESENTS

I Married My Best Friend to Shut My Parents Up

story and art by **KODAMA NAOKO**

TRANSLATION
Amber Tamosaitis

ADAPTATION
Lora Gray

LETTERING AND RETOUCH
Rina Mapa

COVER DESIGN
KC Fabellon

PROOFREADER
Kurestin Armada
Danielle King

EDITOR
Jenn Grunigen

PRODUCTION MANAGER
Lissa Pattillo

MANAGING EDITOR
Julie Davis

EDITOR-IN-CHIEF
Adam Arnold

PUBLISHER
Jason DeAngelis

Seven Seas press and purchase enquiries can be sent to Marketing Manager Lianne Sentar at press@gomanga.com. Information regarding the distribution and purchase of digital editions is available from Digital Manager CK Russell at digital@gomanga.com.

ISBN: 978-1-64275-328-8

Printed in Lithuania
First Printing: June 2019
10 9 8 7 6

FOLLOW US ONLINE: ***www.sevenseasentertainment.com***

READING DIRECTIONS

This book reads from ***right to left***, Japanese style. If this is your first time reading manga, you start reading from the top right panel on each page and take it from there. If you get lost, just follow the numbered diagram here. It may seem backwards at first, but you'll get the hang of it! Have fun!!

1
2
3
4
5
6
7
8
9

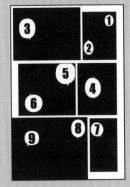

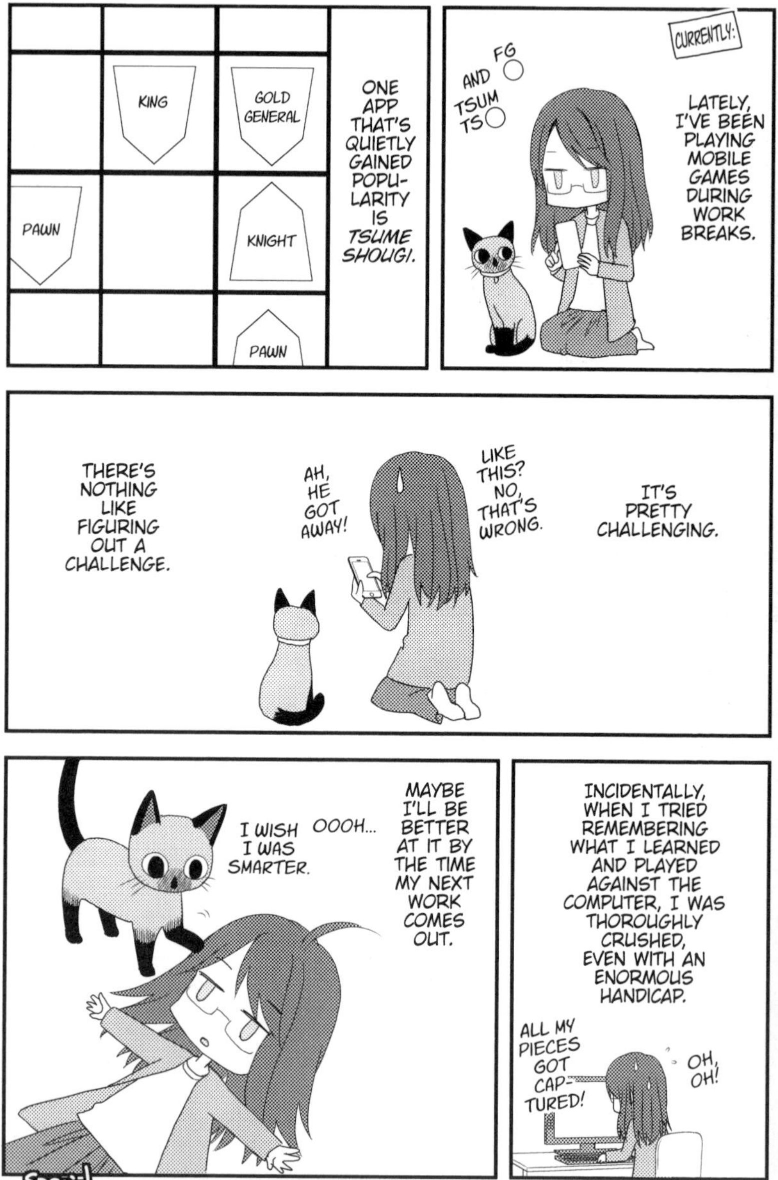
CURRENTLY:
LATELY, I'VE BEEN PLAYING MOBILE GAMES DURING WORK BREAKS.
TSUM TS○
AND FG○
ONE APP THAT'S QUIETLY GAINED POPULARITY IS *TSUME SHOUGI*.
GOLD GENERAL
KING
KNIGHT
PAWN
PAWN
IT'S PRETTY CHALLENGING.
LIKE THIS? NO, THAT'S WRONG.
AH, HE GOT AWAY!
THERE'S NOTHING LIKE FIGURING OUT A CHALLENGE.
INCIDENTALLY, WHEN I TRIED REMEMBERING WHAT I LEARNED AND PLAYED AGAINST THE COMPUTER, I WAS THOROUGHLY CRUSHED, EVEN WITH AN ENORMOUS HANDICAP.
OH, OH!
ALL MY PIECES GOT CAPTURED!
MAYBE I'LL BE BETTER AT IT BY THE TIME MY NEXT WORK COMES OUT.
OOOH...
I WISH I WAS SMARTER.

Special Thanks MY EDITOR, PAIN-SAN; MY ASSISTANTS, H-SAN, G-SAN, AND N-SAN; MY DESIGNER; AND EVERYONE WHO READS THIS MANGA!